Wild West Dragons, Flaming
Space Fossils and Phantom
Automobiles:

An Anthology of American Strangeness, Vol. 2

Wild West Dragons, Flaming Space Fossils and Phantom Automobiles:

An Anthology of American Strangeness, Vol. 2

By

Kevin J. Guhl

Table of Contents

An Introduction to American Strangeness, Vol. 2

So many great stories are lost to us. Thousands of years of oral tradition and early printed works have disintegrated into the sands of time, the deeds of their heroes and villains forgotten forever. Only a sliver of these old histories and adventures, many which held great meaning to our ancestors, survive into the present day. Even within the past few hundred years of written records, much sits on dusty, untouched library shelves, its paper slowly decaying into powder. Today, though, we are fortunate to have easy access to countless volumes of digitized books, periodicals and historical documents. Never before has so much knowledge been available to such a great swath of the population. However, now that we have the luxury of abundance, there is an enormity of untapped materials to review. I find it to be a treasure trove for neglected tales of historical weirdness.

Now, I am by no means suggesting that a Bedouin shepherd tripping into a cave hiding the Dead Sea Scrolls or an archaeologist digging up the Epic of Gilgamesh in an ancient Mesopotamian library is in any way similar to me stumbling upon a crass old newspaper article about a dynamite-eating pig. But I still get excited whenever I find a lost tale from our past that calls out to be revived and explored. Every story contained in American Strangeness, Vol. 2 struck me with that same mix of joy and curiosity.

One trend that fascinates me is how new technology promptly generates its own set of legends and superstitions. Automobiles and TVs, which arrived on the scene in the first half of the 20th century and immediately reshaped society, were from the outset viewed by some as nuts-and-bolts talismans for spiritual forces. Chapters on each explore this phenomenon, with several examples pulled from contemporary reports.

Similarly, as American towns increasingly urbanized in the late 19th and early 20th centuries, fear of the dangers lurking on night-time city streets came into focus. Some of these terrors, like the Blissville Banshee, presented themselves as the apparitions of old set loose in a new environment. Many of these villains were disguised, perhaps reflecting the anonymity that can come with living in a more populous, bustling area. The Lady in Black was an eerie presence on northern streets, while I was shocked to uncover the incredibly long-standing and widespread presence of the nefarious Gown Man and related Hugging Mollies throughout the southern states. The Gown Man, in particular, is a piece of forgotten American folklore (or more...) that I'm proud to have revived and documented in, I hope you will agree, a thorough and thoughtful manner.

The Mystery Airship wave of 1896-97 reads in retrospect as a prototype for the UFO craze that began in 1947, but historically it reflects public anxiety over the inevitable dawn of powered flight just a handful of years before it happened. I was curious how the Mystery Airship phenomenon, so prevalent in newspapers throughout the U.S., affected popular culture, and that is remarkably clear in how it played into celebrations during the Christmas of 1896.

We spend time with a number of historical celebrities in this book. Some are famous, like authors Mark Twain and Edgar Allan Poe, who supposedly encountered monster birds in Pennsylvania (home of the infamous Thunderbird). Other personalities are obscure today but were well-known in their own time, like Broadway star Robert Hilliard, who encountered a sea serpent, and Teddy the Cat, who ruled an Omaha, Nebraska golf course with an iron paw. And then there is Sweeney Todd, a classic character who may be less fictional than you were led to believe. Sarah Whitcher, the lost little girl rescued by a bear, is a celebrated character of Post-Colonial New England folk tales. I was delighted to discover evidence that, not only was she a real person, but her story about a mothering bruin isn't that far-fetched.

Of course, what collection of American Strangeness would be complete without a healthy dose of cryptids? In this volume, we meet the stunning assortment of American Dragons that prowled the Wild West, Ohio's menagerie of reptilian and amphibian monsters, and a very odd year in which The Jersey Devil and Bigfoot battled for attention in The Garden State. It's not every day that a cryptid (mystery animal unknown to science) case gets solved, but you'll find that here as I reveal the true identity of the Monster of Marmotte Street.

Sometimes, I happen upon some historical oddity and then become even more enchanted with the people involved and the surrounding circumstances, compelling me to bring these bizarre pockets of the past back to life. The Flaming Hand of Doom isn't just about a meteor shaped like a gnarled alien appendage that fell to Earth; it's a family tragedy about destructive grief set amidst the glitz of the early 1900's Atlantic City Boardwalk. (There is also a semi-sequel in the Flaming Skull that Fell from Space, which also gave me an opportunity to indulge in my morbid fascination with rumors of dead Cosmonauts orbiting the Earth.) The Wild Girl of Catahoula Parish examines competing backstories behind a feral woman who once resided in the Louisiana swamps. The Prickly Pear Ghost Light is a true account of brutal murder, frontier justice and ghostly apparitions set in 1880's Montana. Haddy the Hadrosaur's Ghost is a tale near and dear to my heart, as it was the first dinosaur skeleton I ever saw, towering over my childhood self at the New Jersey State Museum in Trenton. Little did I know that the poor dinosaur still haunted its place or origin, forever seeking its missing skull! And finally, I tap into my roots as a journalist in examining the case of a Lancaster, Pennsylvania newspaper that never shied away from leaning into the lurid to survive, whether that be tales of headless ghosts, petrified men or river monsters.

Intro to American Strangeness, V.2

I was gobsmacked and humbled by the positive reception and tidal wave of support I received for the release of my first book, "An Anthology of American Strangeness, Vol. 1: Thunderbirds, Lost Temples and Skeleton Ghosts." Family, friends— and friends of family and friends—all demonstrated overwhelming generosity in purchasing copies of the book and leaving glowing feedback. Thank you, everyone!

It was also gratifying to find an audience within the Fortean community (named for groundbreaking paranormal researcher and writer, Charles Fort). In addition to numerous positive and encouraging comments, I enjoyed being invited to speak with Paul Bestall on the excellent Mysteries & Monsters podcast, and Gene Steinberg and Tim Swartz on the venerable Paracast. I hope I was an interesting guest! And then I experienced a surreal moment of personal pride when Nigel Watson reviewed Vol. 1 of American Strangeness for Fortean Times magazine, issue #456, and gave it five stars, no less! If you didn't know, the long-running Fortean Times is like the Time magazine of the unexplained. All in all, it was a very warm welcome, and I am grateful.

One enormous error I need to correct from the first volume of American Strangeness is neglecting to name the paid artists whose work graced Vol. 1. I therefore recognize them here:

Front Cover - Krisnasatriafeb

The Jersey Devil - zettoart, p. 6

The Miami Roc - Ridwan, p. 15

Artists and image sources are noted in this volume. Pictures are otherwise public domain or created/generated by me.

Once again, I hope you find as much pleasure and fascination with the tales in this book as I had in recording them. Thank you for supporting my efforts to continue documenting America's weird history. You can see more of my work at www.AmericanStrangeness.com or reach me at editor@thunderbirdphoto.com.

You can now also listen to my golden voice on YouTube!
www.youtube.com/@AmericanStrangeness

Cheers!

Kevin J. Guhl

July 2025

Dragon Attack on the Southern Pacific Express
(Artist: Robert Jacob Woodard)

The Flying Serpent Who Battled a Train and Other American Dragons

Passengers fired their revolvers at a giant winged monster that attacked their train as it sped along the Colorado Desert in the 1880s. It is one of many fantastic tales of dragons that emerged from the American frontier.

A STARTLING ATTACK ON A SOUTHERN PACIFIC RAILROAD TRAIN NEAR DOS PALMS, CALIFORNIA—AN EXPRESS ATTACKED BY A FLYING SERPENT, AND THE PASSENGERS FIRING AT THE MONSTER WITH REVOLVERS.

"A startling attack on a Southern Pacific Railroad train near Dos Palms, California—An express attacked by a flying serpent, and the passengers firing at the monster with revolvers."—The Illustrated Police News, March 18, 1882.

Imagine for a moment that the year is 1882 and you're a passenger on a Southern Pacific express steam locomotive, barreling across the unforgiving landscape of the Colorado Desert on your way from Yuma, Arizona to Los Angeles. You've just passed the oasis of Dos Palmas, a historically important watering hole so-named for its distinctive pair of palm trees. You gaze out the window and suddenly spot something inexplicable and unsettling. About a half mile ahead, what looks like a column of sand is moving slowly from east to west. It is only a short distance from the railroad track, and traveling at a pace that you calculate will meet the train in certain collision. As you dig your fingernails into your seat and just manage to choke out a gasp, you discern that it's not a column of sand at all, but some kind of strange animal. It is moving perpendicular to the oncoming train, tail dragging on the ground and propelled by two large wings near its head. The bird, snake, or whatever it is, looks to be about 30 feet long and 12 inches in diameter. Your fellow passengers, having noticed this strange and terrifying sight, push their heads out the windows and hang onto the outside railings to get a better look...

According to the Los Angeles Times, this is exactly what happened to a Southern Pacific train on Jan. 17, 1882, relayed by the engineer and fireman and corroborated by passengers when the train arrived in Los Angeles that night. They said that when the flying snake reached the track, the swiftly moving train clipped off a portion of its tail. This painful offense enraged the enormous serpent and it flew after its steel attacker "two miles faster than chain lightning." The angry animal overtook the locomotive in moments and, striking from a position of safety above, "gave the train a lively thrashing, roaring like a cow in distress all the time." As women and children screamed, the beast shattered several windows in its onslaught. The serpent then pulled back and sailed off. Given a moment to recover, several passengers unholstered their pistols and unleased a shower of lead after the beast as wind whistled past the damaged window frames. The bullets, if they hit their target at all, had no effect as the monster winged its way back across the desert sands. "This is vouched for by everyone who was on the train, and is given for what it is worth," stated the Times.

This flying serpent isn't a rare and isolated tale. Rather, it's an early example of a rich tradition of winged reptilian monsters that supposedly terrorized America's western territories and wild environs during the back half of the 19th and early 20th centuries. These "American Dragons," as Strange Magazine editor Mark Chorvinsky dubbed them in a 2000 article, generated numerous headlines across the United States during this period. Chorvinsky didn't give much credence to the editors of Western newspapers when it came to such monster stories or their assertion that the witnesses to such tales were reliable. Indeed, it was an era of American journalism when even major newspapers ran stories of sea serpents, apelike wild men and haunted houses alongside more sober reporting on politics, crime and daily life. It can be hard to discern which articles documenting strange events were spun purely from imagination and which might have been built around a core of truth, possibly sourced from honest yet befuddled eyewitnesses.

Chorvinsky suggested that these American Dragons were an amalgamation of European dragon legends, Native American belief in the Thunderbird as an avian storm deity, and the complicated lore of the Piasa, the pre-European mural of a dragon-like creature once painted on a bluff along the Mississippi River at present-day Alton, Illinois. Fitting America's image as a melting pot, this stew of legends might have solidified into something new.

I think there is another important influence in the composite of the American Dragon—Pteranodon, discovered in 1871 by Yale paleontologist Othniel Charles Marsh within a chalk formation in western Kansas. This was the first discovery of a pterosaur in North America (or outside Europe, for that matter) and it was the largest known genus of the species known at that time, boasting a wingspan of over 20 feet. As evidenced by newspapers of the day, this scientific find captured the public imagination and continued to do so for decades to come. For example, a 1906 San Francisco Examiner article illustrated what this "Most Enormous Bird of All" would have looked like next to a man and a trolley car.

SKELETON OF A PTERANODON IN THE MUSEUM OF YALE UNIVERSITY.

The following American Dragons were reported during the 1800s and 1900s:

The Chile Chimera

An early account emerged from Santiago, Chile in March of 1868, translated and printed in U.S. newspapers. After completing their day at the Garin mine, workers gathered for their evening meal and were stunned by the approach of "an

unknown creature of the air—the roc of the
'Thousand and One Nights' perhaps, or possibly a
Leviathan of the deserts." As it flew over their
heads, the miners witnessed a chimera that had
great wings covered in brown plumage; a

grasshopper-like head "with enormous eyes wide open and brilliant as stars, and covered with something like hair or bristles"; and a long, serpentine body covered with shiny scales that emitted metallic sounds as the strange animal flew. Some but not all of the miners perceived a detestable smell, like burning arsenic. While some of the men called it the devil, others recalled the passage of a similar animal over the mine years earlier.

The Sky Serpents of 1873

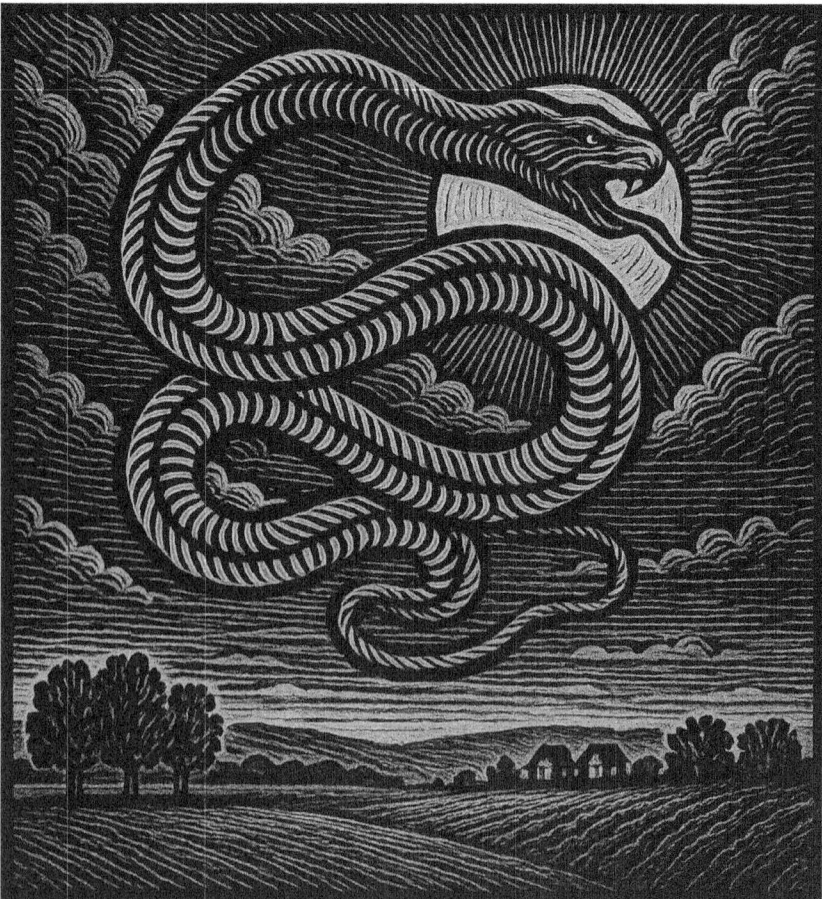

American Dragons

Sky serpents, perhaps ethereal in nature, were reported over Bonham, Texas and Fort Scott, Kansas in June 1873. Witnesses in Texas described something resembling an enormous serpent floating in a cloud, as large and as long as a telegraph pole, and of a yellow striped color. It moved without effort, coiling up, turning over and thrusting its head forward to strike, displaying the maneuvers of a genuine snake. In Kansas, the sky serpent encircled the rising sun and was visible for several moments.

A Flying Crocodile

Thomas Campbell and Joseph Howard, two woodchoppers, were plying their trade in the timber five miles northeast of Hurleton, California on March 10, 1882 when they were startled by the sound of "many wings flapping in the air." Not more than 40 feet above the treetops they saw what looked like a crocodile, 18 feet in length head-to-tail. It flew by means of six fluttering wings along the length of its body, each about 15 inches broad and shaped like a duck's foot. The creature had twelve legs. Howard fired his shotgun at the monster and the bullets bounced off as if striking sheet iron, leaving it uninjured.

The King Snake

In August 1885, farmer James Vincent, Sr. and several friends from nearby Fletcher, Illinois battled a gigantic air serpent that was attempting to devour Vincent's sheep. The massive winged snake worked in unison with three smaller snakes, each 18 to 20 feet in length. The trio snatched a lamb and slithered toward the larger snake, but released their hold when one of the men tossed a fence rail at them. The smaller snakes attacked the men and were repelled, but once again grabbed a lamb. This time they succeeded in depositing it in the hungry king snake's jaws. The men fired several shots at the large snake. It appeared stunned but unharmed, and the smaller snakes retreated into its mouth. The big snake than unfurled its wings and struggled to maneuver around the property's hedge fences before finally gaining enough height to fly away.

The Elizabeth Lake Monster

Elizabeth Lake in California was said to be inhabited by a foul monster whose presence was announced by volcanic rumbling and a penetrating odor arising from the seething, boiling water. In one account, the smell was described as "something between sewer gas and a German bakery." Its roar sounded like the muttering of distant thunder and could have "curdled the blood of a mummy." The slimy beast was about 30 feet long with skin of a warm, reddish color, a long snout and a crooked row of jagged, yellow fangs. It sported enormous bat wings, long hind legs and a barbed tail. A shaggy yellow mane hung over the monster's giant head and neck. Its emerald eyes, the size of dinner plates, gleamed like two horrid fires. A proboscis darted back and forth between the eyes. A prospector was nearly eaten by the beast on July 4, 1886, but he didn't agree with it, and the monster instead dined on three cows and a hog. Peter B. Simpson, an emigrant from Nevada, was camping on the upper end of the lake on July 15, 1886 when the monster gave him and his family a rude awakening. The beast lifted their wagon, carried it about 20 yards and dropped it onto the plain, wrecking the wheels and sending the cattle into a panic. The monster then attacked and bit clean through an antelope with its horrid jaws. Gun in hand, Simpson followed the beast and took a shot, but the bullet rebounded off its

The Elizabeth Lake Monster (Artist: Robert Jacob Woodard)

hide. Simpson later recovered a few round, semi-transparent scales about the size of dinner plates, reddish and glazed like ground glass. Carrying the freshly mutilated antelope in its fearsome mouth, the monster rose into the air and splashed down into the lake like a cannonball. Weeks after news broke of the Elizabeth Lake Monster, the Los Angeles Herald competitively claimed its own amphibious beast had taken up residence and was eating all the large fish in Reservoir No. 5 in East Los Angeles.

Major Horace Bell, a Los Angeles Ranger, soldier, lawyer and newspaperman, expanded the Lake Elizabeth Monster saga in his 1930 book, "On the Old West Coast: Being Further Reminisces of a Ranger." Bell wrote that the monster had been scaring away settlers from its valley since the 1830s, emerging from its muddy home to feast on any horses and cattle that unsuspecting ranchers brought its way. In 1886, a new resident named Don Felipe Rivera emptied his Colt .44 into the monster's side, the shots echoing like they had struck a great iron kettle. Rivera later found his flattened bullets. In this account, the monster was 44-feet long ("as large as four elephants") with a head like a bulldog, wings that sat flat on its back when at rest, and possibly six legs. Bell said that following several sightings between 1881 and 1886, the Elizabeth Lake Monster departed its watery home and flew eastward where it was eventually killed on the desert outside Tombstone, Arizona.

The Tombstone Thunderbird

The Tombstone Thunderbird (Artist: Ridwan)

On April 26, 1890, the Tombstone Weekly Epitaph published what has become the most infamous American Dragon story, titled "Found on the Desert." According to the article, two ranchers traveling on the desert between the Whetstone and Huachuca mountains encountered a winged monster resembling a huge alligator with an extremely elongated tail and an immense pair of wings. Evidently exhausted by a long flight, the creature only flew short distances at a time. The men pursued the animal for several miles on horseback, finally shooting it down with their Winchester rifles. The ranchers cautiously approached the dead monster, measuring its length at 92 feet and its wingspread at 160 feet. Its eyes, large as dinner plates, protruded halfway from its head. The beast's head was eight feet long and its jaws were lined with strong, sharp teeth. Its smooth skin and thick wings, composed of transparent membrane, were devoid of feathers or hair. The men sliced off a small portion of a wingtip to take back to Tombstone as proof of their kill. There, they gathered several prominent men to return and skin the creature, with plans to ship the hide back east for examination by eminent scientists of the day. In the summer 1970 edition of Old West magazine, reader Harry F. McClure insisted in a letter that during his youth in Lordsburg, New Mexico, he knew the ranchers who were involved in the incident outside nearby Tombstone. McClure said the flying monster's wingspan was closer to 20 or 30 feet in reality, and the cowboys had been too far out of range with their low-velocity rifles to kill it. The story also resurfaced in the May 1963 issue of Saga magazine, with the event shifted to 1886 and the dragon replaced by a smaller, yet still enormous, bird of prey with a 36-foot wingspan. This account added the detail that several men in Tombstone were photographed standing in front of the bird, which was suspended from a building for the shot. Decades later, countless people have memories of seeing this photograph, despite it never appearing in the Tombstone Epitaph and no one being able to produce a copy. The creature, whatever its form, has become known as the Tombstone Thunderbird.

The San Diego Dragon

In June 1890, a San Diego boy named Jimmie Dillar was playing on the hills of Balboa Park when he saw an enormous and monstrous half-bird, half-beast flying through the air with bat-like wings, a long bill and a tail twisted like a doughnut. Dillar ducked to the ground, the beast missing him as it flapped overhead and disappeared eastward at great speed. The boy ran home and announced, "Papa, I have just seen the devil!" Upon seeing an illustration of the Tombstone monster printed recently in the San Francisco Examiner, Dillar declared it looked just like the creature he had encountered. A San Diego man named "Mr. Marvin" witnessed a similar monster that very same day over Switzer Canyon near 28th Street and allegedly swore to it on a stack of Bibles.

American Dragons

The Fresno Dragons

A pair of pterodactyls (pair-odactyls?) who survived to the modern age were reported to inhabit the vast swampland around Tulare Lake outside of Selma and Fresno, California in the summer of 1891. Witnesses described them as resembling featherless birds, about six feet long with wingspans of at least 15 feet. Accounts conflicted on whether the creatures had long, wide bills or snouts like alligators, their teeth visible as they flew around and snapped their jaws. They emitted cries somewhat like swans. Their heads were broad and their eyes no less than four inches in diameter. The pterodactyls dined heartily on ducks, mud hens and farm chickens, biting their prey in two. While wading in the water, they looked not unlike gigantic frogs, their folded wings appearing like large knobs on their backs. The creatures left tracks in the mud that revealed their feet to resemble those of an alligator, but more circular in shape. Each foot had five toes and a large claw, with the tracks being 11 inches wide and 19 inches long. This news generated significant debate, with later articles insisting the story was a hoax, an exaggeration, or the misidentification of large, flightless, volatile birds (possibly the Southern Cassowary) imported from Australia by colonists in Sequoia National Park as defense against U.S. Cavalry troops trying to evict them.

The Fresno Dragons (Artist: Zettoart)

The Great White Dragon of Lake Chelan

The indigenous Chelan and Entiat people of Washington state told stories of a deadly dragon who resided in the upper waters of Lake Chelan, attacking any canoe that came near. It appeared again in 1895, with the report of a "great white dragon" that snatched a wader by the leg. The man's companions attempted to free him by dragging the monster's belly over a fire, but it broke free, flew up 200 feet and plunged back into the lake with its victim. The Lake Chelan Dragon

was described as having the legs and body of an alligator and the head and "restless eyes" of a serpent. There were large bat-like wings, ribbed and leathery, on its back and the beast had a scaly tail. The monster was mostly white aside from the under part of its throat and the tips of its wings, feet and tail. Its skin was as soft as velvet. The monster was seen again in 1905, as a 75-foot serpentine creature at the head of the lake. Following a tragic accident in which a school bus plunged into the icy lake in 1945, recovery divers encountered "a fish larger than any man."

The Salt Dragon

Remote Stansbury island in Utah's Great Salt Lake was said to harbor a horse-eating monster in 1903. The creature had a head like an alligator, nearly 15 feet long, with a wide mouth filled with immense, serrated teeth. Its large, round eyes burned with a bright red light. The beast flew via bat-like wings that spanned approximately 100 feet. Its body was between 50-65 feet long head-to-tail and was completely encrusted with salt that caused the dragon to glimmer like a rainbow in the sun.

Bullets had no effect on its armored hide. It had short forelegs and jumped using its hind legs and tail. The aquatic beast possessed a short, fish-like tail, moving quickly in the water and presumably feeding on shrimp. Its cry, half snort and half roar, inspired fear. It left five-toed footprints, like the imprint of a giant hand nearly four feet across the palm. Two hunters, Martin Gilbert and John Barry, tracked the monster to its lair, an immense

The Salt Lake Dragon, pictured in the July 31, 1903 Salt Lake Telegram.

cave near the head of a narrow gulch. Hiding behind boulders to observe the monster, Gilbert and Barry witnessed the creature fly off and return with a horse in its mouth, which it settled down to devour, crunching the equine's bones with each bite.

There might be a connection between the Salt Dragon and the Keith-O'Brien Co. department store in Salt Lake City. The first article about the creature in the Salt Lake Telegram ran alongside an advertisement for the department store's excursion to Provo Canyon and various products. The next day, the newspaper ran an illustration of the Salt Dragon branded with a Keith-O'Brien Co. logo.

The Van Meter Visitor

In the notorious case of the Van Meter Visitor, a winged monster straight out of a horror movie menaced the Iowa town in the fall of 1903. The visitor appeared "half human and half beast, with great bat-like wings," leaping from building to building. It disarmed panicked residents with its stupefying odor and a dazzling light it beamed from a blunt, hornlike protuberance in the middle of its forehead. One night, a Van Meter man saw the creature climb down a telephone pole using its beak like a parrot and then leap away like a kangaroo, finally soaring away on featherless wings. The monster left large, three-toed footprints in the soft earth. Finally, a posse of armed townspeople cornered the monster at an abandoned coal mine. It emerged with a smaller member of its species but both fled back down the shaft when bullets started flying. Residents of Van Meter were apparently incensed by the articles reporting this bizarre incident, which they said was simply an exaggerated account of disruptions caused by a nighttime robber or prankster shining a light in windows. However, Van Meter has now embraced the monster lore and today holds an annual festival in its honor.

OLCOTT BEHELD AN APPALLING MONSTER.

The Van Meter Visitor (had a very shiny nose...). Pictured in the Nov. 19, 1903 Eau Claire, Wisconsin Daily Telegram.

As the American frontier faded into history, the dragons inhabiting its most untamed regions appeared to go extinct. Like old maps that warned European sailors of the gnarling sea beasts lurking in unexplored realms, familiarity sapped away the magic our imaginations assigned to the U.S. unknown. Perhaps these dragons are just dormant in the primitive region of our brains, an instinctual relic protecting us from prehistoric predators. Lest you get too complacent the next time you're on a train speeding through the desert, keep your eyes and ears alert for the strange rippling of sand and the frantic fluttering of leathery wings!

SOURCES:

"An Aerial Monster." *San Diego Weekly Union*, 12 Jun. 1890, p. 8.

Bache, Rene. "Most Enormous Bird of All—Big as a Trolley." *San Francisco Examiner*, 27 May 1906, American Magazine section p. 9.

Bell, Major Horace. *On the Old West Coast: Being Further Reminiscences of a Ranger*, edited by Lanier Bartlett, Grosset & Dunlap, 1930.

Chorvinsky, Mark. "Cowboys & Dragons: Unravelling the Mystery of the Thunderbird Photograph." *Strange Magazine*, Fall 2000. http://www.strangemag.com/strangemag/s

trange21/thunderbird21/thunderbirdintro21.html. Accessed 10 Nov. 2024.

Clark, Ella E. *Indian Legends of the Pacific Northwest.* University of California Press, 1953.

"County Seat Gleanings." *Hanford Journal* [Hanford, Calif.], 11 Aug. 1891, pg. 3.

"Dos Palmas Spring." *Wikipedia*, https://en.wikipedia.org/wiki/Dos_Palmas_Spring. Accessed 10 Nov. 2024.

"A Flying Snake." *Los Angeles Times*, 18 Jan. 1882, p. 3.

"Found on the Desert." *Tombstone Epitaph* [Tombstone, AZ], 26 April, 1890, p. 3.

"A Fresno Mystery." *San Francisco Chronicle*, 3 Aug. 1891, p. 2.

"A Great White Dragon." *Spokane Review* [Spokane, Wash.], 14 Nov. 1892, p. 7.

Guhl, Kevin J. "The Fresno Dragons." *Thunderbird Photo*, 27 Jan. 2023, https://thunderbirdphoto.com/f/the-fresno-dragons. Accessed 13 Nov. 2024.

Guhl, Kevin J. "The Horse-Munching Monster of the Great Salt Lake." *Thunderbird Photo*, 3 Feb. 2024, https://thunderbirdphoto.com/f/the-horse-munching-monster-of-the-great-salt-lake. Accessed 13 Nov. 2024.

Hackenmiller, Tom. *Ladies of the Lake: Tales of Transportation, Tragedy, and Triumph on Lake Chelan.* Point Publishing, 1998.

Hackenmiller, Tom. *Wapato Heritage: The History of the Chelan and Entiat Indians.* Point Publishing, 1995.

"Herbert C. Hensley." *The Journal of San Diego History - San Diego Historical Society Quarterly,* vol. 3, no. 4, 1957. https://sandiegohistory.org/journal/1957/october/hensley/. Accessed 23 Sep. 2021.

"The History and Future of Dos Palmas." *UC Riverside Palm Desert Center,* 20 Jan. 2021, https://palmdesert.ucr.edu/calnatblog/2021/01/20/history-and-future-dos-palmas. Accessed 10 Nov. 2024.

"Holds the Belt." *Examiner* [San Francisco], 8 Jun. 1890, p. 13.

"A Holy Terror." *Los Angeles Sunday Times,* 1 Aug. 1886, p. 3.

Lewis, Chad, et al. *The Van Meter Visitor: A True and Mysterious Encounter with the Unknown.* On the Road Publications, 2013.

"Map Southern Pacific Rail Road and Connections. June 1875." *Stanford Digital Repository,* https://purl.stanford.edu/vc649jy1048. Accessed 10 Nov. 2024.

McClure, Harry F. Letter. *Old West*, Summer 1970, p. 2.

"Monster of Awful Form." *Daily Telegram* [Eau Claire, WI], 19 Nov. 1903, p. 6.

"A Monster of the Air." *Sacramento Daily Record-Union* [Sacramento, CA], 20 Mar. 1882, p. 1.

"A Monster of the Air—A Very Strange Story." *Evening Post* [Chicago], 15 May 1868, p. 2.

"Monster That Swims and Flies Is Sighted on Stansbury Island Shores." *Salt Lake Telegram* [Salt Lake City], 30 Jul. 1903, p. 2.

Pearl, Jack. "Monster Bird That Carries Off Human Beings!" *Saga*, May 1963, pp. 28–31, 83-85.

"Piasa." *Wikipedia*, https://en.wikipedia.org/wiki/Piasa. Accessed 10 Nov. 2024.

"Pteranodon." *Wikipedia*, https://en.wikipedia.org/wiki/Pteranodon. Accessed 10 Nov. 2024.

"Pterosaur: Pteranodon." *American Museum of Natural History*, 3 Apr. 2014, https://www.amnh.org/explore/news-blogs/on-exhibit-posts/thursday-s-pterosaur-pteranodon. Accessed 10 Nov. 2024.

San Jose Daily Mercury [San Jose, Calif.] , 13 Aug. 1891, pg. 4.

"A Sensation Spoiled." *Examiner* [San Francisco], 6 Aug. 1891, p. 2.

"Signs and Wonders: A Serpent in the Clouds." *Monitor* [Fort Scott, KS], 24 Jun. 1873, p. 4.

"Singular Phenomenon." *Monitor* [Fort Scott, KS], 27 Jun. 1873, p. 4.

"Singular Phenomenon." *North Texas Enterprise* [Bonham, TX], 14 Jun. 1873, p. 2.

Smith, Jeff. "I Just Saw a Frightful Monster." *San Diego Reader*, 28 Jul. 2010, https://www.sandiegoreader.com/news/2010/jul/28/feature-i-just-saw-frightful-monster/. Accessed 23 Sep. 2021.

"A Strange Story." *Ventura Free Press* [Ventura, CA], 23 Jul. 1886, p. 4.

"Van Meter, Iowa." *Wikipedia*, https://en.wikipedia.org/wiki/Van_Meter,_Iowa. Accessed 13 Nov. 2024.

"Water Dragons in Los Angeles." *Los Angeles Daily Herald*, 3 Sep. 1886, p. 5.

"A Winged Monster." *Weekly Leader* [Bloomington, IL], 6 Aug. 1885, p. 3.

Phantom Automobiles

Not long after the automobile appeared on American roads, ghostly motorists and spectral roadsters began stalking its moonlit highways and byways.

Phantom Automobile (Artist: Bat Sada)

While the automobile was developed in Europe during the late 1800s, Americans took the steering wheel and dominated the industry throughout the first half of the 20th century. Per History.com, 30 American car manufacturers operated in 1899, with nearly 500 companies emerging over the next decade. Henry Ford debuted the seminal Model T in 1908 and started mass production in 1910, granting Americans an affordable form of freedom to speed down the young nation's wide, open roads. But... they couldn't travel fast enough to escape the latent fears and folklore surrounding this new technology that had altered life so rapidly.

The early years of the automobile in America generated strange reports of phantom vehicles haunting darkened, night-time roads throughout the country. It's hard to imagine today what it must have been like when the car was new. Isolated and tight-knit communities, accustomed to the slower pace of horse-and-carriage travel and the scheduled passage of trains, were suddenly more accessible, the world shrinking in direct correlation to the max line on the speedometer. Strange intruders tore down country streets, elusive and anonymous. Criminals embraced the automobile, enabling them to strike fast and vanish into the night. The anxiety amongst the populace was palpable within historic reports from the turn of the century. And this fear accelerated into the fantastical realm. Soon after the invention of the automobile, ghost stories about these ground-shaking machines began to materialize.

1908 Buick Model 10. Photo by Greg Gjerdingen from Willmar, USA, CC BY 2.0, via Wikimedia Commons.

The more earthly, yet more dangerous, type of phantom automobile was the mysterious transportation that allowed strangers and lawbreakers to appear and quickly disappear like specters along the throughways of unsuspecting towns. Consider these troubling incidents from the dawn of the automotive age:

- A white automobile, thought to be a Buick No. 10, caused a commotion in the vicinities of St. Paul, Wolbach and Cushing, Nebraska one night in July 1909. The mysterious car, carrying two men, tore over the tops of hills and through canyons, with one farmer witnessing the men stop the car and run into his corncrib. He was too afraid to confront them.

- Another ghostly white automobile which traveled "on the wings of the wind" was spotted throughout West Springfield, Massachusetts every night at midnight during a week in May 1911. "It is difficult to estimate the motive power that would admit of so great speed," wrote the Springfield Daily News. Multiple witnesses described the car as being pure white and of unusual length. The headlights were feeble, and all some residents saw was a flash of white as it whirred past. Townspeople suspected that the driver was local and attempting to create a sensation. West Springfield is minutes from Springfield, Massachusetts, where Charles and Frank Duryea built the first gasoline-powered car in the United States and road-tested it on Sept. 20, 1893. Springfield would be home to several independent automobile manufacturers throughout the early 1900s.

- A "Blind Tiger Man" in a mysterious automobile tore through Alabama in January 1914, making midnight trips between Gadsden, Alabama City, Attalla and

Birmingham. So-called "Blind Tiger" operations emerged following the U.S. federal government's passage of the 1913 Webb-Kenyon Act, which regulated the transport of alcoholic beverages across state lines to protect states that had enacted Prohibition. Unable to legally procure liquor within Alabama or legally import it from outside, Blind Tigers would illegally drive it in late at night like prototypical Dukes of Hazzard. Revenue officers were soon on their tail. After National Prohibition was enacted in 1920, one newspaper report noted that rum-runners traveled in the form of "phantom ships" by sea and "phantom automobiles" on land.

- Bandits in a big blue touring car, running without lights or a license plate, invaded South Minneapolis on the night of Jan. 15, 1914. They mugged John A. Hedine, a railroad man who was walking home near the old circus grounds at 25th Street and Hiawatha Avenue. A masked thug relieved Hedine of $46 and his watch at gunpoint before racing away in the phantom car.

- Police in San Pedro, California launched a manhunt on Jan. 22, 1918, with orders to shoot to kill two bands of highwaymen who were terrorizing the area in a gray "phantom automobile" and a black "death car." The villains cruised around in their high-powered machines, leaving a trail of robbery and murder in their wake. The two groups committed five hold-ups, shooting and killing one victim in the back and badly wounding a pedestrian. Police assembled every available rifle, sawed-off shotgun, revolver and cop car, intent on bringing in the robbers "dead or alive." One vacation was to be awarded to officers for every outlaw taken.

Police officers standing alongside a wrecked car and cases of moonshine liquor, Nov. 16, 1922. Courtesy of the Prints and Photographs Division, Library of Congress, Washington, D. C.

Phantom Automobiles

- The Gray Ghost, "a weird phantom of the motor world," glided swiftly along roads in the Los Angeles vicinity in April 1919. The driver dressed in a gray outfit with gray cap and mask, appearing confident that no one could catch them. The car, previously reported in Detroit, was long and gray, displaying great horsepower and speed with a loud boom from its exhaust. The "gray apparition of the road" alerted fellow motorists as it passed with "a low, weird whine, sometimes varied by a piercingly shrill shriek of 'sireno' quality."

- At the close of 1920, authorities were after a well-organized gang of firebugs they believed had set more than 40 structures ablaze over the past few months in Fayette, Washington and Westmoreland counties in Pennsylvania. The arsonists had ignited raging fires at schools, farmhouses, barns, garages and mine shacks. The damage was estimated at three-quarter of a million dollars. Police were making every effort to run down a "phantom" automobile which was seen near many of the largest fires soon after the conflagrations were discovered. "For a time, it was believed that this automobile was myth—a figment of imagination—but when several persons of probity and absolute reliability agreed on the description of the car, the county officials awakened and gave heed," the press reported. Some residents spotted the mysterious automobile on lonely highways at early hours, standing by the roadside with its lights turned off. Others saw it running at breakneck speed immediately following a big blaze, blaring red and green lights. No one could discern a license number, if it had one. After an intense search, state police arrested Albert Smith, 19, the son of a wealthy real estate investor in Fairhope. Smith said that while he set a few of the fires out of personal and family grudges, in most cases "something" told him to do it and he was fueled by his "intense desire to witness flames." Until his arrest, he had never considered the havoc he wrought nor the lives he endangered. Smith denied he was the mastermind directing a group of arsonists, and confirmed that no one (tangible) had helped or ordered him to do it. Smith pled guilty to 13 charges of arson; although responsible for more, he said some of the fires set between late October and Christmas of 1920 were not his handiwork. On Jan. 29, 1921, Smith was sentenced to 42-85 years at Western Penitentiary in Pittsburgh. In 1925, Smith failed in his latest attempt to burn down Western Penitentiary and a judge ruled him insane, sending him to the Hospital for the Criminal

Insane at Fairview. There were indeed fellow or copycat firebugs who continued to burn

ALBERT SMITH

Pennsylvania "Firebug" Albert Smith.

buildings in the Uniontown and Fayette County area after Smith's incarceration. And his influence spread further. Fannie Young, a 12-year-old girl from Fruitville, Pennsylvania, set fire to her foster parents' barn in spring 1926 and then bound and gagged herself, claiming a "wild man" was responsible. This set off mass hysteria for a few weeks with neighbors fearing a "mad monster" was on the loose, attacking children and burning barns. When Young confessed, she admitted she had been inspired by a magazine article about Smith and decided to try arson herself.

Yet there seemed to be just as many phantom automobiles of the second type, the spectral fiend that blended old world spirts with new age innovation. As you will see in the following accounts, ghosts were quick to adapt to the latest technology:

Pittsburgh's Phantom Motorist

In 1905, a phantom motorist flitted about the east end of Pittsburgh at breakneck speeds, hovering around Homewood Cemetery and the dark boulevards of Schenley Park. Policemen patrolling the park told strange tales of a muffled woman in a white touring car who raced through the Bigelow monument every dark night, sending her machine half over the cliffs. Superstitious drivers began carrying rabbits' feet while other motorists gathered to tour the park at midnight in search of the strange apparition.

A road through Schenley Park, 1890s.

Howard Lake Hotrod

In March 1910, a phantom automobile was seen by several supposedly reliable witnesses in the vicinity of Howard Lake in Wright County, Minnesota. The ghostly speedster appeared at the dead of midnight, flying along the public highway at the rate of a mile a minute. It would then vanish into thin air in the center of the roadway.

Devil's Bend

The Pittsburgh Gazette Times reported this hellish story on Jul. 13, 1911: "Washington Irving's Headless Horseman and Wagner's Flying Dutchman had better look to their laurels, or that

Phantom Automobile on the Millvale Road will wrest them away. It is a weird and terrifying tale. Midnight's solemn hour had sounded, and several members of the Society for Psychical Research were returning from a political séance. At Death Dip on the Devil's Bend they encountered the uncanny machine, the lamps of which diffused ghastly white light, while the siren tooted marrow-freezing blasts. A sickening odor of paint on hot metal permeated the air—perhaps it was really brimstone which is thus unscientifically described. Then came the terrifying climax of it all. The motor-car was seen to be occupied by two skeletons, one of which calmly lit a cigarette as the automobile skidded over the embankment, crashed against an oak tree, and disappeared in a flash of flame. The cigarette was found later, but no trace of the motor-car or its infernal occupants. Let not the scoffer set up a facile hypothesis based upon the percentage of breweries in the burg of Millvale."

On-and-Off-Road Phantom

In June 1914, residents of Madison Township, Indiana, near Petersburg, were scared to go out on the highways after nightfall following the sighting of a phantom automobile by half a dozen people in the vicinity of the Barker school. Doug Barker, while sitting in front of his house one night the previous week, saw headlights approaching and stepped out to the road to see who was driving. At a distance of 200 feet, the car suddenly turned into a wooded pasture that was separated from the road by a wire fence, and picked its way through the trees until lost to view. The next week, a little daughter of Joe Barker and their neighbor's daughter were walking along the road when they saw the big lights of an automobile coming toward them. They stepped out of the street to let the car pass, but it abruptly swerved and disappeared into a neighboring field. Jeff Gladish, a neighboring farmer, had a similar experience. On another night, Mrs. Joe Barker was standing in her backyard when she saw the headlights coming over a hill in a neighboring field. Frightened, she ran and told her husband that someone was out driving a car around their property. By the time Joe Barker arrived to look, the mystery car had vanished.

Death Strip

"Death Strip," a 10-mile stretch of road between Twinsburg and Stow Corners in Cleveland, was supposedly haunted nightly by the ghost of Carl Brown, a former test car driver for the B. F. Goodrich Rubber Company in Akron. Brown was killed the previous summer on the Hudson-Twinsburg pike when his car skidded and overturned. There had been so many accidents on the highway since it was paved with brick in 1911 that the span had acquired its notorious nickname. "One life has been sacrificed for every mile of paving," lamented the Akron Times in 1915. Fellow Goodrich test car drivers Gus Anderson and Harry Apple were traveling the same highway one night early in March 1915 when they stopped to get a drink of water and saw the ghost of their old colleague sitting on the edge of the trough. On March 9, Harry Sargeant, a mechanic at the Hudson garage, encountered the spectral chauffer midway between Hudson and Twinsburg. Sargeant heard an auto approaching him at a tremendous rate of speed and swerved his car to the side of the road to avoid a collision. The speeder slowed down as he passed, looking at Sargeant. The mechanic nearly fell out of his seat: the driver was a dead ringer for Brown. They did not exchange greetings. All three witnesses knew Brown well and were positive that his ghost was haunting the pike, breaking all known human speed laws.

Ghostina

A haunted car shattered the nerves of garage employees across Geneva, New York in the steamy August of 1917. Before arriving in the city, the car was supposedly involved in the murder of a young woman in Rochester. Her killer, a prominent young man, was sentenced to 18 years in prison. A Clifton Springs resident acquired the car, which began exhibiting inexplicable behavior, and then sold it to a new owner. Once in Geneva, the big, brown automobile was passed between several garages, as no employee would stay there with it a second night. Multiple garage workers attested that at exactly 2 a.m., the car began to move of its own volition. It didn't leave its parking space, but the fenders waved and the car quivered as though traveling at a high rate of speed. The figure of a big man wearing a heavy overcoat appeared and sat in the driver's seat, along with a vapory white form beside him. They only remained a second before vanishing, the car jolting to a stop. Scotty Cummings, who drove the car from Rochester to Geneva, admitted that during the trip he noticed the form of a woman sitting next to him several times, starting at 2 a.m. Ultimately, the haunted car was moved to a storehouse, the Geneva Auto Company annex on North Main Street (formerly the Burgess Tabernacle). One employee, Hans Hansen, quit his job when ordered to stay overnight in the annex and wash cars. Hundreds of curiosity seekers showed up to observe the spectral manifestations. Although the ghosts did not appear every night, many holding vigil were not disappointed. On some nights, the apparitions performed their brief show at 2 a.m. sharp. The levers in the car began to move, the throttle quivered, and the car jerked as if in rapid motion. One car expert noted that the vibration of the car indicated it was "traveling" at 55 or 60 miles per hour. On one night, the car trembled and all present heard a swishing sound. The automobile then shot out from its position about 20 feet, causing one witness, Mrs. William Scott, to collapse in a dead faint.

THE "HAUNTED CAR."
"Scotty" Cummings and two children are shown in the machine where chauffeur first saw shadowy forms in drive from Rochester.

Ghostina the Haunted Car, driven by Scotty Cummings.

Undeterred by the spooky antics, a Rochester firm expressed interest in purchasing the vehicle for its car collection. Soon after, the car was named Ghostina. Crowds continued to visit the annex at all hours of the day and night to visit the now infamous car, at one point requiring police to disperse them at 4 a.m.

Ultimately, skeptical investigators discovered that Ghostina was the work of "some genius skilled in the art of mischief." She lacked a starter, and an electrical wire ran from the car to the ground. There was a hole in the garage wall through which a prankster could prod the car with a pipe, causing it to wriggle. Because the car "looked as if it had traveled every road in Uncle Sam's wide country," the squeaks and groans were attributed to its rusty parts rubbing together when jostled. One team of debunkers was about to lift Ghostina's hood and cushions when a large cop told them to vamoose or risk arrest. By this point, Ghostina enjoyed her own police protection! Despite the insightful myth-busting, the vaporous forms of the driver and his female passenger, witnessed by many, were beyond the comprehension of the sleuths.

The Phantom "Hearse"

In 1920, the highways adjacent to Los Angeles were haunted by a ghost automobile that had "Kipling's phantom rickshaw absolutely trundled back to the stables." The gasoline-driven ghost never appeared until an unfortunate motorist was killed on the highway. Then it was observed to glide to the spot where the victim laid, and would bear the corpse away at high speed.

Sacramento Valley Highway Haunts

Since about 1923, an eerie automotive phenomenon was seen by many prominent residents of Yuba City and Sutter County in California, in the vicinity of the "Death Curve" at

Lomo, so named for its high number of fatal car crashes. Multiple independent witnesses described seeing a large touring car carrying four men that appeared at dusk and vanished suddenly.

Henry Hook, clerk at the Yuba City post office, was traveling along the highway north of Live Oak when he saw the phantom touring car barreling directly toward him through a cloud of dust. Just as a collision seemed unavoidable, the oncoming car vanished. Hook said that the ghost car appeared suspended a few feet above the roadway, a detail others had reported. Additional witnesses saw the specter near Sunset, just south of Live Oak, and at Berg Station.

Bob Hill, a rancher from Arbuckle, California, claimed to have twice seen a phantom automobile on the state highway below Hershey. He encountered the car the second time on the night of June 24, 1928 while driving home from Sacramento. According to Hill, the automobile had materialized suddenly in his path. Just as he started to slam on the brakes to avoid a collision, the spectral vehicle blinked back out of existence.

Hill penned the following evocative account describing the unsettling apparition encountered by himself and other motorists: "A lonely highway at midnight. To your right a cluster of trees, their branches trembling in wraithlike silhouettes from the wind's soft caresses. To the left a barren, desolate moor, dotted at fitful intervals with the tiny lights of jack-o'-lanterns. You are sitting behind the steering wheel of your car, driving along at a fair clip. Suddenly, and with no vestige of prior warning, there arises from the highway before you the outline of another automobile. It is on your side of the roadway, heading squarely toward you, and a scant 100 feet away. From its radiator and sides it gives forth a soft, strange iridescent light, as though it had been coated with phosphorus, like the famous hound of the Baskervilles. You jam down your brakes and reach for the emergency. With a grinding shriek of protest your car starts to jolt to a stop. But it is too late... A fleeting moment of praying or cussing, and each time the unwilling spectators have all but wrecked their machines and risked their lives in their frantic efforts to avoid a head-on collision with it. But it doesn't. You're stopped, all right, and possibly have skidded half way into the ditch. And maybe you're wondering whether your soul has passed on to its destiny, or whether you're still mortal in this mundane scheme of things. But—There is no other automobile present, or anywhere near you! You've met California's 'phantom automobile'—and it's an experience you'll never forget."

Two nights later, several Arbuckle residents traveled out to the spot in hopes of seeing the ghost car for themselves.

Several phantom automobiles were reported throughout the Sacramento Valley in 1928, with encounters in Colusa, Yuba and Sutter counties. A group of Sutter County youths barely avoided the terrifying specter of the highways, leaving them badly shaken. Later, a Yuba County truck driver sprained a rear axle in dodging a crash with the phantom auto.

The Ghostly Crunch of Gravel

Phantom automobiles weren't exclusive to the early 20th century. In 2004, Sue and Gene Sereno described a ghostly automobile that haunted the 100-yard driveway of their home in Lynchburg, Virginia. It was one of several spooks that inhabited their property, which the Lynchburg News and Advance called "a little patch of urban wilderness." Sue said most of the paranormal activity there was benign, but she found the phantom automobile a bit creepy. For a long time, they rationalized that the invisible car they sometimes heard coming down the driveway was just an echo from the main street. Then the Serenos realized that they were hearing the car's tires crunching gravel, but their driveway and the road were paved. Once, while standing outside waiting for their son to arrive, the couple spotted headlights floating down the driveway. They thought it was their son's car until realizing he had yet to arrive and the phantom lights weren't reflecting on anything the way headlights normally would. The Serenos researched the property's 13 previous owners in city deed records but could find no obvious historical incidents to account for the hauntings. The one exception was the ghostly hoof beats they would hear along the path on which a former resident regularly rode a horse from the farmhouse to the barn.

Faux Phantoms

There is a third type of phantom automobile, one that played on the eeriness of the haunted variety but ended up having a rational, sometimes amusing explanation:

- A "ghost car" that sped through the streets of Tulare, California on July 27, 1925, apparently driverless and uncontrolled, was stopped by a motorcycle cop on the outskirts of the city and its true nature revealed. In the rear of the automobile, piloting it by means of a rope attached to the steering wheel, were two Tulare youths. "They were turned over to their parents to be spanked," it was reported. History repeated itself on Sep. 1, 1948 when five-year-old Daniel Elliott took his 3-year-old girlfriend, Anna Danahy, for a ride in a sedan. The boy turned a switch and stood to peer over the instrument panel while driving, but to spectators it looked like an unoccupied vehicle was driving down the street. The car traveled 350 yards, negotiating two corners in a congested area before hitting a parked trailer and coming to rest just an inch from a gas pump. Anna suffered injuries in the crack-up, but Danny was unscathed. The neighbor who owned the car estimated $300 in damages. The police opined that Danny had a spanking coming to him.

- In July 1955, a "haunted" car on a used auto lot in Schuylkill Haven, Pennsylvania burst into flames, sounded its horn, then slipped into gear and "obligingly moved under its own power away from other cars" for 25 feet before stopping. After extinguishing the blaze, which totally destroyed the car, the fire department revealed that a short circuit had somehow started the engine, put the car in gear and blew the horn, which alerted a bystander to the fire.

- Robert L. Mack of New York City, a former U.S. Navy radio technician, toured California in 1927 and 1928, demonstrating his driverless "phantom automobile." He operated the vehicle by radio control from a separate car. A similar "driverless" remote-control car was demonstrated on California streets in 1934.

Phantom Carriages

A still from the 1921 Swedish silent film "The Phantom Carriage," directed by and starring Victor Sjöström.

The phantom automobile didn't materialize from nothing. In fact, it promptly supplanted an older but thematically similar tradition in English folklore, the phantom carriage. This was a common motif in folk tales from the 19th century and earlier. Typically, the ghost of a deceased landowner or aristocrat rode over the countryside at night in a spectral black carriage, according to "A Dictionary of English Folklore." The horses pulling the carriage could be headless, fire-breathing, luminous or otherwise monstrous. During the Christmas season of 1835, residents of Kelso, Scotland were alarmed by the sounds of a phantom coach that perambulated streets at the witching hour, its horses galloping faster than the swiftest locomotive. An 1882 overview of haunted houses in Washington, D.C. included an old residence on New Jersey Ave., several blocks south of Carroll Manor. Both the house's occupants and neighbors often witnessed "a phantom coach, of the old style, surmounted by a vapory-looking coachman, who drove a pair of ghostly steeds with flashing nostrils and beacon eyes." The specter "drove up to the carriage stone on certain midnights and waited until an ancient-looking pair had entered the house and returned after a few minutes' stay, to be whirled back to spirit-land." A farmhouse in Saunders County, Nebraska, 16 miles north of Lincoln, was afflicted with rampant ghostly activity in 1907, including the spectral galloping of horse hooves along the nearby lane and the apparitions of carriages occupied by dim figures.

Legends can evolve over time to fit the advancements of the era. Folklorist Trevor J. Blank said in a 2014 Library of Congress interview that folklore is adaptive. Humans, as communicative beings, tailor our stories to benefit a particular context and communicate the information effectively.

But what if these tales of supernatural automobiles and carriages aren't just folklore, but represent a real anomalous phenomenon? In his

Phantom Automobiles

1969 book "Passport to Magonia," renowned scientist Jacques Vallée drew a comparison between UFO accounts of modern times and similar tales of mysterious aerial visitors from other realms, like elves and angels, told in ages past. Vallée wrote that one imaginative explanation for this correlation could be that there exists a natural phenomenon or superior intelligence which manifests itself in ways that "border on both the physical and the mental." This entity draws on the human mind to take on forms that "keep pace with human technology" and implements symbolism relatable to the viewer. Perhaps the same old "ghosts" have been wandering America's pathways for generations and simply couldn't resist the high-speed, technical marvels of the automobile!

We've had cars in our lives for nearly 150 years, long enough to take them for granted. For all the joy and convenience offered, though, automobiles can also be terrifying. En masse, we hurry down roads at unsafe speeds as we conduct our daily minutiae, always one split-second mishap from the smashing of steel and churning mortal peril. The 20th century was marked by unprecedented leaps in innovation, the first airplane flight and the first spaceflight separated by only 58 years. But do humans as living organisms really evolve that quickly? We outpace ourselves with inventions, rapidly creating technology that exceeds our ability to safely control it. Such was the case with the automobile, which raced onto the scene, altering the entire American landscape in fundamental ways that our ancestors might not have anticipated. One aspect of humanity the automobile couldn't outrun was our fanciful tendency to create greater meaning and codify our fears. Americans did this by overlaying the ghosts and legends of old onto the freshly debuted "horseless carriage," creating a brand-new phantom menace.

(Yes, Star Wars fans, I went there.)

SOURCES:

"400 Persons Visit Garage and Ghostina Cuts Capers." *Rochester Democrat and Chronicle* [Rochester, NY], 15 Aug. 1917, p. 5.

"Albert Smith, Firebug, Held to Be Insane." *Daily Courier* [Connellsville, PA], 13 Aug. 1925, p. 1.

"Arbuckle Man Says He Saw Phantom Car Twice." *Colusa Daily Sun* [Colusa, CA], 29 Jun. 1928, p. 1.

"Arrest of Firebug Fails to End Fires." *Bedford Gazette* [Bedford, PA], 31 Dec. 1920, p. 1.

"Auto-Ghost Is New Sensation." *Springfield Daily News* [Springfield, MA], 18 May, 1911, p. 2.

"Automobile History." *History*, 21 Aug. 2018, https://www.history.com/topics/inventions/automobiles. Accessed 30 Oct. 2024.

"Automotive Industry in Massachusetts." *Wikipedia*, https://en.wikipedia.org/wiki/Automotive_industry_in_Massachusetts. Accessed 26 Oct. 2024.

"Barn and 2 Homes Burned in Fayette County by Firebug." *Lancaster Intelligencer* [Lancaster, PA], 20 Dec. 1920, pp. 1-2.

"Blind Tiger Men Use Phantom Automobile." *Hearst's Sunday American* [Atlanta], 1 Feb. 1914, p. 3D.

"Bloodhounds Trail Firebugs." *Daily Republican* [Monongahela, PA], 21 Dec. 1920, pp. 1, 3.

"Confession of Incendiarism Startling One." *Punxsutawney Spirit* [Punxsutawney, PA], 2 Feb. 1921, pp. 1-2.

"Couldn't Get a Thrill Out of Haunted Motor Car." *Rochester Democrat and Chronicle* [Rochester, NY], 16 Aug. 1917, p. 16.

"Driverless Car Is Piloted Through Streets of City." *Santa Rosa Republican* [Santa Rosa, CA], 21 Jun. 1934, p. 8.

"Faints When Haunted Car Goes into Weird Action." *Rochester Democrat and Chronicle* [Rochester, NY], 13 Aug. 1917, p. 3.

Fernandez, Julia. "Understanding Folk Culture in the Digital Age: An interview with Folklorist Trevor J. Blank, Pt. 1." *Library of Congress Blogs*, 30 Jun. 2014, https://blogs.loc.gov/thesignal/2014/06/understanding-folk-culture-in-the-digital-age-an-interview-with-folklorist-trevor-j-blank-pt-1/. Accessed 31 Oct. 2024.

"Fifty Geneva Brave Ones Watch the 'Haunted' Car." *Rochester Democrat and Chronicle* [Rochester, NY], 7 Aug. 1917, p. 5.

"Firebug Still Active; Another Man Victim." *Daily Republican* [Monongahela, PA], 7 Nov. 1921, p. 1.

"Firebug, Trying to Burn Hotel, Is Gun Target." *Pittsburgh Press*, 29 Dec. 1920, p. 10.

"Get Bandits Dead or Alive Orders Butler." *San Pedro Daily Pilot* [San Pedro, CA], 22 Jan. 1918, p. 3.

"'Ghost Car' Case Solved: 5-Year-Old Boy Takes Girl Friend for Ride in Auto." *Long Beach (Calif.) Press-Telegram*, 2 Sep. 1948, p. B-8.

"Ghost Car Drivers Properly Spanked." *Ventura Free Press* [Ventura, CA], 27 Jul. 1925, p. 4.

"'Ghostina'" Enjoys Police Protection." *Rochester Democrat and Chronicle* [Rochester, NY], 18 Aug. 1917, p. 11.

"Ghost Locks Doors in Lincoln, Neb." *Portland Sunday Telegram* [Portland, ME], 6 Jan. 1907, p. 2.

"Girl, 12, Admits She is 'Wild Man' of Terror Region." *Harrisburg Telegraph* [Harrisburg, PA], 6 May 1926, p. 1.

"Girl Firebug Gets Inspiration from This County." *Morning Herald* [Uniontown, PA], 7 May 1926, p. 9.

"Gray Ghost Motor Car Mystifies Southland." *Los Angeles Evening Express*, 5 Apr. 1919, p. 1.

"'Haunted' Car Drives Away.'" *Journal and Courier* [Lafayette, IN], 14 Jul. 1955, p. 25.

"Haunted Car Now Named 'Ghostina.'" *Rochester Democrat and Chronicle* [Rochester, NY], 14 Aug. 1917, p. 3.

"A 'Haunted Car' Shatters Nerves of Geneva Garages." *Democrat Chronicle* [Rochester, NY], 6 Aug. 1917, p. 9.

"Haunted Houses." *Atlanta Constitution*, 23 Jul. 1882, p. 5.

James, Henry. "Comment on the Day's News." *Pasadena Evening Post* [Pasadena, CA], 13 Nov. 1920, p. 4.

Laurant, Darrell, "Local Woman Loves Halloween but Her Ghosts Don't." *News and Advance, Lifestyle section* [Lynchburg, VA], 31 Oct. 2004, pp. D1, D8.

"Manipulator of Driverless Auto Arrives." *Los Angeles Times*, 22 Aug. 1927, p. 17.

"Mysterious Automobile Has Been Seen." *Vincennes Sun* [Vincennes, IN], 12 Jun. 1914, p. 1.

"Neighborhood News the County Over." *Central City Record* [Central City, NE], 22 Jul. 1909, p. 8.

"Once Again Hudson Man Sees Ghost." *Akron Times* [Akron, OH], 10 Mar. 1915, p. 1.

"Phantom Auto Again Reported at Lomo Curve." *Marysville Appeal* [Marysville, CA], 11 Jul. 1926, pp. 1, 8.

"Phantom Auto Creates Stir on Tri-County Road." *Bulletin* [San Francisco], 3 Jul. 1928, p. 2.

"'Phantom Car' Is Seen Again." *Colusa Herald* [Colusa, CA], 30 Jun. 1928, p. 2.

"Phantom Cars and Planes." *Pomona Progress Bulletin* [Pomona, CA], 16 Feb. 1928, p. 4.

"The Phantom Coach." *Welshman* [Carmarthen, Wales], 25 Dec. 1835, p. 4.

"Phantom Motorist." *Motor Age* [Chicago], Vol. 3, No. 22, 30 Nov. 1905, p. 24.

Phantom Automobiles

"Pipe Supplies Mysterious Power to Haunted Auto." *Democrat Chronicle* [Rochester, NY], 17 Aug. 1917, p. 19.

Princeton Union [Princeton, MN], 3 Mar, 1910, p. 4.

"Radio Car Is to Be Seen in Action." *Whittier News* [Whittier, CA], 29 Aug. 1927, p. 1.

"Real Firebug Is Thought Captured." *Daily Republican* [Monongahela, PA], 27 Dec. 1920, p. 1.

"Rum-Running at Sea." *Bristol Herald Courier* [Bristol, VA-TN], 4 Aug. 1921, p. 4.

"Satan as Chauffeur." *Pittsburgh Gazette Times*, 13 Jul. 1911, p. 4.

Simpson, Charles A., and Jacqueline, and Steve Roud, editors. *A Dictionary of English Folklore.* Oxford University Press, 2003.

"Think They Have Seen Ghost on 'Death Strip'." *Mansfield News* [Mansfield, OH], 25 Mar. 1915, p. 1.

"Thugs Raid in Phantom Car." *Minneapolis Morning Tribune*, 16 Jan. 1914, p. 1.

"Two Claim They Set Schoolhouse Fire." *Evening Sun* [Baltimore], 29 Dec. 1920, p. 1.

"Undertaker Sees Geneva Car Spooks." *Democrat Chronicle* [Rochester, NY], 8 Aug. 1917, p. 3.

Vallée, Jacques. *Passport to Magonia: From Folklore to Flying Saucers*. Daily Grail Publishing, 2014.

"Webb-Kenyon Act." *Wikipedia*, https://en.wikipedia.org/wiki/Webb%E2%80%93Kenyon_Act. Accessed 25 Oct. 2024.

"Wish to Own 'Haunted Car.'" *Rochester Democrat and Chronicle* [Rochester, NY], 7 Aug. 1917, p. 14.

The Flaming Hand of Doom Falls to Earth

A cursed meteorite in the shape of a petrified alien hand became a star attraction on the Atlantic City Boardwalk and a tragic omen for the family that discovered it.

February 1916—Henry Prantl, his wife and children sat forlornly on their farmhouse's porch, numb to the lateness of the hour or the chill of the winter air. Exactly one month earlier, Rudolph, the youngest son, had perished in a battle with pneumonia. Gottlieba, his mother, couldn't reconcile how this fate befell her rugged 18-year-old, who stood six-feet-two, weighted 182 pounds and had never been sick a day in his life. Rudolph had been dealt a one-two punch of illness, first suffering a severe bout of influenza, then often called the grippe. He regained his health enough to feel confident embarking on an adventure into the frigid woods, an ill-advised decision which resulted in a deadly fever and lung infection. Despite these events, Rudolph's mother believed the fatal blow had been an excess of morphine administered by the attending nurse. The once strapping lad now laid in the little Methodist churchyard on Zion Road, his grave marked with bricks and bottles containing flowers. The family hoped to place a monument once they had the money. Clara, 16 and the youngest child, had been running a harrow through the fields to try and fill Rudolph's absence on their Bargaintown, New Jersey farm.

The family was shaken from their grief at 10 p.m. by a loud boom and a great white light that shot across the nighttime sky. A fiery projectile crashed down onto the farm, landing on the very spot where Rudolph had worked most of his days, and less than 100 feet from the room where he died.

John, 22 and the oldest son, rushed over to the fallen object and was shocked to discover what he described as a hand, a writhing piece of "mystic material" which lay on the ground burning off at the wrist. John attempted to pick it up, but scalded himself as the hand was sizzling hot. Squinting at the smoldering, glowing appendage, John could see the imprint of its fingernails and imagine the smell of its burning flesh. The family waited hours for the hand to cool and then carried the strange arrival into the house for further examination.

The "Flaming Hand," as it became known, was evidently a meteorite but of a composition that no one initially studying it recognized. It was light in weight, had no smell, and resembled the right hand of a human being grasping something in anguish. The thumb and little finger were unusually long. Nails indeed showed on some of the fingers. The first, middle and ring fingers were drawn closely together as though in pain, and curved slightly inwards. The wrist was abnormally small. It was burnt off with blackened, charred edges that, with a stretch of the imagination, might be called scorched bones.

In the coming days, hundreds of visitors filed into the Prantl residence in Egg Harbor Township to lay eye on the Hand of Flame. Work on the farm had to go on, but the family found themselves lagging behind as they continually granted requests to see the hand and describe how it fell. While scientists evaluated its mineral properties, a murmur arose among neighbors that the meteorite was much more, an omen or a message from the deceased Rudolph. Some thought the meteorite was a plea for help from the boy, while others imagined it to be a "hand of vengeance." Mrs. Prantl was among those who discerned a missive from beyond.

"I know it never was intended he should die yet," the mother told a reporter between sobs. Since the funeral, she had visited Rudolph's grave every day and praised her son for all he had been in his short life. Gottlieba took the gruesome thing from the stars in her hands and looked it over lovingly. "There's some who say Rudolph has not reached the other side yet. They do say as this hand may be a message from him," said Gottlieba, who was noted in the press as being prone to superstition. "This 'hand' had a peculiar meaning to me," she explained. As time went on, Mrs. Prantl would come to believe it was a different kind of message from her son, one that pointed a seared, accusing finger at the medical practitioners she believed had failed him. Clara offered a more optimistic interpretation, hinting that the meteorite was a sign that her brother wanted to help, or give a helping "hand," to those he left behind.

The Prantls planned to acquire a glass case in which to display the hand for posterity. Though far from wealthy, the family turned down an offer of $1,000 for the falling star from two men from Philadelphia who arrived in an automobile. "I will not part with it for all the money in the world," said Mrs. Prantl.

However, that didn't mean they wouldn't profit from it. Bargaintown was only minutes from the glitz and glimmer of the Atlantic City Boardwalk, after all. Though retaining ownership of the Flaming Hand, the Prantl family soon made a deal with two amusement men, C. Wistar Grookett and Thomas Irish. Grookett had managed Young's Million Dollar Pier for several successful years. He was an early pioneer of Skee-ball on the Atlantic City Boardwalk, installing the venerable game at the Ocean Pier in 1915. In early 1916, Grookett partnered with Irish, a partner in the Heenan-Irish Company, furniture dealers, to form the Arcadium Amusement Company. Grookett and Irish leased the amusement corner at Missouri Avenue and the Boardwalk, renovated the building, and planned to open the Arcadum, which would feature a carousel, Skee-ball and a Kentucky Derby game. But its marquee attraction would be the Flaming Hand, and the amusement men hawked its wonder throughout the spring and summer of 1916 in the Atlantic City press.

The Sunday Gazette proclaimed on May 28, "Messrs. T. Wistar Grookett and Thomas Irish have brought the 20th century wonder to Atlantic City at an enormous expense, placing it to the view of thousands at a nominal admission. The origin of this [phenomenon] remains the question of the day, but the problem will likely be solved soon now as it has become ready access for thousands." After paying 10 cents to view the ominous hand, visitors could listen to Henry Prantl give a lecture on "the strange circumstances and striking coincidences accompanying the appearance of the gruesome yet interesting meteor on its fiery plight to Earth."

The Million Dollar Pier at the Atlantic City Boardwalk, approx. 1916.

"Superstitious ones regard it as an omen and letters now in the hands of Mrs. Prantl beg her to exhume the body of her boy," claimed the Sunday Gazette. Albert Miller of Philadelphia wrote, "Do you not think the flaming hand might carry the message that the Prantl boy has been buried alive? It may have been the mission of the hand, suggesting agony, that this has really happened, and there may yet be time to restore him to life. Why not have him exhumed?"

The advertising-like coverage in the Sunday Gazette boasted that the transfixed public returned to view the Flaming Hand time and again, and that laymen and scholars engaged in animated conjecture as to its nature. Scientific experts believed the object to be either a meteorite, possibly a siderolite (stony-iron meteorite), a fulgarite (aka "fossilized lightning," or a mass of earth fused by a lightning strike), or a siderite (a valuable iron ore commonly found in hydrothermal veins). "It was an unusual specimen of meteor, probably the only one of its kind in the world," opined a University of Pennsylvania professor who toured the exhibit.

A photograph of the Flaming Hand and an article describing its descent onto the Prantl farm was syndicated in newspapers across the United States in the summer of 1916. However, this coverage omitted any details about the object being displayed on the Atlantic City Boardwalk. In fact, some articles confused the location entirely, placing the Prantl farm in locations such as the "Middle West," Cleveland and "Bakersville, New Jersey" or "Bakersville, New York."

It does not appear that the Flaming Hand's starring role at the Arcadum lasted more than a single summer season. In July, Grookett and Irish were among several amusement men cited for violating city noise regulations by running their venues on a Sunday. Irish was fined $15 for the Arcadum and Grookett was fined $15 each for the Arcadum, his Skee-ball alleys on Almac Pier at the foot of Tennessee Avenue, and his Magic Waltz ride at 2019 Boardwalk. By spring 1917, Irish was out and Grookett was alone in leasing the merry-go-round at Missouri Avenue and the Boardwalk, slightly renamed to the Arcadia. There was no mention of the Flaming Hand in that year's Boardwalk ads.

One might conjecture that the entire story of the Flaming Hand was planted in the newspapers by Grookett and Irish in the spring of 1916 to drum up excitement and anticipation for the new Arcadum and its (falling) star exhibit. And certainly, some of the articles that ran in different Atlantic City newspapers sound like slight variations of the same press release. However, the tragedy of Rudolph Prantls' death was real, and the cursed legacy of the Flaming Hand persisted during and after its money-making run as a summer diversion, primarily in court. The media continued to cover the saga, always referring back to the infamous Flaming Hand.

By July 1916, Mrs. Prantl was convinced that her son had sent the Flaming Hand from the heavens as an accusation of malpractice against Dr. Halvor Harley, the Pleasantville physician who had treated him for pneumonia. Early coverage of this story, apparently erroneously, cited tuberculosis as the affliction. Mr. Prantl refused to pay the doctor's $30 bill for the house call, although he clarified that he had decided this before the meteorite fell. Harley sued to claim the unpaid fee.

The entire Prantl family arrived with Henry on July 5 to combat the charge in a courtroom at Atlantic City's City Hall. The trial was conducted before Magistrate D. D. Martz and a 12-man jury. Gottlieba was highly agitated throughout the trial, eventually fainting and needing to be carried out of the courtroom. Harley testified that he knew Rudolph's life was in danger but had to leave partway through the night against the family's wishes as he had been called to another case of equal urgency. It was this refusal that Mrs. Prantl said she blamed for the loss of her boy's life on Jan. 3. However, there were two other physicians in attendance with Rudolph after Harley departed. After what amounted to "a battle of technicalities" between the opposing attorneys, Martz ordered the bill paid.

Henry Prantl was back in court late that October, seeking $200 damages from a neighbor, carpenter Josiah R. Smith, who the farmer alleged shot and killed his dog without cause. The shooting was said to have occurred on Prantl's own property, on the very spot where the "Flaming Hand" had fallen. Smith was arrested and charged with malicious mischief. In a district courtroom, Prantl testified that his deceased pet was a hound dog of the most select breed with unusual qualities as a domestic hunter. On the other hand, Smith and supporting witness Williams Collins said that the dog was "a mongrel of the lowest type... an egg sucker" who had invaded Smith's poultry yard and killed marketable chickens. The men sneered that the Prantl dog was not worth the powder it had taken to blow him to kingdom come. Judge Frank Smathers ruled in favor of the defendant and dismissed the case.

The Prantls, still dissatisfied that justice hadn't been served for Rudolph, sued Dr. Harley and the attending nurse, Emma Thompson, for $20,000 in a New Jersey Supreme Court action in May 1917. The malpractice lawsuit alleged that Harley suggested an untrained nurse be employed despite the Prantls' objections and that the doctor tried to prevent other physicians from visiting Rudolph until it was too late. Rudolph died eight days after being stricken. The matter was ultimately heard in circuit court at May's Landing before Judge

Howard Carrow beginning Nov. 9. Harley testified that he had followed the regularly prescribed treatment for pneumonia with the family's cooperation, and without any alleged delay in his response. Sensing dissention as Rudolph grew worse, he offered to withdraw in favor of any other physician but the family retained him until the end.

DR. HALVOR L. HARLEY,
New Member of the Pleasantville
Board of Education.

Dr. Halvor L. Harley, 1917.

While Mrs. Prantl had opined months earlier that Thompson had administered too much morphine, resulting in her son's death, Henry's position during the trial was that the nurse had run out of medicine and not provided it promptly. Thompson asserted this was untrue, and explained that the night before Rudolph died, she had given him an injection of morphine to ease his pain. She recalled that Henry wanted a second administration of morphine, which she did not have. For the record, Thompson clarified that she was not a professional nurse but had considerable practice. Thompson at one point claimed that Henry had placed a shotgun behind the door and declared that if his son died, he intended to "get even" with Dr. Harley.

Four local doctors testified that Harley had provided the proper treatment to Rudolph. Prantl's lawyer, Attorney General John Westcott, brought in his own brother, Dr. William Westcott, to give expert medical testimony against Harley. However, the contrarian doctor could not state definitively that Harley's treatment was incorrect.

It took the jury only six minutes to return a verdict to the packed courtroom that there was "no cause for action." Harley declined to bring a counter suit for damages. However, Dr. Westcott was severely censured that December by the Atlantic County Medical Society for unethically impugning Harley's professional care as an expert witness for the plaintiff, a clear conflict of interest that was standard practice for the brothers.

Throughout the 1917 malpractice trial, the oft-reported story of the Flaming Hand oddly flipped to state that the meteorite had fallen a year *before* Rudolph's death, thus serving as a warning of the tragedy. It is not clear what happened to the Flaming Hand following its showing at the Arcadum, other than Henry retained possession of it.

There is another possible inconsistency as pertains to the two publicized images of the Flaming Hand. A photograph included in early Atlantic City articles about the mystery, though of low quality, appears to reveal an object with the size and appearance of a doll's hand, held up by the wrist between the thumb and forefinger of a much larger human hand. A completely different photograph, copyrighted to H.B. Smith from news photo bureau Underwood & Underwood, appeared in national syndication of the story. It depicted an object that matched the description from the articles of what sounded like a meteorite in the shape of a charred and petrified alien hand. The hand is secured to a base, possibly a brick, with a metal bracket, although there is nothing else in the image to provide a sense of scale.

*Arcadum ad for the Flaming Hand, published in the
May 28, 1916 Atlantic City Sunday Gazette.*

The Prantls experienced two years of woe and
failed to obtain any satisfaction for the death of
their son, or even their dog. Despite this, history
suggests they were able to make peace with the
tragedy that had visited their lives. On Feb. 28,
1949, Henry and Gottlieba quietly observed their
57th wedding anniversary. Forty-seven of those
years had been spent in Bargaintown, and they
still resided there, on Delaware Avenue. Their
other three children—John, Lizzie and Clara—
were still alive and had given the Prantls three
grandchildren and two great-grandchildren. Henry
died, age 88, on April 20, 1951; Gottlieba passed
away, age 84, on July 9, 1952. The curse of the
Flaming Hand, it seems, was finally extinguished.

"Flaming Hand" Baffles Scientists

The "flaming hand" meteor.

*Photo by H.B. Smith from the Underwood &
Underwood press agency, included with articles
about the Flaming Hand meteorite that were
published throughout the U.S. in the summer of
1916.*

**However, there is a spiritual sequel to the
Flaming Hand. Could the grasping meteorite
actually have been a broken-off body part from
a petrified extraterrestrial astronaut orbiting
the Earth?? Read Chapter 14 to learn about
the Flaming Skull!!**

*Huge thanks go out to Odd Old News, who first
discovered an article about the Flaming Hand and
shared it with this author.*

An uncropped, though still murky, newspaper photo of the Flaming Hand.

SOURCES:

"$20,000 Court Action Instituted as Sequel to 'Flaming Hand' Case." *Sunday Gazette* [Atlantic City, NJ], 13 May 1917, p. 1.

"Amusement Men Summoned for an Open Sunday." *Atlantic City Daily Press* [Atlantic City, NJ], 15 Jul. 1916, p. 1.

"Appeal Will Be Taken in 'Flaming Hand' Case." *Atlantic City Gazette-Review* [Atlantic City, NJ], 25 Jul. 1916, p. 1.

Flaming Hand of Doom

"Atlantic City Amusement Men's Association Supplying the Principal Mirth Spots Along the Boardwalk." *Atlantic City Daily Press* [Atlantic City, NJ], 7 Apr. 1917, p. 6.

"Bargaintown." *Atlantic City Press* [Atlantic City, NJ], 4 Mar. 1949, p. 3.

"Boardwalk Amusements to be Censored by William H. Dentzel." *Atlantic City Daily Press* [Atlantic City, NJ], 7 Apr. 1917, p. 4.

"Boardwalk Gets the 'Flaming Hand.'" *Atlantic City Daily Press* [Atlantic City, NJ], 26 May 1916, p. 3.

"Court Echo of 'Flaming Hand.'" *Atlantic City Gazette-Review* [Atlantic City, NJ], 16 Nov. 1916, p. 8.

"Deaths." *Atlantic City Press* [Atlantic City, NJ], 23 Apr. 1951, p. 21.

"Deaths." *Atlantic City Press* [Atlantic City, NJ], 12 Jul. 1952, p. 18.

"Doctor Scored for Testimony in Prantl Case." *Atlantic City Gazette-Review* [Atlantic City, NJ], 15 Dec. 1917, pp. 1-2.

"Dr. Harley Defendant in Large Damage Suit." *Pleasantville Press* [Pleasantville, NJ], 19 May 1917, p. 3.

"The Flaming Hand." *Atlantic City Daily Press*, 29 May 1916, p. 3.

"'Flaming Hand' Baffles Scientists." *Akron Beacon Journal* [Akron, OH], 2 Jun. 1916, p. 2.

"'Flaming Hand' Bit of Meteor Baffles Scientists." *Buffalo Courier* [Buffalo, NY], 18 Jun. 1916, p. 3.

"Flaming Hand Falls from Sky to a Farm in the Middle West." *Atlanta Semi-Weekly Journal*, 20 Jun. 1916, p. 3.

"The 'Flaming Hand' Figures in Suit Brought by Doctor." *Atlantic City Gazette-Review* [Atlantic City, NJ], 6 Jul. 1916, p. 1.

"'The Flaming Hand Now on Exhibition.'" *Sunday Gazette* [Atlantic City, NJ], 28 May 1916, p. 13.

"'Flaming Hand' Is Shown Here." *Atlantic City Gazette-Review* [Atlantic City, NJ], 26 May 1916, p. 2.

"'Flaming Hand' Shooting from Sky Alarms the Superstitious." *Huttig News* [Huttig, AR], 24 Jun. 1916, p. 2.

"Flaming Hand's Weird Effect." *Atlantic City Gazette-Review* [Atlantic City, NJ], 30 May 1916, p. 2.

"Fulgurite." *Wikipedia*, https://en.wikipedia.org/wiki/Fulgurite, Accessed 26 Dec. 2024.

"Hand of Flame Excites a Town." *Atlantic City Daily Press*, 20 May 1916, p. 2.

"Henry Prantl, United States Census, 1910." *FamilySearch*, https://www.familysearch.org/ark:/61903/1:1:MK18-TLM. Accessed 18 Dec. 2024.

"Hound Dog Is Shot on Site Where Flaming Hand Fell." *Atlantic City Gazette-Review* [Atlantic City, NJ], 21 Oct. 1916, p. 1.

"How Much Is this Dog Worth?" *Atlantic City Daily Press* [Atlantic City, NJ], 9 Nov. 1916, p. 1.

"Mainland Doctor Emerges a Victor in Damage Action." *Atlantic City Daily Press* [Atlantic City, NJ], 22 Nov. 1917, p. 1.

"Man of 'Flaming Hand' Fame Sues." *Atlantic City Daily Press* [Atlantic City, NJ], 14 May 1917, pp. 1, 6.

"New Amusement Company on 'Walk." *Atlantic City Daily Press* [Atlantic City, NJ], 4 Apr. 1916, p. 5.

"Owner of 'Flaming Hand' Complainant." *Atlantic City Daily Press* [Atlantic City, NJ], 21 Oct. 1916, p. 1.

"Physician Wins Verdict in 'Flaming Hand' Litigation." *Atlantic City Gazette-Review* [Atlantic City, NJ], 22 Nov. 1917, p. 1.

"Prantl Asks $200 Damages for Death of Valuable Dog." *Atlantic City Gazette-Review* [Atlantic City, NJ], 4 Nov. 1916, p. 1.

"Rank Discrimination in Amusement Cases." *Sunday Gazette* [Atlantic City, NJ], 6 Aug. 1916, pp. 1-2.

"Says Plaintiff Concealed Gun Behind a Door." *Atlantic City Daily Press* [Atlantic City, NJ], 17 Nov. 1917, pp. 1,2.

"Seeks $200 Balm for Loss of Dog." *Atlantic City Daily Press* [Atlantic City, NJ], 4 Nov. 1916, p. 1.

"Siderite." *Wikipedia*, https://en.wikipedia.org/wiki/Siderite. Accessed 26 Dec. 2024.

"Suit Recalls Flaming 'Hand.'" *Atlantic City Gazette-Review* [Atlantic City, NJ], 10 Nov. 1917, pp. 1, 10.

"Uncanny Mystery of Flaming Hand." *Atlantic City Gazette-Review* [Atlantic City, NJ], 29 May 1916, p. 7.

"Underwood & Underwood." *Wikipedia*, https://en.wikipedia.org/wiki/Underwood_%26_Underwood. Accessed 27 Dec. 2024.

"Warrants Out for Five 'Walk Amusement Men." *Atlantic City Gazette-Review* [Atlantic City, NJ], pp. 1, 10.

"Wistar Grooket Branches Out in Amusement Deal." *Atlantic City Review* [Atlantic City, NJ], 20 Mar. 1916, p. 2.

The Monster of Marmotte Street

AKA The Frankenstein of Fisher's Alley, a fearsome nocturnal beast terrorized an Alabama community during the winter of 1938.

In late January 1938, police related stories of cruel attacks by a "monster," dubbed by them the "Frankenstein of Fisher's Alley," in North Mobile,

Alabama. Approximately 300 men in the predominately Black community armed themselves with shotguns, knives, clubs, razors and ice picks as they patrolled their neighborhood for the dangerous creature. Police cars rolled down the streets in search of the nocturnal beast.

The creature lunged at a group of women as they were leaving services at the Truvine Church one night. Men from the congregation grabbed their guns and headed into the street after the monster but were unable to locate it. Several days later, an ice truck driver told the press he heard that two policemen had shot at the animal, but the bullets bounced off and it had slowly walked away, unscathed. One resident, Johnny Boykin, opened his front gate and was shocked when the monster bit his fingers, requiring bandaging of his hand.

On Jan. 28, S. L. Bowman arrived at police headquarters with lacerations about his neck, which he told Sergeant J. J. Convy were inflicted by the monster's claws. Bowman, who needed medical attention, said the creature had emerged from Three Mile Creek swamp and leapt at him on Fisher's Alley. Bowman described the monster as being six feet long, with thick black fur and a white mark around its neck. Bowman was rescued only when his cries summoned his father, who beat the creature with an axe until it fled. Alex Herman, who lived along the alley, stated he fired a pistol at the animal but it jumped through a fence and escaped. In a conflicting but slightly later account, Bowman's heroic savior was reported to have been neighbor Henry Johnson, who blasted away at the fleeing creature with buckshot that merely bounced off its back. Johnson described the monster as being six feet long, wooly and larger than a police dog. He said the "Frankenstein" had a broad head, a six-inch-wide ring of white fur around its neck, and tracks Johnson thought looked like they belonged to a lion.

Residents developed a number of potential theories for the identity of the beast stalking the neighborhood. Perhaps "Frankenstein" was actually a ghost, the spirit of a woman who was killed by her unfaithful husband. Or the thing might be a madman, a forest animal, a dog gone wild from living in the swamp, or a tame lion from a circus that passed through Mobile the previous fall.

Witnesses offered a variety of conflicting descriptions of what some residents were now calling the "Monster of Marmotte Street," after the roadway parallel to Fisher's Alley. Some said the creature had "scales like a dinosaur," "phosphorescent hair" and attacked people and animals, often dogs, but only after sundown. It was described as a cross between the "Hound of the Baskervilles" and a werewolf, perhaps the legendary "loup-garou" that supposedly haunted the swamps. Estimates of the creature's size ranged all the way from that of a rat up to an elephant. Some versions had it breathing fire and leaving blood-stained tracks. There was talk that a hunter had gone into the swamp and returned speechless with fright and minus his dogs. Newspapers were flooded with hundreds of calls reporting rumors like the monster had just been killed, had returned to the Truvine Church and "wrecked the place," or had "just bit a little girl's ear off."

The area of Fisher's Alley, Marmotte Street and Three Mile Creek in North Mobile, Alabama, present day. Map data ©2025 Google.

City Commissioner Charles A. Baumhauer joined a crowd of citizens and rushed to a spot where the monster supposedly had been cornered. On arrival, the group found that the creature in question was only a large hog, cornered in a pig pen. Baumhauer then offered a $2.50 reward to anyone who bagged the monster.

Investigating officers who rushed to the scene of Bowman's attack had discovered large tracks in the sand. They expressed their belief, based on the tracks, that the rogue animal was a bear, which had been known to roam the swampland north of the city in recent years. Alternatively, they postulated it could be a black panther or huge dog. Police firmly denied "tall tales" of bullets bouncing off of the monster's "shell-like exterior."

The next morning, children were afraid to attend school and curfew was declared at dusk. Tales of terror spread fast along Fisher's Alley and the nearby main street, Davis Avenue (today, Dr. Martin Luther King, Jr. Avenue). Not since the notorious "Gown Man" of Davis Avenue had there been such a scare in North Mobile. The Gown Man had turned out to be a thief who frightened the wits out of his victims by dressing in white and shouting, "Boo!" He had since been arrested and was serving a sentence in the penitentiary for his exploits. (But more on him in Chapter 16.)

After nearly 48 hours of responding to calls about the monster, police grew weary of the chase. They decided to disperse the vigilante search party after finding a 13-year-old boy carrying a revolver. When police asked what he was doing, the boy replied, "I am hunting for that monster."

Chief of Police Warren Burch announced on Jan. 29 that any man found carrying a firearm without a permit would be arrested. The crowd complied, although several arrests were reported. Two men, Robert Walker and R. L. Johnson, received $10 fines, Johnson for firing several shots at what he thought was the Monster of Marmotte Street.

Just before Valentine's Day, city fireman Charles Ardoyno was awoken in the dark of early morning by what he thought were stray dogs fighting outside his house. He went out to investigate and discovered his own dog, a collie, in a precarious situation.

"As I came on the back porch, I saw our dog knocked clear across the yard by the animal. I didn't know what the thing was, but I called to my wife to send somebody for a shotgun and ran to help the dog," said Ardoyno. "My wife, thinking I was kidding, paid no attention. As I came into the yard, the animal started at me. I stopped and told the dog to 'go get him.' The thing had already mauled the dog badly and had bitten a piece from his nose but the collie didn't stop a minute. He tore between me and the animal and they battled again. The fight started at 6:30 a.m. Twenty minutes later, Gene Sullivan, who lives down on the corner, got there with his gun. We herded the animal into the yard next door and killed it. But the dog gets all the credit."

Ardoyno obtained permission from Baumhauer to exhibit the fallen Frankenstein of Fisher's Alley publicly on Valentine's Day, charging 10 cents a head. Baumhauer said the reward he offered would be paid, although it is not clear if Ardoyno, Sullivan or both would be the recipient. However, both Ardoyno and Sullivan were promptly summoned to inferior court by Game Warden A. Z. Oberhaus to face charges of shooting an animal out of season and illegally displaying it. Oberhaus criticized Baumhauer for allowing the exhibition to happen, with curiosity seekers streaming through Ardoyno's yard well into the night.

And the reason Oberhaus set his sights on the men was that the Monster of Marmotte Street wasn't a monster at all, but an otter. The animal weighed 30 pounds and measured four feet from its head to the tip of its tail. The otter had apparently left a nearby swamp to forage in the city, and met its fate after it slithered through Ardoyno's fence. The dog confronted it near a cage of pet rabbits belonging to Ardoyno's son, Charles, Jr. Sullivan, Ardoyno and the latter's collie were pictured in newspapers posing with the dead otter.

Charles Ardoyno, holding the "Monster of Marmotte Street" and standing with his son, Charles, Jr., and his collie dog that fended off the beast. Gene Sullivan, who killed the otter with his shotgun, stands immediately to the right of the box.

Inferior Court Judge Tisdale J. Touart quickly rejected the game warden's request for a warrant to arrest Ardoyno and Sullivan. "The way I look at this thing, this otter had invaded this man's property and was shot. They had a perfect right to shoot him," said the judge. "Otters belong in swamps and woods—not on people's property, especially at night."

Monster of Marmotte St.

The Frankenstein of Fisher's Alley was big enough news to appear in papers across the United States. A Wisconsin headline declared upon the monster's death, "There Otter Be Peace Now."

The animal shot by Sullivan was within the normal dimensions of a North American river otter. Males average 25 pounds with a length of 48 inches, although larger specimens have been recorded at 33 pounds and 54 inches. The otter's long, tapered tail accounts for one-third of its body length. The river otter inhabits freshwater bodies throughout North America, with a presence in 45 states and all Canadian provinces aside from Prince Edward Island. They are residents of Alabama's coastal region, with populations recorded in Mobile and Baldwin counties, including waterways adjacent to the Mobile Bay estuary. Three Mile Creek, home to the Frankenstein of Fisher's Alley, discharges into the Mobile River, a tributary of Mobile Bay.

WARNING: Close-Up Photo of Dead Otter

On Next Page

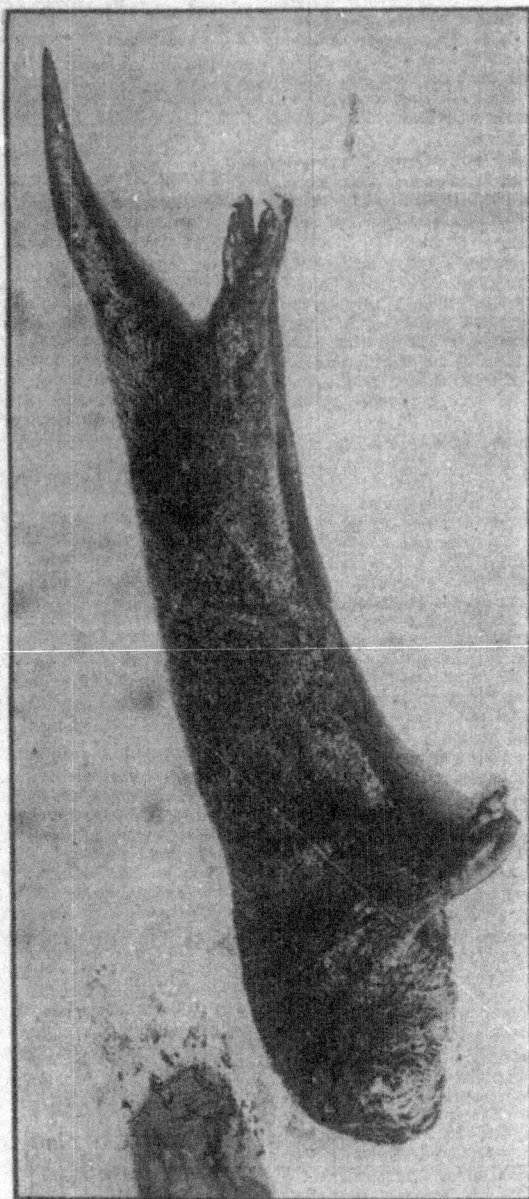

The monster, himself, with his head blown away by the shotgun blast, does not appear so formidable in death, but Charles Ardoyno, Mobile city fireman who killed it with the aid of a neighbor and his collie dog, declared it "looked as big as a house" when it invaded his yard and started towards him. The monster, a 35-pound otter, as it turned out, had wandered far from its natural habitat into the heart of the city where it met its fate Sunday, after a reign of terror in Mobile for the past month.

The Monster of Marmotte Street

Three Mile Creek, which passes north and immediately east of Marmotte Street, flows 14 miles through Mobile and was the city's main source of drinking water until the mid-20th century. Urbanization deteriorated the water to Alabama's lowest quality standards. "Sometimes, I think there are places on Three Mile Creek only the devil and I have seen," Mobile Press-Register columnist Bill Finch wrote in 2014. "I can imagine when it was the creek nature gave to us... Now, Three Mile Creek swamp is caught between the city's hindquarters and the railroad tracks, and we all turn our backs on it." Starting in 2014 and continuing into the present, the Mobile Bay National Estuary Program has targeted the Three Mile Creek watershed for water quality restoration and transformation into a recreational destination. While North American river otters are categorized as "Least Concern" on the International Union for Conservation of Nature (IUCN) Red List of Threatened Species, they are vulnerable to water pollution.

Most people think of otters as playful, curious creatures, holding paws as they backstroke through the water. And they are that. But they are also wild animals, and have been known on several occasions to attack human beings. In 2011, following a rash of incidents in Florida, IUCN conducted an historical review of violent or fatal otter attacks on humans. IUCN collected 39 anecdotal reports and four scientific reports between 1875 and 2010, with 38% of them occurring in Florida. Rabies was confirmed in 36% of the anecdotal cases. According to the IUCN, North American river otters are known to be territorial in nature, with human expansion and encroachment on their natural habitat possibly being the underlying cause for aggression.

Otter violence against people and dogs has been reported in the years since the IUCN inventory. On July 19, 2017, a group of otters swarmed Linda Willingham's family dog and dragged it underwater at American Lake in Lakewood, Washington. The two-year-old Labrador retriever, Gracie, was able to struggle free and dash back to her owners' home, safe aside from some bite wounds and a new fear of the water. There was a spate of encounters in 2023. In July, actress Crystal Finn was bitten on her leg and backside while swimming in Feather River in northern California. On Aug. 2, an otter attacked and injured three women on innertubes who were floating down the Jefferson River near Three Forks, Montana. A Montana Fish, Wildlife and Parks official said otter attacks were rare although the animals might act aggressively to protect their young and food sources. The Washington State Standard joked that the women "stood about a near-equal chance of being charged by an angry unicorn." In September, another California swimmer, Matt

Leffers, experienced the horror of being chased and bitten more than a dozen times by two otters as he frantically tried to swim back to shore at Serene Lakes in Placer County. On Sept. 27, Joseph Scaglione was feeding ducks at a pond near his home in Jupiter, Florida when an otter scattered the waterfowl. Scaglione, 74, tried to back away while facing the aggressive otter but it attacked before he could close the gate to his yard, biting him 41 times. The otter later attacked a dog on a walk with its family and residents managed to trap the animal under a recycling bin secured with cinderblocks. The otter tested positive for rabies.

While primarily interested in fish, a river otter can consume a varied diet that includes fruit, aquatic plants, reptiles, amphibians, birds (especially molting ducks that are flightless and easier to capture), aquatic insects, small mammals, and mollusks.

The case of the Frankenstein of Fisher's Alley is a reminder that monster reports, especially those in old newspapers, can often be greatly exaggerated due to the excitement of the witnesses, public hysteria, and a story that grows more vivid in detail with each retelling. Surely, the otter did not breathe fire or have a six-foot long body covered in dinosaur scales. But the "phosphorescent hair" might be an interpretation of the sheen of a river

"Your Worst Nightmare" North American River Otter. Photo by Thomas from USA, CC BY 2.0, via Wikimedia Commons.

otter's thick, water-repellent coat of fur. While normally content to emerge from their dens at night and hunt for fish, river otters are known to enter residential neighborhoods seeking food and adventure, especially in areas where their natural habitat has been disrupted. This sounds like what happened in 1930s North Mobile. Perhaps the individual otter was rabid, although it wasn't indicated in the original news reports. But what the Monster of Marmotte Street also pointedly demonstrates is that these wild tales from the past just might contain glimmers of truth, not to be summarily dismissed as mere journalistic invention.

Sea otters holding hands. Photo by Joe Robertson from Austin, Texas, USA; cropped version by Penyulap., CC BY 2.0, via Wikimedia Commons.

SOURCES:

"Alabama Town Terrorized by Mysterious 'Monster.'" *Waco Sunday Tribune-Herald* [Waco, TX], 30 Jan. 1938, pp. 1-2.

Belanger, Michael, et al. "A Review of Violent or Fatal Otter Attacks. *IUCN Otter Specialist Group Bulletin*, vol. 28, no. 1, 2011, pp. 11-16.

Blanchet, Brenton. "Swimmer Attacked by Otters in Northern California Says It 'Felt Like They Wanted to Kill Me.'" *People*, 3 Nov. 2023, https://people.com/swimmer-attacked-by-otters-northern-california-terrifying-experience-8386912. Accessed 7 Jan. 2025.

Ehrlick, Darrell. "Recent Otter Attack in Montana (Almost) Unheard of." *Washington State Standard*, 11 Aug. 2023, https://washingtonstatestandard.com/2023/08/11/otter-attack-montana-not-common/. Accessed 7 Jan. 2025.

"Excited Townsmen Shoot 'Frankenstein' of Mobile." *Johnson City Press* [Johnson City, TN], 14 Feb. 1938, p. 3.

Finch, Bill. "Mobile's Three Mile Creek: Beauty's Refuge Hidden in the Refuse." *AL.com*, 20 Apr. 2014, https://www.al.com/living/2014/04/three_mile_creek_beautys_refug.html. Accessed 5 Jan. 2025.

"'Fisher's Alley Frankenstein' Brings 'Terrible Fate' Threat." *Miami Daily News*, 30 Jan. 1938, p. 7D.

Haven, Rose Ann. "Caught on Camera – Otter Sighting in Mobile Bay." *WKRG*, 12 Mar. 2019, https://www.wkrg.com/baldwin-county/caught-on-camera-otter-sighting-in-mobile-bay/. Accessed 5 Jan. 2024.

Hill, Edward P. "River Otters." *Internet Center for Wildlife Damage Management*, Archived: https://web.archive.org/web/20151224112941/http://icwdm.org/handbook/carnivor/RiverOtters.asp. Accessed 5 Jan. 2025.

"How to Keep Otters Away." Wildlife Education & Directory of *Wildlife Experts*,

2024, http://www.wildlifeanimalcontrol.com/otter keepaway.html. Accessed 7 Jan. 2025.

Kooser, Amanda. "When Otters Attack: Experts Weigh in on Spate of Incidents." *Forbes*, 21 Aug. 2023, https://www.forbes.com/sites/amandakooser/2023/08/18/when-otters-attack-expert-weighs-in-on-spate-of-incidents/. Accessed 7 Jan. 2025.

Larivière, Serge and Lyle R. Walton. "Lontra canadensis." *Mammalian Species*, No. 587, 1998, pp. 1-8.

"Mobile Bay." *Wikipedia*, https://en.wikipedia.org/wiki/Mobile_Bay. Accessed 5 Jan. 2025.

"Mobile -------, Armed to the Teeth, Hunt Scaly Monster Which Attacks Man or Beast." *Knoxville News-Sentinel* [Knoxville, TN], 30 Jan. 1938, p. 3.

"Mobile River." *Wikipedia*, https://en.wikipedia.org/wiki/Mobile_River. Accessed 5 Jan. 2025.

"Mobile Terror." *Montgomery Advertiser* [Montgomery, AL], 30 Jan. 1938, p. 20.

"Mobile's 'Monster' Just an Otter After All." *Birmingham News* [Birmingham, AL], 14 Feb. 1938, p. 2.

"Mobile's Monster Slain, Puzzling Mystery Solved." *Shreveport Times* [Shreveport, LA], 14 Feb. 1938, pp. 1,7.

"'Monster' Bites a Man in North Mobile Alley." *Chattanooga Times* [Chattanooga, TN], 29 Jan. 1938, p. 11.

"'Monster' Hunted by Armed Patrols in North Mobile." *Shreveport Journal* [Shreveport, LA], 29 Jan. 1938, p. 15.

Munoz, Rob. "Dog Attacked by Otters in Lakewood, Homeowners Say." *KIRO 7*, 20 Jul. 2017, https://www.kiro7.com/news/local/dog-attacked-by-otters-in-lakewood-homeowners-say/566482890/. Accessed 6 Jan. 2025.

"Mysterious Marauder of Alabama Brings Police Reserve Call." *Nevada State Journal* [Reno, NV], 31 Jan. 1938, pp. 1-2.

National Oceanic and Atmospheric Administration. "Taking and Importing Marine Mammals; Taking Marine Mammals Incidental to Alabama Department of Conservation and Natural Resources Fisheries Independent Research Programs." *Federal Register*, 26 Dec. 2024, https://www.federalregister.gov/documents/2024/12/26/2024-30726/taking-and-importing-marine-mammals-taking-marine-mammals-incidental-to-alabama-department-of. Accessed 5 Jan. 2024.

Neely, Samantha. "Florida Man, Dog Attacked by Rabid Otter. How Dangerous are These Cute, Beloved Animals?" *Naples Daily News*, 28 Sep. 2023, https://www.naplesnews.com/story/news/2023/09/28/river-otter-bites-jupiter-florida-man-attacks-why-attack/70988887007/. Accessed 7 Jan. 2025.

"----- Section Terrorized by Night Stalking Monster." *Pensacola Journal* [Pensacola, FL], 29 Jan. 1938, p. 10.

"No More Gun-Totin' for 'Monster.'" *Dothan Eagle* [Dothan, AL], 31 Jan. 1938, p. 1.

"North American River Otter." *Wikipedia*, https://en.wikipedia.org/wiki/North_American_river_otter. Accessed 5 Jan. 2025. Accessed 5 Jan. 2025.

O'Neil, Patrick E. and Maurice F. Mettee, editors. *Alabama Coastal Region Ecological Characterization, Volume 2: A Synthesis of Environmental Data*. Bureau of Land Management, 1982.

"Remembering the Avenue." *Alabama Contemporary Art Center*, https://www.alabamacontemporary.org/events/the-avenue/. Accessed 7 Jan. 2025.

"Restoring Three Mile Creek: One Neighborhood at a Time." *Build Mobile*, https://www.buildmobile.org/uploads/Thr

eeMileCreekWatershedSummary.pdf. Accessed 5 Jan. 2025.

Reynier, Whitney. "Restoring Three Mile Creek via a Comprehensive Watershed Management Plan." *CAKE*, 24 Oct. 2024, https://www.cakex.org/case-studies/restoring-three-mile-creek-comprehensive-watershed-management-plan. Accessed 5 Jan. 2025.

Serfass, T. "North American River Otter." *IUCN Red List*, 2021, https://www.iucnredlist.org/species/12302/164577078. Accessed 5 Jan. 2025.

"Slayer of Mobile's 'Monster' Escapes Game Law Warrant." *Daily Herald* [Gulfport, MS], 14 Feb. 1938, p. 1.

"There Otter Be Peace Now." *Wisconsin State Journal* [Madison, WI], 14 Feb. 1938, p. 2.

"Three Mile Creek." *Mobile Bay National Estuary Program*, https://www.mobilebaynep.com/watersheds/three-mile-creek-watershed. Accessed 5 Jan. 2025.

"Too Many with Guns; 'Monster' Hunt Ended." *Chattanooga Times* [Chattanooga, TN], 30 Jan. 1938, p. 3.

Toole, Daniel. "North American River Otter." *Outdoor*

Alabama, https://www.outdooralabama.com/carnivores/north-american-river-otter. Accessed 5 Jan. 2024.

Tweedy, Aislin. "FWP: Otter Attacks Three Women." *Daily Montanan,* 3 Aug. 2023, https://dailymontanan.com/2023/08/03/fwp-otter-attacks-three-women/. Accessed 7 Jan. 2025.

Terror of the Black Ghost

Ethereal Ladies in Black presaged tragedy at the dawn of the 20th century, predicting a miner's demise in Pennsylvania and literally scaring a New Jersey woman to death.

*"She appears at the most unexpected times; she haunts certain localities; she conceals her face beneath a thick veil and her form with heavy folds of black; she comes and goes alone and no one is ever able to trace her movements; she is often the harbinger of misfortune, and there are clear-headed business men who aver that they have been pursued by this 'woman in black,' who has exercised a baleful influence upon their lives." - **San Francisco Chronicle, 1912**

The Black Ghost, or Woman in Black, haunted America's darkened streets throughout the late 1800s and early 1900s. Numerous accounts describe encounters with this feminine phantom, clad in black mourning clothes and her face concealed by a veil. She glided soundlessly through the shadows of moonlit avenues, her presence sometimes an omen for pending disaster. Today we focus on a pair of these tales, which, though divergent in details, both had fatal outcomes.

The Woman in Black (Artist: Orila Id)

The Black Ghost's Third Visit

The ghost of a woman, dressed head to foot in black, appeared three times throughout January and February 1892 in the mining town of

Carbondale, Pennsylvania, always just past midnight. The New York Sun reported that a caller for the Erie Railway Company, tasked with awakening railroad workers whose shifts started at night and early morning, saw the mysterious Woman in Black standing in the street near the train depot. Concerned that she was alone in that part of town at a late hour, the caller and a co-worker approached the woman. She abruptly headed away from them toward the city. Although the woman appeared to be moving slowly along the street, the men could not catch up to her no matter how rapidly they walked or ran. She consistently kept a few yards ahead of them despite advancing with the same apparent slow movement. Suddenly, she vanished from sight entirely. A few nights later, the Woman in Black was spotted in another part of Carbondale and led two citizens on a similarly weird chase, disappearing in the same uncanny way. Soon after, she performed the same trick near the old Coal Brook mine entrance.

Old miners said the same black ghost had appeared three times under identical circumstances 50 years earlier, shortly before the disastrous cave-in at the Delaware and Hudson Canal Company's old No. 1 mine. At about 8 a.m. on Jan. 12, 1846, a nearly 50-acre section of the mine's roof collapsed and imprisoned many workers. Although most of the men were rescued,

14 lives were lost, with eight of the bodies never recovered.

Twenty-eight years earlier, the Woman in Black's trio of spectral visits presaged the black fever plague that struck northeast Pennsylvania, killing about 400 people in Carbondale over the winter of 1863-64. According to one contemporary account, the black fever congealed the blood of its victims in that outbreak, causing their skin to turn black. This ghastly symptom is associated with what is today called black fever (Visceral leishmaniasis, or VL), a disease caused by protozoan parasites, although blackening of the skin was noted in instances of the disease in India and does not occur with most strains of VL. Spread by sandflies in tropical climates, it seems unlikely that VL was the cause of the Carbondale epidemic. The 1863-64 outbreak was also referred to as spotted fever, and was compared to a similar disease that afflicted Vermont from 1812-14. The medical consensus of the time was that "black fever" was actually cerebrospinal meningitis. Meningococcal meningitis, a bacterial cause for the disease, is specifically noted for a rapidly spreading rash of purple or red spots.

Needless to say, superstitious residents were on edge following the Black Ghost's ominous and physics-bending midnight strolls early in 1892. They didn't have to wait in suspense for long.

On Feb. 19, 21-year-old Thomas Caviston was working alone in a chamber in the mines of Coal Brook colliery at the Delaware and Hudson Canal Company when a mass of 14-inch vein fell on him, crushing him to the ground. A fellow miner found Caviston alive, but the sharp coal had sliced an artery, causing the man to bleed out and perish before his rescuer could carry him out from the mouth of the mine. Caviston's family revealed that the young man had a disposition to bleed easily and dangerously, which suggested he was a hemophiliac.

Bear in mind that the article about the Black Ghost materializing before disasters was published on Feb. 8, obviously sans foreknowledge of the deadly collapse that would occur just 11 days later. And the Lady in Black was seen on her third and final appearance at the entrance to the Coal Brook mine, which is where Caviston would soon after meet his tragic fate. This eerie sequence of events certainly gave this author pause when he discovered them.

Not to dampen a good story, but it should be said that the local Carbondale Leader newspaper told a somewhat more grounded account of the railroad caller's encounter with the Woman in Black compared to what was printed in the Sun. The caller saw the woman in the same locality on three consecutive nights in January 1892. Resolving to

Terror of the Black Ghost

Delaware and Hudson Canal Company Coalbrook Breaker, Carbondale, Pennsylvania.

solve the mystery, the caller and an acquaintance met on the night of Jan. 14 on the Seventh Avenue bridge. They eagerly awaited the arrival of the Boston Express, as the Lady in Black and the train tended to appear in unison. "With the very first toot of the engine's whistle the somber robed figure came in sight and swung gracefully along in the direction of the Seventh Avenue crossing." The men obtained a good view of her as she waited for the train to pass. They described the woman as being of medium height, wearing an old-fashioned slat bonnet that hid her face, and clad in a heavy dress and ulster coat. She carried a short stick not unlike a policeman's club in her right hand and an old-fashioned enamel leather traveling bag in her left hand.

As the train flashed by, the woman disappeared "as if the earth had opened to receive her." Utterly bewildered, the caller and his cohort resolved to try again the next night. They met again at Seventh Avenue for the passage of the 10:50 p.m. train, but the specter failed to appear. Laughing at their folly, the two men walked along the depot platform. As they were about to turn toward River Street, they glimpsed the Woman in Black walking up the railroad track. The pair gave chase but the woman eluded them up-track to the train depot, then down Dundaff and River streets to Seventh Avenue before once again disappearing. More determined than ever, the caller and his companion attempted to catch the ghost over the next two nights. She evaded them on Saturday, vanishing at the gravity railroad trestle on Dundaff Street, and then on Sunday, appearing again promptly with the 10:50 train signal before losing the men on Seventh Avenue and Mill Street.

The slippery phantom left footprints in the mud, which convinced the railroad caller and his acquaintance that she was human, even if they could not explain her ability to vanish so suddenly.

The Woman in Black had also pestered Carbondale and nearby Scranton in 1886, although the news reports did not connect her to any disasters at that time.

An unveiled Woman in Black, depicted in the San Francisco Chronicle.

The Greenville Ghost, Terror in Skirts

Jersey City, New Jersey's Woman in Black struck fear and hysteria amongst the populace of the city's Greenville and Bergen sections during the winter of 1901-1902. She was a menacing and dangerous character who managed to avoid nightly patrols of armed young men and frustrated police officers hellbent on catching her.

Shortly before Christmas 1902, "a mysterious creature, dressed like a woman, but possessing the figure of a man," was seen loitering on streets throughout Jersey City's Greenville and Bergen sections. The figure was six feet tall and clothed in deep black, its face entirely covered by a heavy black shawl or veil. A soft black hat surmounted its head. On several occasions, it was seen standing on the Ocean Avenue bridge, gazing down into the abyss. The being often halted in front of women and girls, muttering a few incoherent sentences before the accosted females fled in terror. Witnesses believed it was a man, six-feet tall and heavily built, dressed in woman's attire, with children calling the figure "The Veiled Man." Residents debated whether the Black Ghost was a supernatural being, a lunatic (male or female), a prankster, or someone who did not wish to be recognized while seeking a lost female relative.

After taking a rest at the end of the year, the Black Ghost returned in bolder form during the first week of January 1903. The ghost proved it was "more substantial than air" on the night of Jan. 3 when it seized a young woman on Randolph Avenue and half-led, half-dragged her beneath a street lamp. There, the ghost peered intently into her face. The stunned girl regained her voice and let out a piercing shriek, causing the ghost to hurry away toward the Newark and New York Railroad. A young man ran to the girl's aid and, hearing what had happened, ran off in pursuit of the black-clad figure. Catching up, the courageous young man grabbed the ghost by its arm. Quietly, the ghost turned and delivered a stiff punch beneath the man's left ear, knocking him senseless to the ground. When the rescuer recovered, the ghost was gone. Oher Jersey City residents suffered similar experiences. Miss Arndt, a cashier, was grabbed from behind by the ghost and dragged 10 feet to a streetlight on Kearney Avenue. The phantom scrutinized her features and then released her.

A driver for Borden's Condensed Milk Company jumped from his wagon and attempted to capture the Black Ghost on Virginia Avenue, only to receive a powerful punch to the head that knocked him down in a daze. He staggered up and attempted to tackle the ghost, only to be tossed aside once again following a short, rough-and-tumble brawl. The daring milkman wisely conceded the fight and retreated from the scene, leaving the Black Ghost to its slow and stately march across Jersey City's nighttime streets. On another occasion, the ghost picked up a little girl and fled when neighbors hurried over to her rescue. The preternaturally athletic specter at one point outran a crowd of 30 pursuers across half a mile and vanished into a vacant lot.

"The Black Ghost is more effective than any curfew in the Greenville and Bergen sections of Jersey City. Folks in those parts get indoors early o'nights, and even then go in shaking lest the black terror shall knock at their doors and summon them out. The Black Ghost gets bolder every night. At first he merely chased women along the lonelier streets. Of late he has appeared in the more frequented highway," wrote the New York Sun on Jan. 6.

In some reports, particularly in the Jersey City News, the Black Ghost's assaults were described as being more vicious. It accosted 19-year-old Margaret Cash of Randolph Avenue and asked her to have a drink. When Cash declined, the ghost seized her by the throat to prevent her from screaming, then released its hold and struck her in the face. The ghost was said to have "brutally assaulted several young girls" in addition to simply frightening others. Meanwhile, the ghost was nicknamed "Jack the Hugger" because it embraced some of the girls instead of injuring them. It was also suspected that the "Black Ghost" was one and the same as "Jack the Knocker" (alternatively, "Jack the Tapper"), another nocturnal character who rapped on doors and windows along Jackson, Bergen and Bramhall avenues, then disappeared by the time anyone answered.

Growing tired of these incidents, the police were not "averse to trying the efficacy of cold lead on the anatomy of the black masquerader." Patrolmen from the Ocean Avenue and Communipaw Avenue precincts, several in plainclothes, hit the streets looking for the culprit but came up empty. All the assaults had occurred within a half-mile of each other. Vigilance committees of concerned citizens also assembled to track down the Black Ghost. A mother of two small boys on Claremont Avenue nervously questioned her children as they prepared to leave the house one night after supper, one holding a hatchet and the other a cleaver. "Oh, we belong to the vigilant committee and are going out to capture the 'Black Ghost,'" explained the boys. They joined a posse upward of 1,000 searchers armed with clubs, baseball bats, sticks and shovels.

After a couple weeks of havoc, Greenville police reported in the Jan. 10 Evening Journal that they had finally identified the Black Ghost as a man who lived on Kearney Avenue (and happened to be Black). The police didn't release the man's name, but said he had a penchant for practical jokes and was warned to cease his activities or be arrested. This seems extremely lenient if the Black Ghost was as violent as described in the Jersey City

News, but is in line with the more benign activities reported in the competing Evening Journal as well as the New York Sun. (The Evening Journal [1867-1909] and Jersey City News [1889-1906] co-existed during this era as political alternatives in the city; the News was created as a Democratic counterpart to the Republican-leaning Evening Journal.) However, a contradictory story in the Feb. 10 Sun included a different outcome from the Jersey City police: "The nearest we ever got to him, or it," said Chicf Murphy last night, "was in the arrest of an insane man living in Lafayette, about two weeks ago, for hugging a woman in Greenville. We followed up the 'Black Ghost' stories carefully and couldn't find anybody who had ever run across it."

Whoever the Black Ghost really was, its disruptive adventures had reached their conclusion. However, it was too late for 22-year-old Mary Sheehy, who resided on 107 Kearney Avenue. Sheehy's co-workers at the Standard Watch Company factory told scary stories of the Woman in Black, inflaming her anxiety. Sheehy became hysterical, refusing to go out after dark. Afraid the Black Ghost was chasing her, she ultimately sunk into delirium. Sheehy was taken to the Jersey City hospital, where she tragically died on Feb. 9, attributed to mortal hysteria. While this might sound like a tall tale, Sheehy's death notice was published in the Feb. 10 Jersey City News, and her remains lie today at Holy Name Cemetery and Mausoleum in Jersey City. "So far as could be learned, Miss Sheehy never had any personal experience with the mysterious stranger in black," reported the Sun. "The police say that there has never been any 'Black Ghost.'"

The New York Standard Watch Co. at 401 Communipaw Avenue, Jersey City, New Jersey, 1906. Image from Jersey City Public Library Postcard Collection.

It is notable that the Jersey City News published Women in Black stories from elsewhere in the country in March and April 1902, less than a year before Jersey City's own Black Ghost appeared. Could these articles have inspired both the perpetrator and mass panic surrounding the specter?

According to 1902 articles in the Jersey City News:

- A ghostly woman robed in deepest mourning stalked the streets of Bushnell, Illinois at all hours of the night. Although seen once in a flowing white dress, she most often donned long black robes and a veil. She appeared suddenly and vanished noiselessly. No one could catch her, and sometimes the ghost herself chased pedestrians, who only escaped on their fleetest foot. A theory arose that she was the spirit of a woman who died recently after months of great suffering and had returned to harass the city.

- H.S. Wetherald, editor of the Alma Journal in Nebraska, was working at night in his office when a breeze from an open window blew out the flame in his kerosene lamp. Wetherald looked up and saw the tall figure of a woman in black standing outside. He raised the window and was surprised when she "disappeared—melted" away. A few evenings later, he stepped outside his office and the woman brushed by him, traveling about 30 feet before disappearing into thin air. Wetherald shared his experiences with Bank of Alma founder and Congressman Ashton C. Shallenberger (later governor of Nebraska), who in turn confessed to his own encounter with the ghost. Shallenberger had finished work at the bank about 10 p.m. one night and was strolling home when he felt a sudden rush of air. A black-garbed figure, that of a woman heavily veiled, darted out of the alley and passed him with a long, swinging stride. Ten paces ahead, she vanished completely from sight. A dozen different men witnessed the Black Ghost over the following week.

U.S. Congressman & Nebraska Governor Ashton C. Shallenberger, witness to the Woman in Black.

"Haunted Ohio" author Chris Woodyard catalogued a rash of Woman in Black hysteria that spread across the U.S. from about 1865-1915. These ominous ghosts shared the common attributes of being tall, thin and dressed head-to-toe in Victorian widow's garb, including a thick veil. They generally glided silently through the night, evasive and intangible. Solutions such as child pranksters, lunatics or men in drag were sometimes proffered in the sensational news articles. Woodyard noted a large spate of these sightings in Pennsylvania's coal-mining towns.

"Tales of a mystery woman in black were going the rounds here today," wrote an Indiana newspaper in 1923. "Nearly every town at some time or another has had its woman in black mystery, but Boonvillians assert their woman in black in the 'real stuff.'" Like many other towns, Boonville's late-night specter was wisp-thin and wore deep black, stared with vacant eyes, and disappeared before she could be approached. As in other communities, the Black Ghost's visitation was tied to historical tragedies, in this case a mine accident 25 years earlier and a husband-wife murder-suicide just three years in the past.

A few more examples of Black Ghosts during this era:

- A Black Ghost, "funereal" in appearance, stalked the streets of Albia, Iowa in the late-night hours of September 1892. The ghost appeared in the form of a woman, dressed in the deepest black and heavily veiled. She pointed a long, black finger at strolling lovers, sending them running. The shade often followed unaccompanied women, standing and gazing wistfully at them when they finally fled. The ebony specter was traced to a rickety house in the south part of the city, where a female resident had mysteriously disappeared years earlier. No one could be persuaded to venture in and explore the house after nightfall.

- W. J. Jones, an oyster shipper in the village of Cold Spring Harbor, Long Island, New York, awoke at 4 a.m. on Dec. 10, 1900 to check on his business and ensure that no one was stealing his wares. Finding everything secure, Jones strolled homeward under the moonlit sky. Suddenly, a black form that looked like a woman appeared before Jones, sending shivers down his spine. He sprang back and the ghost turned and glided up Main Street. The oyster shipper followed at a respectful distance. Jones thought he heard a noise behind him and looked back. Nothing was there, and when he turned to follow the apparition, he saw that it had vanished. A woman residing on Main Street also witnessed the ghost glide up the street and disappear. Sometime earlier, a villager named Robert Donohue saw a similar ghost in white.

- An eight-foot-tall "black ghost" wearing a white shroud and black mask, that belched fire and roared like a lion, spent two weeks in November 1902 frightening the residents of New Rochelle, New York as they traveled along the highway in the vicinity of the Thomas Paine monument. The ghost drove Mrs. Paulson nearly to hysterics and spooked the horses of several Manhattan residents with country homes in the area. Finally, the ghost sprang from behind a wall to scare a local farmer, who instead of running lashed the fiend with a sharp blow from his whip. The ghost fell with a yell of pain and scampered away. It left behind a sheet, its black mask and five-foot stilts. Investigation revealed that some of the mischievous neighborhood boys had been impersonating the powers of darkness.

In 1912, the San Francisco Chronicle asserted that the "somber veiled figure" was an international phenomenon that preceded numerous historical crises. An appearance of the "Black Lady of the Castle of Darmstadt" was said to indicate the impending death of a member of the Bavarian royal family or a relative of the Grand

Duke of Hesse. She was also said to appear in the halls of U.S. Congress during national scandals and crises.

Black-clad widows were a normal sight in American communities during the 1800s and early 1900s. The anonymity of the concealing outfit and the cultural empathy for widows, however, made it an attractive costume for criminals. Woodyard has collected numerous examples of women, and some men, who dressed in widow's weeds to commit crimes from pickpocketing and burglary up to kidnapping and murder. Cross-dressing was a cultural taboo, even illegal in numerous U.S. cities, wrote Woodyard. For men who wished to do so in public without risking legal repercussions or institutionalization, a mourning veil offered an adequate disguise. However, the era's distrust of cross-dressers filtered into news stories about the Women in Black.

While the Woman in Black has a nebulous motive or serves as an omen in some tales, one tradition is that she functioned to ward off men from cavorting late at night and to hasten home to their wives. A 1902 Tazewell, Virginia newspaper ad from The J. F. Hurt Insurance Agency explained how the Woman in Black would "appear to the belated man without warning, [and] slap him to the earth with a swish of her phantom garments." J. F. Hurt warned, "Fire, like the Woman in Black, comes without warning...There is only one protection against fire known to man. We sell this protection. Fire Insurance."

Alan Murdie, who prepared the 2024 edition of ghost hunter Andrew Green's classic book, "Phantom Ladies," floated the possibility that the parallel spectral phenomenon of the "White Lady" might not represent the spirit of a once-living person. Rather, Murdie suggested it could be "a symbolic form or exotic imitation of a female, one displaying superhuman characteristics, operating independently of the normal constraints of time and space." That description certainly evokes the portentous Black Ghost of Carbondale and similar dark phantoms.

Whoever these Women in Black were, inscrutable shades or masquerading criminals, they terrorized American streets at the dawn of the 20 century, ethereally slipping through the grasp of anyone who dared try to catch them. They prowled each city's darkest corners, both a symbol of an uncertain future and an echo of a past striving to hold on as the modern world callously dared to forget it.

SOURCES:

"About The Evening Journal. [Volume] (Jersey City, N.J.) 1867-1909." *Chronicling America*, https://chroniclingamerica.loc.gov/lccn/sn84026060/. Accessed 16 Oct. 2024.

"About The Jersey City News. (Jersey City [N.J.]) 1889-1906." *Chronicling America*, https://chroniclingamerica.loc.gov/lccn/sn87068097/. Accessed 16 Oct. 2024.

A. D., M. D. Letter. *Medical and Surgical Reporter* [Philadelphia], Vol. 11, No. 13, 26 Mar. 1864, p. 199.

Atlantic City Daily Press [Atlantic City, NJ], 15 Jan. 1903, p. 5.

"A Black Ghost." *Camden Daily Courier* [Camden, NJ], 9 Apr. 1902, p. 2.

"Black Ghost a Holy Terror." *Sun* [New York], 6 Jan. 1903, p. 5.

"'Black Ghost Is a Practical Joker.'" *Evening Journal* [Jersey City, NJ], 10 Jan. 1903, p. 1.

"'Black Ghost Is Being Hunted.'" *Evening Journal* [Jersey City, NJ], 6 Jan. 1903, p. 1.

"Black Ghost Killed Her." *Buffalo Evening Times* [Buffalo, NY], 13 Feb. 1903, p. 7.

"Black Ghost That Appears Only to Men." *Jersey City News* [Jersey City, NJ], 26 Apr. 1902, p. 6.

"A Black Ghost's Third Visit." *Sun* [New York], 8 Feb. 1892, p. 8.

"Black Robed Ghost Haunts Illinois Town." *Jersey City News* [Jersey City, NJ], 8 Mar. 1902, p. 7.

"A Colored Individual." *Republican* [Valentine, NB], 23 Sep. 1892, p. 6.

"Conductor Sees a Ghost." *Jersey City News* [Jersey City, NJ], 13 Jan. 1903, p. 2.

"Died." *Jersey City News* [Jersey City, NJ], 10 Feb. 1903, p. 1.

"The Female Ghost Still Abroad." *Carbondale Leader* [Carbondale, PA], 2 Dec. 1886, p. 4.

"'Ghost' in Black Takes a Rest." *Evening Journal* [Jersey City, NJ], 23 Dec. 1902, p. 1.

"'Ghost in Black Walks the Streets.'" *Evening Journal* [Jersey City, NJ], 22 Dec. 1902, p. 11.

"Greenville 'Ghost' Becoming Bolder." *Evening Journal* [Jersey City, NJ], 5 Jan. 1903, p.4.

Hitchcock, Frederick L. *History of Scranton and Its People, Vol. I.* Lewis Historical Publishing Company, 1914.

"Hunt for 'Black Ghost.'" *Morning Call* [Paterson, NJ], 9 Jan. 1903, p. 7.

"Is 'Black Ghost' 'Jack the Tapper'?" *Evening Journal* [Jersey City, NJ], 9 Jan. 1903, p. 1.

"Jack the Knocker." *Jersey City News* [Jersey City, NJ], 9 Jan. 1903, p. 1.

Keenan, Charles M. *Historical Documentation of Major Coal-Mine Disasters in the United States Not Classified as Explosions of Gas or Dust, 1846-*

1962. Bulletin 616, U.S. Department of the Interior, Bureau of Mines, 1963.

"Live Notes About Town." *Jersey City News* [Jersey City, NJ], 8 Jan. 1903, p. 2.

"Max Seeger Saw the 'Black Ghost.'" *Evening Journal* [Jersey City, NJ], 7 Jan. 1903, p. 1.

"Meningitis." *Wikipedia*, https://en.wikipedia.org/wiki/Meningitis. Accessed 31 Oct. 2024.

Murdie, Alan. "Women in White: The Mystery of Phantom Ladies." *Fortean Times*, Nov. 2024, pp. 30-35.

"A Mysterious Apparition." *Carbondale Leader* [Carbondale, PA], 20 Nov. 1886, p. 4.

"The Mystery Solved." *Jersey City News* [Jersey City, NJ], 5 Jan. 1903, p. 5.

"A New Disease." *Luzerne Union* [Wilkes-Barre, PA], 13 Jan. 1864, p. 2.

"New York Standard Watch Co.," *Jersey City Public Library Postcard Collection*, https://jcfplpostcards.omeka.net/items/show/21. Accessed 19 Oct. 2024.

Null, III, H. H. "The Rev. George Peck, D.D." *Lackawanna Historical Society Bulletin*, vol. 6, no. 2, 1972.

Rumrill, Alan F. "The 'Spotted Fever' Epidemic of 1812." *Historical Society of Cheshire County*, Feb.

2021, https://hsccnh.org/wp-content/uploads/2021/02/The-Spotted-Fever-Epidemic-of-1812-by-Alan-F.-Rumrill.pdf. Accessed 31 Oct. 2024.

"Southwest Virginia News: Tazewell." *Roanoke Times* [Roanoke, VA], 17 Jan. 1909, p. 4.

"Tales of Mystery Woman in Black, Who Fades Away, Stir Boonville." *Evansville Press* [Evansville, IN], 18 Jun. 1923, p. 1.

"Terror in Skirts." *Jersey City News* [Jersey City, NJ], 6 Jan. 1903, p. 8.

"Thomas Caviston Killed." *Carbondale Leader* [Carbondale, PA], 19 Feb. 1892, p. 4.

"Visceral leishmaniasis." *Wikipedia*, https://en.wikipedia.org/wiki/Visceral_leishmaniasis. Accessed 15 Oct. 2024.

"Woman in Black." *Carbondale Leader* [Carbondale, PA], 19 Jan. 1892, p. 4.

"The Woman in Black." *Clinch Valley News* [Tazewell, VA], 2 May, 1902, p. 4.

"The Woman in Black!" *Carbondale Leader* [Carbondale, PA], 4 Dec. 1886, p. 2.

"'The Woman in Black': International Spectre." *San Francisco Chronicle Sunday Magazine*, 7 Apr. 1912, p. 2.

"Woman in Black (Supernatural)." *Wikipedia*, https://en.wikipedia.org/wiki/Woman_in_Black_(supernatural). Accessed 16 Oct. 2024.

"Woman Killed by a Myth." *Sun* [New York], 10 Feb. 1903, p. 1.

Wood, Pat. "Mary J. Sheehy." *Find A Grave*, 4 Nov. 2009, https://www.findagrave.com/memorial/43920283/mary-j-sheehy. Accessed 17 Oct. 2024.

Woodyard, Chris. "Mistresses of the Dark: The Ghost Wore Black." *Haunted Ohio*, 21 Sep. 2013, http://hauntedohiobooks.com/news/mistresses-of-the-dark-the-ghost-wore-black/. Accessed 16 Oct. 2024.

Woodyard, Chris. "Source File for Pennsylvania's Women in Black." *Academia*, 2021, https://www.academia.edu/60166519/Source_File_for_Pennsylvanias_Women_in_Black_9_. Accessed 16 Oct. 2024.

Woodyard, Chris. "The Woman in Black – Victorian Mourning as Criminal Disguise." *Haunted Ohio*, 25 Mar. 2017, http://hauntedohiobooks.com/news/the-woman-in-black-victorian-mourning-as-criminal-disguise-10250/. Accessed 16 Oct. 2024.

The Wild Girl of Catahoula Parish

Multiple theories emerged about the identity of a feral lady living on the Louisiana bayou during the late 1800s, but the mystery was never conclusively solved.

A "Wild Girl" was frequently encountered in the woods of Catahoula Parish, Louisiana during the late 1880s and early 1890s. "She is perfectly nude and has no shelter of any kind, but has survived several severe winters," one Louisiana newspaper described her in 1887. The girl was "so fleet of foot that all efforts to capture her have failed." Despite numerous sightings and a few disparate theories regarding her identity, the case was never solved and the Wild Girl disappeared into Louisiana legend.

Catahoula Parish had about 13,000 residents in 1890. Today, it's even less. The parish was formed in 1808, shortly after the Louisiana Purchase. The stomping grounds of the Wild Girl were described as "the desert of Catahoula Parish," an area of 45,680 acres north and west of Bayou Funny Louis, a name derived from the Choctaw words "fani" (squirrel) and "lusa" (black), meaning Black Squirrel Bayou. Located on the western edge of Catahoula Parish, this section broke away as LaSalle Parish in 1910.

The report set the scene: "There are three roads running through it from Centerville, one to Columbia, one to Castor Springs and the other to Simmon's Ferry, at the head of Little River. There are no habitations on this vast tract of land, yet it is covered with a dense forest of spruce, or short leaf pine, mixed with post oak, white thorn huckleberry bushes and sedge grass."

In 1886, several families lived just south of this "desert," on the northern border of Funny Louis Stream. One of these residents was Jack Francis, who had several children. That December, one of Francis' daughters, who was 14 or 15, ran into the house and declared that she had seen a wild girl while driving home the cows. The teen said the girl, who was naked and had long, black hair, had broken a parsley haw bush and run away upon seeing her.

"The wild girl, it is claimed, has been repeatedly seen, and several times by persons on horseback, who pursued her at full speed, but her extraordinarily fleetness enabled the strange creature to outstrip their horses and escape," stated a June 1887 news article in New Orleans' Daily Picayune.

Mr. A. Dukes, who lived near White Sulphur Springs in Catahoula Parish, at this point offered **Theory #1** about the Wild Girl's identity: A "wretched and degraded white woman" named Madam Duck used to tramp through the country with her three children. One, a seven-year-old girl, was pretty but had a club foot, for which Madam Duck often threatened to abandon her. Dukes soon afterward noticed Duck accompanied by only two children. He suspected that the woman had made good on her threat to abandon the child, who managed to survive the miseries of the situation and was running wild in the forests and swamps. Tracks left by the girl showed one clubbed or otherwise deformed foot. How she achieved great speeds with the disability wasn't questioned. People in the countryside were planning to conduct a systematic search for the "wild waif."

In July 1888, about a year after the previous news report, the Wild Girl was sighted again, in the Swilley neighborhood about 15 miles west of Harrisonburg in Catahoula Parish. Several groups claimed to have encountered her multiple times over the course of three weeks. Mrs. Swilley, her two sons and daughter-in-law said they were not more than 30 or 40 steps from the girl. At one time she was seen catching a goose, then picked it up and carried it away with her. The Wild Girl was also seen by two of Mr. Taylor's grown sons. The witnesses all gave the same description of her and were of the opinion that she frequented the local waterways and subsisted mostly on fish. Based upon the last time the girl was seen with Madam Duck, the townspeople guessed she was between 12 to 14 years of age. The neighbors turned out several times en masse with the goal of rescuing the girl but failed to capture her, only finding her tracks. Jay Ellis, the source for the story, said he did not originally believe in the Wild Girl but changed his opinion after so many citizens of unimpeachable veracity told him the same story.

Soon after this latest article appeared in the Daily Picayune, Funny Louis resident J. R. Adams wrote to the paper to declare the Wild Girl "a probable creature of the imagination." Adams lived within two miles of the Francis family, and Lou (as she was called), the girl who first reported the Wild Girl, was his wife's niece. Lou was actually between 10 and 12 years old, not a teenager. Adams confirmed that the whole neighborhood searched fruitlessly for the lost child, only finding the same tracks Lou had discovered near her father's house.

Adams wrote, "Of course all this excited neighbor after neighbor and on all sides would come some unreasonable story, such as men seeing and chasing on horseback, dogs running it, tracks all over the woods for miles away, child seen at gates in snow storms, etc., every one of them resembling in possibilities. Where it is said the child was first seen there is absolutely nothing to subsist on at that time, fall and winter. The clubfoot signifies that the little waif had lost a foot during its wanderings. What an absurdity! It is about all we can do to make a living in this country with all the advantage of our little civilization and both feet, with houses and clothes and parental care added."

Some local women who desperately wanted to help the lost girl told Adams and others that they were cruel not to believe the story. The search party, unsuccessful, had returned to the Francis home for lunch, Adams recalled. Lou and her sister were sent outside to gather firewood, but soon came back and reported fresh tracks.

Adams wrote, "Upon this news one of the ladies, Mrs. Emily Cockerham, had her faith shaken and went out in pretended search again, but was on the alert watching Lou, and finally saw her step one foot down into a little ravine or muddy place and make a track, then turning to the parties behind, said: 'Aunt Emily, I have found another track.' The truthfulness of this statement can be verified by Mrs. Cockerham's oath. Since this nothing more has been seen or heard of the lost child... I do not pretend to say but that Mr. J. C. Francis honestly believes his child saw a wild girl."

Adams said he was also acquainted with Duck; she passed by his place often and still had all her children intact, both before and since the rumor of the wild girl began. Captain M. Dempsey, who had urged townspeople to conduct a search for the unfortunate girl on July 4, 1887, was a nice man with a generous heart who had nonetheless been taken in by the rumors, said Adams. Meanwhile, he learned from the brother of Mrs. Swilley that the family had heard something but was too timid to investigate. The story then became exaggerated to include more tracks and the presence of the Wild Girl. Ellis had then reported the tale, building upon the previous summer's news coverage. "I have been so disgusted with this stuff I feel it my duty to write what I have written," Adams explained.

Despite this attempt at a thorough debunking, the Wild Girl was seen again just one week later.

During the third week of July 1888, two men from Alexandria, Louisiana were walking through Trinity near Hemp's Creek when they stumbled upon "one of the most ferocious looking beings that the human eye was ever cast upon." The men at first thought the girl was on a jaunt through the woods and not far from home. They stopped to ask her a few questions but could not get nearer than 50 feet. Fleet as a deer, she cleared a large root seven feet high as she fled. Had the men been on horseback, they say it would have still been almost impossible to capture her. They surmised she could "conquer any three men in the neighborhood" and were terrified to sleep near the woods for fear of encountering the girl again.

The men said the girl appeared to be about 16 and spoke only gibberish. She was clothed in nothing but what nature gave her. The girl had immense eyes and brown hair that hung down to her waist. She stood about four-foot-six and weighed about 125 or 140 pounds, "with no surplus flesh." Her arms were long, brawny and muscular. She walked with a limp, but they could not get near enough to distinguish whether she had a deformed foot. The girl carried an old knife about eight inches long. A dead calf found in the neighborhood with pieces cut out was suspected to be her handiwork.

"A great many who have heretofore doubted the existence of this girl are now more convinced that it is a truth, the information coming as it did from two men who had never been in the parish before," reported the Trinity Herald. "The country is aroused." A committee of 15 men with provisions for two weeks was to be organized to capture her.

The posse was apparently unsuccessful, as another witness claimed to have run into the Wild Girl in September near the mouth of Little River. She did not appear vicious and wasn't carrying her knife, seemingly engaged in fishing or goose hunting.

In late September, the Wild Girl was seen by Captain J. M. Ball, a large planter near Alexandria; John C. Goulden, a leading scenic artist and house and sign painter; M. W. Calvitt, city marshal; and Charles Goldenberg, bookkeeper at the Levino lumber yard. The quartet were fishing at Gum Springs on Clear Creek, about 18 miles from Alexandria in Grant Parish near the line of Rapides and Catahoula parishes. Ball heard squealing and a ruckus amongst their pigs and asked Goulden to accompany him to investigate. They soon discovered a woman standing on a log with a young pig she had killed in one hand and a short knife in the other, intent on avoiding the enraged adult hogs around her. When she first saw the two gentlemen at about 30 yards off, she did not seem to be half as much afraid as they were. Ball and Goulden backed away, keeping their eyes on the Wild Girl. When the men were far enough, she absconded into the bushes with the pig she had killed. Ball said she was a naked white female, appeared to weigh about 140 pounds, and was "as active as a cat." She "was covered with hair varying in length in different parts of her," said Ball. In a separate article that ran the same day, Ball further explained that the girl "had a brushy, matted head of hair, and long hair on feet and hands." Ball said he would be willing to make an affidavit as to the truth of his testimony. Calvitt and Goldenberg said they both examined the tracks of the woman and the spilled blood of the pig, and had never seen two men more frightened.

The Wild Girl became the town talk in Alexandria once Daily Picayune readers read about the incident on Clear Creek. R. W. Bringhurst, parish surveyor, thus proposed **Theory #2** about the Wild Girl's origins: She might be the daughter of the late Captain Dave Wilson, who lived for several years on the east bank of Flaggon Creek, where it empties into Little River. Wilson kept a woodyard on the river. In 1853 or 1854, Wilson sent his little daughter, aged six or seven, alone to a neighbor's house. She did not return, and after diligent searching it was considered that she had been devoured by some wild beast or alligator and was given up as lost. Bringhurst learned of the tragedy from Wilson himself when visiting his house a few days later. The woman seen by Captain Ball the previous Monday was only three or four miles from the old Wilson home. Ball had estimated the Wild Girl was about 35 (making her more accurately a Wild *Woman*), placing her in the same age range of Wilson's daughter had she somehow survived. Bringhurst said that Ball was unaware of the Wilson girl and her disappearance. The Picayune said it contacted a celebrated detective in Marshall, Texas to make arrangements for him to travel to Catahoula Parish with his hound dogs and lead a posse of citizens in search of a solution to the mystery once and for all.

That October, Francis paid a pleasant visit to the office of the Town Talk newspaper in Alexandria, accompanied by his daughters, Mrs. Price and Alice Francis. Alice was the young lady who, two years earlier, has seen the Wild Girl. (It is unclear if she was nicknamed Lou, as Adams had claimed.) Alice informed a journalist that she had indeed seen the "creature," and her description tallied with Ball's account from a few weeks earlier. Francis informed the paper that he and neighbors had tracked the Wild Girl for miles, through dense and almost impregnable places, but never could catch her. He did find a place in the top of a tree where she slept at night. Long before the Wild Girl was first seen, neighbors had been losing all their young pigs and could not account for it. The Wild Girl had been killing and eating them, Francis explained.

On Oct. 26, the Lake Charles Echo in Calcasieu Parish published **Theory #3** about the Wild Girl's origins, at least as it pertained to the encounter at Clear Creek: A few shrewd businessmen from Alexandria (presumably Ball, Calvitt and Goldenberg) took note of all the press the Wild Girl of Catahoula was receiving. They conceived the idea that an illustration of her might make an attractive mascot for patent medicine advertisements, perhaps even taking the place of the alligator on matchboxes and patent medicine almanacs. They enlisted the aid of Goulden, "one of the finest artists in the state," who joined them on their fishing excursion to Gum Springs as the set-up to the tale. Upon returning to Alexandria, they told their made-up story to the press in order to generate free advertising. Goulden then secluded himself to work on the painting. "This seems to be the most plausible story yet related. After so much free advertising on the subject certainly a picture of the description above written, protected by a patent, ought to bring big money," opined the Lake Charles Echo. The "wild girl with a knife in one hand and a pig in the other would certainly be a great relief to the eye, especially to the blizzard-stricken immigrant, who has been educated, as it were, to the belief that Louisiana was literally alive with alligators."

The regional press was divided on the reality of the Wild Girl. The Bunkie Blade complained, "Why is it that an intelligent press, whose duty it is to teach truth and educate the people, will parade such nonsense before their readers, is more than we can divine. The papers must be hard pressed for news items to even allow themselves to entertain for an instant any such 'bosh'... Don't cram us with myths any longer."

One newspaper declared the idea that a child could survive for so long in the wild "too revolting and silly even for a plausible yarn." Another paper reminded readers of 50-year-old woman in Rapides who, in 1875, had been trapped in the swamps due to overflow from the Red River. Hunters passing through in September 1876, after the flooding receded and the swamp dried, were surprised to find the barefoot tracks of a woman along the streambanks. It caused great excitement in the vicinity. That fall, two men riding through the swamp found the woman, nude but for a string around her waist from which hung the remains of a squirrel she had killed. She had survived by creating a log raft and living on raw frogs, crayfish and anything she could find. "Now if a woman who never perhaps camped out before, could go through a winter, and at least four months high water on a raft, with nothing but crayfish to support life, I can see no reason why we should doubt there being a wild girl living on *terra firma* in the hills, and who can occasionally enjoy 'pig on a log,'" argued the paper.

Another reporter insisted that Ball and Goulden were "gentlemen of well-known veracity" who would not "tell such a yarn and stick to it so long if it really had no foundation." Goulden reinforced that he really did see the Wild Girl, who he described "as being of medium height, well formed and very active; her body was covered with long brown hair."

The Wild Girl was seen again on a Friday afternoon in November about three miles west of Black Gum Springs and 12 miles from Trinity. A group of witnesses gave chase but came to a creek, which the girl jumped in and swam across to the opposite shore, cutting off further pursuit. "At one time we thought this a myth, but are now becoming convinced that such a thing as a wild girl in Catahoula is a reality," wrote the Trinity Herald.

The Meridional newspaper of Abbeville, Louisiana printed **Theory #4** about the Wild Girl's identity on Nov. 17: In 1873, Mr. McDonald, a resident of Calcasieu Parish, left Louisiana to establish himself in Texas and was never heard from again. It was generally believed that he had drowned in a marsh adjoining the parish. His only companion was his seven-year-old daughter, who was also assumed to have perished on the journey. However, it was soon reported that "a wild white child, in a nude condition, had been seen in the neighborhood of Dr. Mims' residence. The child, it would seem, was ignorant of the existence of any being of its kind, and had partaken of the wild nature that surrounded her; for, on the appearance of the person who saw her, she ran in the opposite direction, pursued by his dogs, which he called off, when she disappeared and has never been heard of since in that section. Frequently since that epoch the woods in that section have been searched by experienced swampers; the most secret recesses were hunted, but all efforts have proven of no avail whatever."

J. D. Stanfield, a resident of Pinchburg in Calcasieu Parish, offered some support for this theory in a letter published in the Town Talk on Jan. 19, 1889. Stanfield was among the party that fruitlessly searched for the Wild Girl reported near the residence of Dr. L. N. Mims in western Calcasieu, which he said occurred in the spring of 1874. A 10-year-old boy, the son of William Lyons, had seen the Wild Girl. A few days later, the daughter of Joe Harden said she saw a little white girl run through an old field about two miles from where the Lyons boy had spotted her.

The recent connection drawn between the Wild Girl and the vanished McDonald reminded Stanfield of an incident from February 1874. He and a few boys had headed down a river in Calcasieu Parish for the purpose of deadening (culling) undesirable cypress timber. About five miles downriver and two or three miles from the nearest settlement, they discovered the body of a man that had drifted against a log projecting from the west bank of the river. They returned with a large group of citizens, including Dr. Mims. The group removed the corpse from the water and examined it but found no marks of violence. They buried the body the best they could and sent a signed report to the Lake Charles Echo. The closest police officer was 40 miles away in Lake Charles.

"Whether this was the man McDonald or not, I cannot say. He was not recognized by any of the Jury of Inquest. It is only recently that I heard of McDonald's disappearance," wrote Stanfield. "How the body of the man spoken of ever got where it was found has always been a mystery to this settlement. It must have been two or three months after the body was found and buried, when the child was said to have been [seen] by Mr. Lyons' boy... I do not believe a child could go wild and live on what it could catch in the woods, but if it so, I would like to see it proved."

According to "street gossip" reported in the Town Talk on Jan. 26, 1889, the Wild Girl had been captured, but not until after she had killed half a dozen dogs and a man.

In spite of this previous evocative yet likely spurious account, the Daily Picayune reported another appearance of the Wild Girl, this time in Pineville, in its June 21, 1890 edition:

"Yesterday J. Hardtner, one of Pineville's prominent merchants, and his daughter Alice, aged 16 years, were in one buggy, and Emmet Walker, a merchant of Fishville, and Miss Jennie Hamilton, also of Fishville, in another buggy, were coming from Fishville to Pineville. When they arrived within about eight miles of Pineville, they saw a white female, aged apparently about 30 years, weighing about 125 pounds, about five feet high, near the road. She was dressed in a faded homespun dress and barefooted. As soon as the wild woman saw them, she retraced her steps at right angles with the road, at a speed, all say, they never saw a human being run at. On reaching about 300 yards, she stepped behind a tree, but as soon as the buggies stopped, she started to run again, and they could all see her for about a half-mile stretch. The two gentlemen and one of the ladies were interviewed separately by the Picayune's correspondent, and all gave about the same account. It is proposed by our citizens to organize a party and attempt to capture the wild girl of Catahoula."

However, the Town Talk soon after doused reality on this latest claim, stating that this Wild Girl was actually Old Mrs. Smith's grandchild, a mute little girl who became lost and ran in fear from the strangers she saw coming up the creek. How the witnesses mistook a child for a 30-year-old woman is anybody's guess.

"The wild girl of Catahoula is out again this season. She has no new dress and takes to the woods, which appears to be full of her," wrote the amused Daily Picayune on July 10, 1891.

Wild Girl sightings appear to have died off at this point, although she lived on in local legend. Louisiana papers recounted the old tales periodically over the next 100 years. In a 1940 article, the son of little Alice Hardtner of Pineville, by then Mrs. C. F. Crockett of Alexandria, had supplied the Town Talk editor with a presumably yellowing clip of his mother's sighting of the Wild Girl in 1890.

The Wild Girl accounts are reminiscent of European traditions of "Wild Men of the Woods," humans who fled society to live as hermits in the wilderness and ultimately regressed into an animal-like state, foraging for food and growing a thick coat of hair over their bodies. Feral children who lived like animals in the woods and lacked human language skills were also a motif of European folklore, although actual accounts were documented starting in the 1600s. Settlers likely carried stories of wild people to the Americas, and 19th century newspaper accounts of these strange and terrifying individuals living in the untamed wilderness were prevalent. Many of the news articles described eccentric loners living on the edge of society, while others depicted Sasquatch-like creatures. A number of these Wild Men existed somewhere in-between, still human but covered with hair and possessed of enormous strength and agility. Some of the Wild Girl sightings fit this pattern, ascribing to her superhuman athletic abilities and long hair covering her hands and feet or entire body.

The Wild Girl of Catahoula persisted in Louisiana news columns for five years, with healthy debate and several witnesses coming forward. It seems unlikely to have been a straight-out hoax. Could she have been real, one or more of a number of missing girls who managed against all odds to survive amidst the parish's wetlands and woodlands? Or did it all begin with one little girl's imagination, spinning out into a regional legend that at times reached mass hysteria? The truth, whatever it may be, lies submerged in the murkiness of the Louisiana bayou.

SOURCES:

Bartholomew, Robert E. and Brian Regal. "From Wild Man to Monster: The Historical Evolution of Bigfoot in New York State." *Voices: The Journal of New York Folklore*, vol. 3-4, 2009, pp. 13-15.

"Catahoula Parish, Louisiana." *Wikipedia*, https://en.wikipedia.org/wiki/Catahoula_Parish,_Louisiana. Accessed 10 Sep. 2024.

"The Catahoula Wild Girl." *Weekly Town Talk* [Alexandria, LA], 15 Sep. 1888, p. 3.

"Catahoula's Sensation." *Daily Picayune* [New Orleans], 20 Jul. 1888, p. 6.

"Catahoula's 'Wild Girl' Legend Gets Publicity Again." *Alexandria Town Talk* [Alexandria, LA], 27 Jun. 1940, p. 1.

Guhl, Kevin J. "Bigfoot Sightings of the 1800s." *ThunderbirdPhoto.com*, 9 Aug. 2024. https://thunderbirdphoto.com/f/bigfoot-sightings-of-the-1800s. Accessed 13 Sep. 2024.

Jarman, Michelle. "Feral Children." *Britannica*, https://www.britannica.com/topic/feral-children. Accessed 13 Sep. 2024.

"LaSalle Parish, Louisiana." *Wikipedia*, https://en.wikipedia.org/wiki/LaSalle_Parish,_Louisiana. Accessed 11 Sep. 2024.

"More About the Wild Girl of Catahoula—A Search to be Made for Her." *Daily Picayune* [New Orleans], 29 Sep. 1888, p. 1.

"News and Notes from Our Exchanges." *Weekly Town Talk* [Alexandria, LA], 26 Jan. 1889, p. 1.

"Not a 'Wild' Woman." *Weekly Town Talk* [Alexandria, LA], 17 Nov. 1888, p. 2.

Opelousas Courier [Opelousas, Parish of St. Landry, LA], 8 Dec. 1888, p. 3.

"Our Picayunes." *Daily Picayune* [New Orleans], 10 Jul. 1891, p. 4.

Read, William A. "Louisiana Place-Names of Indian Origin." *University Bulletin: Louisiana State University and Agricultural and Mechanical College,* vol. 19, no. 2, 1927.

"Southern News by Mail: Louisiana." *Times-Democrat* [New Orleans], 20 Jun. 1887, p. 7.

"State Gleanings." *Weekly Louisiana Review* [New Orleans], 2 Jul. 1890, p. 1.

"Terrible, If True." *Weekly Town Talk* [Alexandria, LA], 28 Jul. 1888, p. 1.

"Was the Wild Girl the Child of McDonald?" *Weekly Town Talk* [Alexandria, LA], 19 Jan. 1889, p. 2.

"Wild Child of the Woods." *Meridional* [Abbeville, LA], 17 Nov. 1888, p. 2.

"The Wild Girl." *Weekly Town Talk* [Alexandria, LA], 20 Oct. 1888, p. 3.

"The Wild Girl." *Weekly Town Talk* [Alexandria, LA], 27 Oct. 1888, p. 4.

"The Wild Girl." *Weekly Town Talk* [Alexandria, LA], 10 Nov. 1888, p. 2.

"The Wild Girl." *Weekly Town Talk* [Alexandria, LA], 28 Jun. 1890, p. 2.

"The Wild Girl Again." *Weekly Town Talk* [Alexandria, LA], 29 Sep. 1888, p. 3.

"The Wild Girl of Catahoula." *Daily Picayune* [New Orleans], 21 Jun. 1887, p. 4.

"The Wild Girl of Catahoula." *Daily Picayune* [New Orleans], 3 Jul. 1888, p. 4.

"The Wild Girl of Catahoula." *Lake Charles Echo* [Lake Charles, Calcasieu Parish, LA], 26 Oct. 1888, p. 1.

"The Wild Girl of Catahoula Appears Again—This Time Near Pineville." *Daily Picayune* [New Orleans], 21 Jun. 1890, p. 1.

"The Wild Girl of Catahoula Makes Her Appearance in Rapides." *Daily Picayune* [New Orleans], 27 Sep. 1888, p. 4.

Ohio's Strange Menagerie of Reptilian and Amphibian Monsters

The Loveland Frog, the Crosswick Monster and the Red-Eyed Reptile of Bellbrook all lurk in the same fertile corner of the Buckeye State.

The Red-Eyed Reptile of Bellbrook

Southwestern Ohio has a mysterious predisposition for oversized herpetofauna (reptiles and amphibians) lurking in the vegetation along its waterways. The most famous of these creatures is the Loveland Frog, but it is joined by its "relatives," the Crosswick Monster and the Red-Eyed Reptile of Bellbrook. These three oddities, though seemingly unconnected, all managed to haunt an approximately 343-square-mile region between Cincinnati and Dayton, in the vicinities of the Little Miami and Great Miami rivers. Today, you're looking at about a 76-mile drive of under two hours to pass through all the towns involved. Sightings date back to at least the mid-19th century.

The Red-Eyed Reptile of Bellbrook

In the fall of 1865, farmer "Uncle Tommy" Cramer was keeping his cows in a swamp pasture by the banks of the Little Miami River near Bellbrook. While searching for the cows one evening, Cramer found the entire herd running in a circuitous route through the tall swamp grass and high weeds, looking terribly scared. Investigating further, Cramer discovered that his cows were being hotly pursued by what he supposed was a large snake, its head sticking up about four feet above the grass and undergrowth. The reptile spotted Cramer and lowered its head before disappearing into the swamp. Cranmer persuaded some friends to accompany him in search of the beast, and they anxiously followed him back to the swamp. The party failed to find the reptile but did see the place where it had passed through the grass.

Excitement about the creature died down until the next encounter in 1868. David Raper was mowing the grass with a scythe on a farm adjoining Cramer Swamp. As Raper swung the scythe, he suddenly noticed what appeared to be a huge snake sticking its head above the grass a few feet away from him. Frightened, Raper dropped the scythe and fled to town. Once again, a group searched for the monster and failed to track it. Raper was in such prostration over the incident that he laid in bed sick for weeks.

The enormous reptile stayed hidden until 1876. One day, a young boy named William Murphy discovered his dog barking ferociously at what looked like a log on the edge of a dense thicket. Assuming that the faithful canine had cornered a rabbit or mouse in the hollow of a log, Murphy headed over to render assistance. The lad had only advanced a few feet when the supposed log raised its head four feet in the air and vanished into the forest. The terrified dog ran off in the other direction and never returned to its master. Once more, the townsfolk were riled but could not locate the creature.

That was until 1879, when William Dill encountered the beast "lying secreted behind a drift along a branch." This was about two miles distant from where it was first seen. Dill, not willing to cultivate any further acquaintance with the creature, made a hasty retreat. Fearing physical abuse from his friends, Dill kept his sighting secret for several weeks.

Nothing more was seen of the monster until January 1884, when it made several appearances in the four-mile span between Bellbrook and Gandertown,* along a small stream known as Possum Run. On these occasions, witnesses finally obtained a full view of the fearsome animal. They described it as being 15 feet long in total with a serpentine head and neck the size of a man's body, around six feet in length. It glared at surprised locals with large, red eyes and produced a hissing sound. Its body was about nine feet long and resembled that of an alligator. When walking, the animal carried its head erect, but would coil its long neck and head on its back when still and alert for intruders. It displayed no aggressive tendencies toward people, and ran with terrific speed. Dogs refused to give chase. Residents supposed the beast subsisted on rabbits and fowls, as on Jan. 24 Frank Dunkin shot at the creature while it was running with a portion of a rabbit in its mouth.

Ohio Monsters

On Jan. 20 at about 3 a.m., Eli Hower was returning from Xenia when his horse became terribly frightened upon passing a stable near his home. Hower was noted in the 1880 U.S. census as a 53-year-old farmer living in Bellbrook. There was an uproar among the chickens, and Hower suspected that a thief was in the process of stealing them. After unhitching the horse, the farmer inspected the stable and found feathers scattered over trampled snow. Tracks extended in the direction of Possum Run. Hower roused his neighbor, John Webb, and the armed men set off to follow the trail. They hadn't gone far when they spied the monster at 300 yards distant, devouring a chicken near a plank fence. The excited Webb fired his rifle, causing the creature to flee. It burst through the fence, demolishing the two bottom boards. The men followed, stopping briefly to obtain the assistance of Calvin Lansinger, an old hunter. The trio tracked the monster until after daylight, when it entered a crevice between the rocks in Huston's stone quarry. Soon after, a party began setting up a deadfall trap outside the hole with hope of capturing the creature when it emerged. We never learn if this plan succeeded.

All of the eyewitnesses described the monster as having a head resembling a snake's and as large as a calf's head, with large, fiery-looking, red eyes.

Historical note: Gandertown, listed on maps today as Auburn, was a village along Lick Run in Butler

County, west of Xenia and immediately west of
Millville, positioned at the corners of Ross,
Morgan, Reily and Hanover townships.
Gandertown (named for wild geese that inhabited
the area) appears to have experienced a rough-
and-tumble past. A Hatfield-McCoy-style feud
erupted between Gandertown's neighboring Owen
and Flenner clans in February 1876, resulting in
gunplay and the arrest of several family members
for assault with intent to kill. In November 1878,
the Xenia Gazette noted that, "Gandertown has
determined that they will not have peace, for when
one tribe stops hostilities another begins. This
time the quarrel commenced on a foraging
expedition." On Jan. 29, 1885, two young men
named Newland and Real were returning home
from church when they began to argue and
Newland shot Real in the breastbone with a No. 22
(bean-blower). Though non-fatal, a doctor had to
dig the lead out piecemeal from Real's chest. The
name of Gandertown for this village seems to have
become an obscurity.

The Bellbrook/Gandertown monster is a mind-
boggling mystery. Was it a myth, a
misidentification of an out-of-place reptile, or an
animal lost to science and history? It bears some
resemblance to the Komodo Dragon, although this
large Indonesian lizard wasn't even discovered by
the Western world until 1910. Despite the fear
engendered by the Red-Eyed Reptile of Bellbrook,

one truth is clear -- it just wanted to be left alone, far away from the much more terrifying humans that repeatedly invaded its swampy abode.

The Crosswick Monster

In 1882, residents of the long-established neighborhood of Waynesville, Ohio were used to seeing black snakes, garter snakes and even rattlesnakes. But once in a while, someone reported a monster serpent that went beyond the norm. For several years, various people claimed to have spotted the track of a snake of unusual size that had crossed the dusty pike above town.

One fearsome encounter took place on May 26 of that year in the village of Crosswick, about one mile north of Waynesville. Several citizens, including Judge J. W. Keys, vouched for the truth of the story. Crosswick residents Ed Lynch, 13, and Joe Lynch, 11—the sons of John Lynch—were fishing in a small creek that meandered through the south side of the village along the Little Miami River. After sitting on the bank for a short time, the brothers heard a stir amongst the reeds, grass and brush behind them. Turning around, they were shocked to see a huge monster approaching rapidly. The boys screamed and, after a fleeting moment of paralyzed horror, began to run. The monster, snakelike but with limbs, ran down Ed and seized the boy in the slimy embrace of its long forelegs. It simultaneously produced two additional legs, each about four-feet long, from some hiding place in its body, and dragged the boy some 100 yards down the creek to a large sycamore. The tree was 26 feet in diameter at the base, hollow, and had a large hole on one side. The monster attempted to pull Ed, by this time in shock and unable to resist, into the large hole in the tree.

The Crosswick Monster

Three men—Rev. Jacob Horn, George Peterson and Allen Jordan—were quarrying stone a short distance away and heard the screams from the creek. They raced down to help and saw the monster. Alarmed at their approach and having failed to drag Ed into the tree trunk, the creature dropped the half-dead child and bared its horrible fangs. The group snatched away the boy and carried him home, where Dr. L. C. Lukens of Waynesville was summoned to attend him. Though badly bruised, scratched and afraid, the doctor expected Ed to recover fully within a few days.

That afternoon, a posse of about 60 men armed with clubs and axes, accompanied by dogs, gathered around the sycamore tree and began chopping it down. Roused by the commotion, the monster leapt out of the tree, stood up about 12-14 feet on its hind legs, and tore across the creek with the velocity of a race horse. It ran up a small hill and climbed over a rail fence, shattering it. Some of the men and dogs were so terrified that they backed away, but the braver among them pursued the animal for a mile as it fled north. Reaching a hole beneath a heavy ledge of rocks on a large hill, the monster retreated underground. The posse planned to watch for the beast's re-emergence and to slay it, if possible.

The serpentine monster was described as being 30 to 40 feet long, 16 inches in diameter, and covered in scales. The head was about 16 inches wide with a deep red mouth and a long, black, forked tongue. The legs were four feet long, with 12-inch feet that resembled a lizard's. At least the legs (due to ambiguity in the description) were black and white in color with large, yellow spots. The monster appeared to utilize its hind legs to stand erect and propel itself forward with its tail.

The Loveland Frogman

Most online sources trace the Loveland Frog back to a night around May 1955, although the details have the sparseness of a generalized urban legend. According to the story, an unnamed businessman was driving through Loveland when he saw a trio of three or four-foot-tall bipedal frog creatures near a bridge or along the road, one holding a sparking metal wand. The facts of this story, however, have melted somewhat in the fiery passage of time.

What actually happened was that Robert Hunnicutt, a short-order chef in a newly-opened Loveland restaurant, was driving northeast on the Madeira-Loveland Pike in the sparsely populated vicinity of Hopewell Road at Branch Hill in Symmes Township. It was May 25, 1955, and Hunnicutt was returning home from work at about 3:30 a.m. As he topped a rise in the road and came down a slight grade, his headlights revealed what he at first thought were three men kneeling down in the grass on the right side of the road. Hunnicutt parked about 10 feet away and got out to investigate, the headlights illuminating what he quickly realized weren't human at all.

The Loveland Frogman

The beings were about 3.5 feet tall, their heads and garments a uniform shade of gray. Hunnicutt found them repulsive. Mouths that were large, straight and appeared to lack lip muscles crossed nearly the entire width of their faces. The creatures' mouths reminded Hunnicutt of those belonging to frogs, which is the only detail in the original report that referenced the amphibians.

They had indistinct noses and lacked eyebrows, although their eyes looked human. The beings had bald heads with rolls of fat running across the top, resembling "the corrugated effect of a doll's painted-on hair." Their torsos were strangely lopsided and asymmetrical, with a larger right arm and a bulge swelling out from the right armpit down to the waist. Although not stated in the original report, this bulge is reminiscent of the balloon-like vocal sac possessed by most male frogs and toads. The chef couldn't discern if they wore shirts, but noticed that they were clothed in loose-fitting pants and had heavy waists and hips. The nearest creature held up a rod or chain that emitted blue-white sparks two or three at a time, which jumped back and forth from one hand to the other just below the device. When Hunnicutt stepped out of the car, the being lowered the device and appeared to tie it around one of its ankles. Hunnicutt's impression was that the forward figure had been signaling someone or something in the woods on the opposite side of the road.

Hunnicutt stepped nearer and the creatures did likewise with a peculiar, graceful motion. But the man gleaned a strong impression that he should not come any closer. As Hunnicutt returned to his car and pulled away, he suddenly experienced an extremely strong and penetrating odor that he compared to "fresh-cut alfalfa, with a slight trace of almonds." Although it was 4 a.m., Hunnicutt drove directly to the home of Loveland Police Chief John K. Fritz, frantically pounding on the front door to awaken the officer. Fritz listened patiently to the frazzled man's tale and, not detecting any alcohol on his breath, dressed and proceeded alone to the location of the sighting. The chief didn't spot anything there out of the ordinary, but stated that he "felt peculiar" as well as that he might be "the biggest fool in Loveland."

If you think the trio of creatures Hunnicutt described sound more like descriptions of extraterrestrials than frog people, that would be an astute observation. Prolific UFO investigator Leonard Stringfield and his colleague Ted Bloecher investigated this case in late summer 1956. It took place in the wake of the famous Hopkinsville-Kelly encounter that occurred one year earlier, in which residents of a Kentucky farmhouse were allegedly terrorized by a group of gremlin-like aliens from a flying saucer. Bloecher directly interviewed Hunnicutt and Fritz. He also learned that there had been a UFO sighting from the Loveland Ground Observer Tower on Lebanon Road at 7:48 p.m. on May 24, 1955, about eight hours before the chef's encounter with the little men. The UFO sighting was verified by an article printed in the June 2, 1955 edition of the Loveland Herald newspaper. Furthermore, pungent smells, like ammonia, are an oft-reported aspect of numerous alleged close encounters with alien beings.

Creatures about 3½ ft. tall.
witnessed by Robert Hunnicott
May 25, 1955

about 4 ft apart →

← 5 feet apart →

ROAD

142

Drawn by Len Stringfield
Sept. 1-'56 under direction

PREVIOUS PAGE: *UFO investigator Leonard Stringfield's 1956 sketch of the strange little men that Robert Hunnicutt encountered at Branch Hill in Symmes Township near Loveland, Ohio on May 25, 1955. Hunnicutt described them as having wide mouths that reminded him of frogs, and this incident has since been folded into the legend of the Loveland Frog. Also, is it just me, or does the guy in the middle look like he's trying to win back his lost love à la John Cusack in "Say Anything..."? Drawing shown here on a Fair Use, educational basis.*

There were additional witnesses to the strange little men in Loveland, according to Bloecher. Early in July 1955, a 19-year-old man identified only as C. F., then an auxiliary policeman with Civil Defense, was driving his work truck over a bridge in the Loveland area (likely the one crossing the Little Miami River from Claremont County) when he noticed four small figures on the river bank beneath the bridge. An awful odor blanketed the area. C. F. drove immediately to police headquarters to inform Fritz, his superior, but the chief wasn't there and those present treated the man's claim with great derision and skepticism. There were, however, rumors that police had cordoned off the bridge and that the FBI had investigated. Fritz was reluctant to discuss this incident with Bloecher and denied direct knowledge of any official activity at the bridge.

However, he did offer to take the investigator to meet C. F. at his farmhouse. It wasn't a very productive visit. The young man refused to discuss his sighting in any detail, and blamed the ridicule and abuse he received for his decision to quit his job at Civil Defense. Fritz later explained to Bloecher that C. F. had resigned since he wanted more responsibility that the chief felt he wasn't ready for, and that the sighting had nothing to do with it. Bloecher did manage to elicit an important factoid when he showed C. F. drawings of the pointy-eared humanoids seen in Kelly, Kentucky. The young man stated that the beings he witnessed looked nothing like them, and were instead "four more-or-less human-looking little men about three feet high" that were "moving about oddly" under the bridge, accompanied by "a terrible smell." The encounter only lasted about 10 seconds.

Around the same time as C. F.'s experience, Emily Magnone and her husband were awoken one night by their dog continually barking outside their Loveland Heights home. The couple looked out the window for prowlers and saw nothing, but were met with a foul, penetrating odor "like a swamp" that lingered throughout the hot summer night. The next morning, the Magnones' neighbor told them she had also been awoken by the dog's barking. When she looked outside, there was a diminutive little man about three feet in height, covered in what looked like twigs and foliage, standing motionless about 15 feet from her back porch. Strangely, the creature disappeared when she flicked on the porch light and immediately reappeared when she turned the light off, repeating this process multiple times.

The next step in the evolution of the Loveland Frogman legend occurred early in March 1972. Loveland police officer Ray Shockey, 23 at the time, was cruising along the Little Miami River on Riverside Drive in Loveland when he spotted "an animal two to three feet tall with dark green or blackish scaly skin." The creature ducked over the bank and descended into the river. Shockey only told his immediate superiors about the incident, not wanting to alarm Loveland residents.

A few days later at 6 a.m., patrolman Mark Matthews, 21, was driving home from duty along the same road (Riverside Drive/Kemper Road). He was near Loveland's city limits, about a quarter mile from where Shockey's encounter took place but still near the river. Matthews spotted "the same type of creature" and swung his vehicle so the headlights illuminated it. The officer said the monster appeared irritated at the interruption and stuck out its forked, serpent-like tongue at him. It had a face like a frog. The patrolman exited his car and observed the animal, which he estimated stood two to four feet high. The creature hopped at Matthews but didn't display any aggression.

A news report published about two weeks after Matthews' sighting, on March 27, stated that the patrolman fired three shots and presumably missed, with the creature running off toward the river. However, an April 12 report clarified that Matthews had actually shot and killed the animal with four bullets from his .357 magnum because it was running away and he wanted to see what it was. But his attempt to examine the creature was for naught, as it managed a final hop into the river and was washed away.

The Loveland PD decided to keep the matter quiet for the public good and to spare the department any embarrassment. Shockey and Matthews did ask an artist friend to draw the creature they had both seen, which supposedly bore resemblance to the titular star of the 1954 film, "The Creature from the Black Lagoon." Parry Wakeman, a zoologist at the Cincinnati Zoo, examined the composite sketch. While it didn't resemble any known animal, Wakeman opined that it could have been an otter or woodchuck since the weather was too cold for an amphibian or reptile. He likewise ruled out the goliath frog, native to central Africa.

Matthews said in April 1972 that he thought what he shot was an iguana, and he maintained that identification when interviewed decades later in 2016 following another sighting (see below). He also revealed that Shockey had called him after the earlier sighting. While Matthews didn't believe that Shockey had seen a monster, he sensed from his fellow officer than something he saw had upset him. Later that month, Matthews saw the puzzling creature cross the road on four legs and crawl under the guardrail (not walking on two legs and climbing over the guardrail as urban legend stated). Matthews also admitted in 2016 that he had recovered the creature's body and placed it in the trunk to show Shockey, who agreed it was the same animal he had witnessed. Matthews said it was a large iguana about 3-3.5-feet long and was missing its tail, which is why he initially failed to recognize it. Likely a pet that escaped or was released when it got too large, Matthews said the sickly reptile was already half-dead when he shot it. He postulated that the cold-blooded animal might had survived into the winter by keeping warm near pipes that released water used for cooling ovens at the nearby Totes boot factory.

Despite its demise, the Loveland Frog lived on. During the night of Aug. 3, 2016, Sam Jacobs and his girlfriend were playing the mobile game "Pokémon Go" between Loveland Madeira Road and Lake Isabella when they recorded photos and video of what resembled a real-like Pokémon. According to Jacobs, it was an actual giant frog near the water that astonished the couple when it stood up and walked on its hind legs. The shaky video displays what looks like two bright lights in the darkness, although FOX 19 Now news lightened a frame to reveal what does indeed look like a humanoid frog with glowing eyes standing half-submerged near the edge of a lake.

In 1985, University of Cincinnati folklore professor Edgar Slotkin said that local stories of the Loveland Frog had "survived for several decades." It might be pertinent to note that the majority of the supposed encounters, in both 1955 and 1972, involved the Loveland police department. It is not hard to imagine that the earlier stories about little men with frog-like mouths persisted within the department and fed into the later tales of a frog man, spurred on by a tailless iguana on the loose.

Overall, it's fascinating that there is a history of strange herpetofauna lurking throughout a contiguous slice of southwestern Ohio. There are certainly some good-sized reptiles and amphibians resident in this region, like the snapping turtle, broad-headed skink, gray ratsnake, Eastern Hellbender salamander and American bullfrog, but none of those come close to the large dimensions of the bizarre creatures described above. Is it possible that an animal like an escaped pet iguana, the prime suspect in the 1972 Loveland Frog case, had any role in the earlier incidents in Gandertown or Crosswick? In 1890, a cigarette manufacturer on upper Broadway in Manhattan was notable for keeping an iguana in a big bird cage. The reptile had stowed away on a Brazilian steamer and was gifted to the cigarette maker by the captain. So, it's not impossible that an iguana or some other exotic reptile could have escaped from a menagerie and lived briefly along Ohio's waterways. The green iguana, native to Central and South America, can reach an impressive length of around six feet. Meanwhile, the Crosswick creature's ability to run on its hind legs and its black, white and yellow markings are reminiscent of the common collared lizard of the American Southwest. But that animal only grows to a length between 8-15 inches and can hardly carry off a small boy! The Bellbrook/Gandertown monster, with its crocodile body and serpentine head and neck, is even more inexplicable. It and the Crosswick beast sound like nightmares pulled from prehistory, while the Loveland Frog straddles the line between cryptid and extraterrestrial.

Once again, we're left with paradoxical puzzle pieces that don't quite match up. But we can say for certain that one corner of Ohio is unsettlingly dense with legends of oversized, potentially nefarious, reptilian and amphibian enigmas.

SOURCES:

Amphibians of Ohio Field Guide. Ohio Division of Wildlife, 2012.

"Bellbrook." *Xenia Gazette* [Xenia, OH], 8 Nov. 1878, p. 4.

"A Big Brazilian Lizard." *Springfield Daily Republic* [Springfield, OH], 20 Jul. 1887, p. 2.

"Common Collared Lizard." *Wikipedia*, https://en.wikipedia.org/wiki/Common_collared_lizard. Accessed 10 Dec. 2024.

Cornell, Si. "Loveland Monster." *Cincinnati Post*, 27 Mar. 1972, p. 7.

Davis, Isabel and Ted Bloecher. *Close Encounter at Kelly and Others of 1955*. Center for UFO Studies, 1978.

"Eli Hower, United States Census, 1880." *FamilySearch*, https://www.familysearch.org/ark:/61903/1:1:M8MJ-YSJ. Accessed 10 Dec. 2024.

Globe-Republic [Springfield, OH], 1 Feb. 1885, p. 4.

Goldstein, Jan. "Frog'll Boggle Minds." *Journal Herald* [Dayton, OH], 12 Apr. 1972, p. 25.

"Green Iguana." *Wikipedia*, https://en.wikipedia.org/wiki/Green_iguana. Accessed 10 Dec. 2024.

"Hamilton." *Cincinnati Daily Star*, 14 Feb. 2024, p. 3.

"Hamilton." *Cincinnati Enquirer*, 27 Jul. 1880, p. 7.

Haupt, Ryan. "The Loveland Frog." *Skeptoid*, 30 Jun. 2015, https://skeptoid.com/episodes/4473. Accessed 8 Dec. 2024.

A History and Biographical Cyclopaedia of Butler County, Ohio, with Illustrations and Sketches of Its Representative Men and Pioneers. Cincinnati, Western Biographical Publishing Co., 1882.

"Komodo Dragon." *Wikipedia*, https://en.wikipedia.org/wiki/Komodo_dragon. Accessed 20 May 2025.

"Kwin the Eskimo." "Classic Cryptid: The Legend of Ohio's Loveland Frogmen." *Week in Weird*, 24 Jul. 2012, http://weekinweird.com/2012/07/24/classic-cryptid-legend-loveland-frogmen/, Archived: https://web.archive.org/web/20160624003152/http://weekinweird.com/2012/07/24/classic-cryptid-legend-loveland-frogmen/. Accessed 8 Dec. 2024.

Leggate, James. "Officer Who Shot 'Loveland Frogman' in 1972 Says Story Is a Hoax." *WCPO ABC 9*, 5 Aug. 2016, https://www.wcpo.com/news/local-news/hamilton-county/loveland-community/officer-who-shot-loveland-frogman-in-1972-says-story-is-a-hoax. Accessed 9 Dec. 2024.

"Loveland Frog: Did It Croak?" *Iowa City Press-Citizen* [Iowa City, IA], 18 Oct. 1985, p. 6.

"Loveland Frogman." *Kook Science Research Hatch*, https://hatch.kookscience.com/wiki/Loveland_Frogman. Accessed 9 Dec. 2024.

Reptiles of Ohio Field Guide. Ohio Division of Wildlife, 2018.

Scott, Jason. "Local Legend: Does the Loveland Frogman Live On?" *Fox 19 Now*, 4 Aug. 2016, https://www.fox19.com/story/32688947/legend-of-loveland-frogman-lives-on/. Accessed 9 Dec. 2024.

"Snaix." *Cincinnati Enquirer*, 29 May 1882, p. 2.

"Vocal Sac." *Wikipedia*, https://en.wikipedia.org/wiki/Vocal_sac. Accessed 9 Dec. 2024.

"What Is It?" *Cincinnati Enquirer*, 27 Jan. 1884, p. 13.

The Case of the Exploding Pig

Why dynamite and farm animals <u>do not</u> mix.

So, I have to share this story, because apparently I'm a horrible citizen and laugh like a looney tune every time I read it. My friend "Odd Old News" discovered this article and posted it on his <u>Substack</u> and <u>X</u>. It was originally published in the St. Louis Globe-Democrat on Aug. 16, 1887. And I include the whole sordid tale here for your demented enjoyment:

A Hog Explodes on Being Kicked by a Mule.

[From the Henderson (Ky.) Journal.]

A remarkable case of dynamite explosion is related by Henry Simpson, a resident of the Point. Simpson has been using dynamite for the purpose of blowing several old stumps out of the ground. Yesterday he carelessly left the dangerous compound lying by the side of a stump, on which he intended to begin operations this morning. The dynamite was mixed with sawdust and gave an exceedingly pleasant odor, which attracted the attention of two of Simpson's hogs, which soon had converted themselves into gigantic cartridges. The stuff, when eaten, creates a peculiar sensation, which annoyed one of the hogs to such an extent that it entered Simpson's stables and began rubbing its side against a post at the mouth of a mule's stall. The mule remained passive for but a few moments, when it gave the hog a terrific kick in the side. A tremendous explosion followed, and after the clearing away of the smoke and dust, the hog was to be found only in detachments, while an enormous aperture marked the spot where it had stood. The mule received a tremendous shock, but was still intact. The other hog is now running at large, greatly to the terror of the entire neighborhood. Neither of these hogs belongs to Mr. Joseph Mulhatton.

For those that don't know, Joseph Mulhatton was a prolific newspaper hoaxer in the late 19th century. He concocted numerous weird and imaginative tales and managed to get them published in newspapers across the U.S., gaining him fame and notoriety. Mulhatton embodied the devil-may-care style of journalistic tall tales that were so entertaining and prevalent in his day, a true American institution.

Most of Mulhatton's work has been identified, such as (to name a few examples) the opening of George Washington's tomb at Mount Vernon, revealing his body was now petrified to stone; the discovery of a cave containing hieroglyphics, pyramids and Masonic emblems in Litchfield, Kentucky; the innovative use of monkeys to harvest hemp; and the giant Magnetic Saguaro Cactus of Arizona, which uses its attractive powers to pull victims—animal and human alike—onto its impaling spines and into its carnivorous grasp. But during this era, many similar tales of Munchausenistic whimsy were attributed to Mulhatton or compared to his work, I'd say lovingly. An exploding hog would have fit seamlessly in his oeuvre.

Watch those mule kicks!

SOURCES:

"A Hog Explodes on Being Kicked by a Mule." St. Louis Daily Globe-Democrat, 16 Aug. 1887, p. 4.

"Joseph Mulhatton." Kook Science, https://hatch.kookscience.com/wiki/Joseph_Mulhatton. Accessed 24 Apr. 2025.

The Real Sweeney Todd

The Demon Barber of Fleet Street was just a fictional character, wasn't he? Maybe not. A 17th century North American explorer recounted a supposedly true and harrowing tale that perfectly matched the events of the Penny Dreadful published 200 years later.

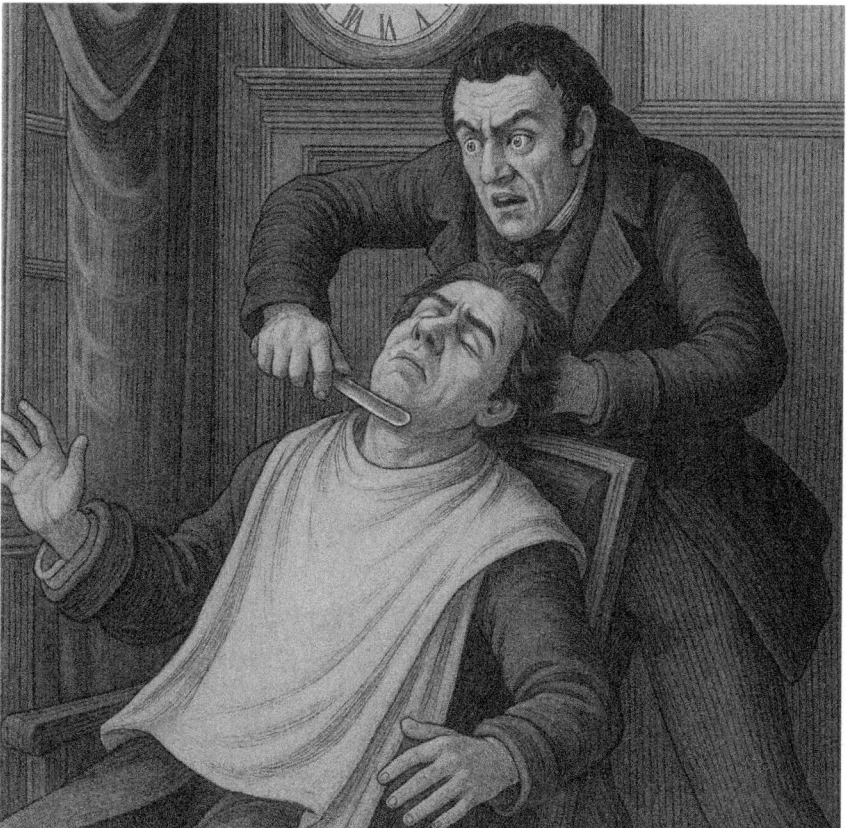

Like Sherlock Holmes, Sweeney Todd, the Demon Barber of Fleet Street, is a Victorian Age literary character whose worldwide popularity and longevity might lead one to believe he was a real person. While in London, after all, you can visit Holmes' "residence" on 221B Baker Street (in actuality the Sherlock Holmes Museum) or (if you dare) take a stroll looking for Todd's barbershop at 186 Fleet Street, in literary tradition beside St. Dunstan-in-the-West Church (186A Fleet Street).

First serialized as a Penny Dreadful from 1846-1847, "The String of Pearls: A Romance," set in 1785, explained how Todd killed his customers by dropping them via trick barber chair through a trapdoor into his cellar, which broke their necks. If needed, Todd slit their throats with a straight razor to polish them off. The barber collected their valuables, dismembered the remains and gave them to baker Mrs. Lovett, who used the human flesh as ingredients in her meat pies. Todd is undone when a young sailor comes searching for his friend, last seen in the barbershop, a saga that unravels the barber's dark secret. Todd is finally exposed with the discovery of hundreds of victims stashed in a crypt beneath St. Dunstan's church. In one last act of malice, the barber poisons Lovett before being captured and sent to the gallows.

As early as the first collected volume of "The String of the Pearls" in 1850, publisher E. Lloyd proclaimed the tale's veracity:

The Real Sweeney Todd

In answer to the many inquiries that have been, from time to time, made regarding the fact of whether there ever was such a person as Sweeney Todd in existence, we can unhesitatingly say, that there certainly was such a man; and the record of his crimes is still to be found in the chronicles of criminality of this country.

The house in Fleet Street, which was the scene of Todd's crimes, is no more. A fire, which destroyed some half-dozen buildings on that side of the way, involved Todd's in destruction; but the secret passage, although, no doubt, partially blocked up with the re-building of St. Dunstan's Church, connecting the vaults of that edifice with the cellars of what was Todd's House in Fleet Street, still remains.

(The original Medieval Period St. Dunstan's was demolished and replaced by the current structure in the 1830s.)

OLD ST. DUNSTAN'S CHURCH, 1814 (see page 135).

Old St. Dunstan's Church in 1814, Fleet Street.

Modern scholarship isn't so sure about Sweeney Todd's existence as a real person. "There are no clear answers," states PBS. "No public records substantiate the existence of a London barber named Todd in the late 18th century or, for that matter, of a barber shop located on Fleet Street." According to Londonist, "It has been generally accepted that Todd never actually existed and that, like Bram Stoker's Count Dracula, he is an amalgam of different sources, a composite of obscure horror tales, known murderers, folklore and the very human fear of cannibalism."

Sweeney Todd's gruesome crimes would be best contained to lurid Victorian literature but the truth is that there IS a historical precedent—only it took place about a century earlier, and not in England, but in France.

To find the origin of Sweeney Todd, you must look in an unexpected place—the autobiography of Peter Mårtensson Lindström, a Swedish engineer "specializing in the science of fortification" and an adventurer who voyaged from Stockholm to the colony of New Sweden on the Northeast American coast in 1653/1654. During his two-year stay in the New World, Lindström mapped the Delaware River and befriended the native Lenni Lenape. Lindström's written account, completed late in life, was translated into English by Amandus Johnson and published as "Geographia Americae with An Account of the Delaware Indians" by the Swedish Colonial Society of Philadelphia in 1925.

The "Geographia" begins with Lindström's voyage aboard the Öhrn from Stockholm to New Sweden, starting in October 1653. After a stay in Gothenburg, the Öhrn departs for New Sweden on Feb. 2, 1654 and sails directly into "cracking cold winter" and a great storm, the ship nearly becoming frozen in by ice. Once the crew successfully navigates to sea, they take course along the Scottish and English coasts. Adrift in darkness and violent, blowing storms for two weeks, the passengers and crew of the Öhrn are both surprised and delighted when they realize they have shot far off-course and reached the French coast. As the sun rises on Feb. 16, the Öhrn drops anchor in the port of Calais [which Lindström spells "Cales"]. Passengers and crew spend the morning onshore, leaving just past noon and continuing along the English Channel.

But those few hours in France were long enough for Lindström to glean the following tale:

The Real Sweeney Todd

At that time, here in Cales, many delicious, palatable and rare pies were baked, which were widely cried out [for sale]. [I] will relate a story which happened then in Cales, concerning an affair between a barber and a pie-baker, which took place thus: The barber had a front chamber in his house in front of his [own] room. Below that chamber-floor he had made for himself a secret cellar and above the floor was a square trap-door, so nicely made that one who did not look for it closely could not see where it was joined, and the said trap-door shut so hard that a person could sit on a chair on it and [it] did not go down by it. But when one stamped once hard on it with the foot, it fell down immediately. Now when any traveler, who was of a foreign nation, came to this barber to be shaved, then he took him into this said chamber, placed a chair on the aforesaid trap-door for him to sit upon, while he was to shave him. The stranger did thus. When now the barber began to shave him and came to shave him under his chin, he cut his throat, stamped thus while he cut him on the said trap-door with his foot, by which the trap-door with the man and chair fell down into the cellar and immediately thereafter he robbed him. And because the said barber and pie-baker were in company and council together in this [affair], the former sold the human flesh to the latter of which he baked the above mentioned rare pies. These were at last discovered and betrayed in this manner, namely: Two traveling students from a foreign country arrived there, and in going along the street came right before the barber's [house]. Then one companion said to the other: "Brother go and engage good lodgings for us somewhere, where you can find some good people. I will, in the meantime, go into this barber to get shaved, where I will wait for you so long, until you return here to me again." However, the barber did away with him, after his usual aforesaid manner and custom with others. Now finally the other one returned and asked the barber after his companion. He answered that he went his way immediately after he had been shaved. But this companion of his did not believe it, rather considered his companion's word to be more creditable, upon which he relied, but did not [yet] know what he should do. Nor would he risk to accuse this barber right away, although he might have his suspicion, but went away at first everywhere about the city and sought for him, but did not find him. He therefore went back to the same barber again and began to quarrel with him, telling him that he must produce his companion, "for here in the house I must have him again," he said. At this the barber waxed angry and wanted to treat him with striking and beating. The other [one] then made a complaint before a magistrate of the city, stating the nature of the case concerning his comrade, with the request that he might get some good men to go with him to search the barber's house for his companion, which was granted him. Now when those arrived there, who *were ordered to search [the barber's house], they searched everywhere, but did not find him. Finally, they came into the said chamber, where the sergeant stepped on the trap-door, saying in an angry tone: "According to the word and account of this comrade of his, we must really find the man here in the house," and with this he stamped on the trap door. Thereby the sergeant fell down into the cellar on the comrade of the other, who had not yet been undressed. Here the cellar was as full of skulls and skeletons as a charnel house in a churchyard. Thus both the barber and the pie-baker were arrested and locked up and soon afterwards received as a reward a miserable departure [from this life]. This account is written with the object of [instructing] him who intends to travel and gain experience, in the first place that he may herefrom be able to see how very necessary it is for him to have a good and faithful companion and secondly that he may know how to guard himself against such villains in similar and other cases and instances.*

In translating this story, Johnson made no reference to Sweeney Todd in his footnotes. Had he been familiar with the tale, he surely would have mentioned the glaring fact that the entire premise of "The String of Pearls," never mind a few details like the anonymous barber's name and the gender of the baker, is present in this historical account dated to 1654. Did Lindeström record second-hand news of a killing spree, which crossed the Channel and survived in oral tradition, inspiring "The String of Pearls" decades later? Maybe, but Johnson doubted the tale of the killer barber and saw another inspiration. "This story is found in a number of variations. Human flesh is relished by many tribes and the basis for Lindeström's story, told by some seaman, may have had a foundation of truth," he wrote, citing his own ethnography of certain Bantu tribes of West Africa.

Johnson called the "Geographia" "an interesting document from our Colonial period" but cautioned that, "It is not always reliable, in this respect sharing the failings of other and similar treatises of the age." He suggested that certain passages were based on fancy, like Lindeström's reports of encountering mermaids and sirens while traversing the Eastern Passage from the Canary Islands to North America. The adventurer said these channels contained more mermaids and sirens than "any other places in the Western Ocean," their appearance heralding storms. Lindeström claimed to have seen a mermaid floating on the water with gold, glittering hair of "10 or 12 fathoms in length," holding a mirror. Meanwhile, the alluring songs of sirens caused men who were sick and delirious to leap overboard the Öhrn, only some able to be rescued.

A mermaid depicted in The New York Herald, July 17, 1842.

According to Johnson, 17th century sailors did not look upon mermaids and sirens as creatures of the imagination, but as living beings of flesh and blood. "Their reality was taken for granted; they were something every seaman had encountered; something every seaman could vouch for," he wrote.

"We must not, therefore, class these narratives as mere inventions. They had a basis of truth in them to this extent that some unexplained phenomena or some weird creature of the sea was transformed into mythological characters of fantastic shapes by minds steeped in superstition, feeling themselves surrounded by unseen forces of the spirit world and momentarily expecting hobgoblins and what not to throw off their veil and monsters of evil to raise their heads out of the treacherous deep, especially in those far-off waters which ships seldom sailed. The head of a sea-cow, seen at a respectful distance among floating weeds, would be a sufficient and true evidence of the existence of mermaids, with long golden hair, to a man 'who knew such things existed,' although these 'charming maidens rarely appeared at close quarters, except to the chosen few,'" Johnson said of Lindeström's testimony. "The same can be said of his flying fish that could go ten miles at a stretch, and the pie-baker of Calais, who waxed prosperous by preparing delicious pies of human flesh. These stories were partly based on 'tales of sea-faring men' and adopted as gospel truth."

The Real Sweeney Todd

Lindeström was "a child of his time" and believed what he wrote, glowing with the "enchanted memories of childhood" as he penned his memoirs in later years, the translator suggested. Lindeström also presented the Calais story as a parable about the dangers of traveling unwary and alone in a foreign place.

So, can we chalk up the seed of Sweeney Todd's origin to a Swedish author's imaginative flourishes? Well, there is a noticeably big difference between Lindeström's references to mystical sea people and his story about the Demon Barber of France—the level of detail. The mermaid and siren accounts are mere sketches, while the Calais murders are given a few dedicated pages. It certainly appears that Lindeström heard a vivid tale, strongly told, and exciting enough news to reach the young Swede's ears during the few short hours he spent in Calais. Yes, the drama of the murderous barber and the baker of human pies might just be folklore that has persisted for close to 400 years. But it would be logical for a story with so much staying power to have a basis in fact.

You know, I'm pretty convinced...

Sweeney Todd was real!

Do you think he would approve of his portrayal by Johnny Depp?

203

SOURCES:

"221B Baker Street." *Wikipedia*, https://en.wikipedia.org/wiki/221B_Baker_Street. Accessed 22 May 2025.

"Contact & Visiting." *St. Dunstan-in-the-West*, https://www.stdunstaninthewest.org/contact-details-and-visiting. Accessed 22 May 2025.

"Did Sweeney Todd Actually Exist?" *Londonist*, 16 Oct. 2017, https://londonist.com/london/history/did-sweeney-todd-actually-exist. Accessed 22 May 2025.

Ganillero, Elon. "The Demon Barber of Calais, a 17th Century Sweeney Todd." *Leeds's Singing Organ-Grinder*, 13 Nov. 2006, https://elorganillero.com/blog/2006/11/13/the-demon-barber-of-calais-a-17th-century-sweeney-todd/. Accessed 21 May 2025.

Lindström, Peter. *Geographia Americae with An Account of the Delaware Indians*. Translated by Amandus Johnson, Swedish Colonial Society, 1925.

"Newspaper, Novel, Blood." *PBS*, https://www.pbs.org/kqed/demonbarber/penny/newspaper.html. Accessed 22 May 2025.

"St Dunstan-in-the-West." *Wikipedia*, https://en.wikipedia.org/wiki/St_Dunstan-in-the-West. Accessed 22 May 2025.

"The String of Pearls." *Wikipedia*, https://en.wikipedia.org/wiki/The_String_of_Pearls. Accessed 21 May, 2025.

The String of Pearls; or, The Barber of Fleet Street: A Domestic Romance. London, E. Lloyd, 1850.

"Sweeney Todd." *Wikipedia*, https://en.wikipedia.org/wiki/Sweeney_Todd. Accessed 21 May 2025.

"True or False?." *PBS*, https://www.pbs.org/kqed/demonbarber/penny/index.html. Accessed 22 May 2025.

The Ghost of Haddy the Hadrosaurus Seeks Its Missing Skull

Paleontology's most famous dinosaur is said to stalk the streets of Haddonfield, New Jersey, searching for its long-lost head.

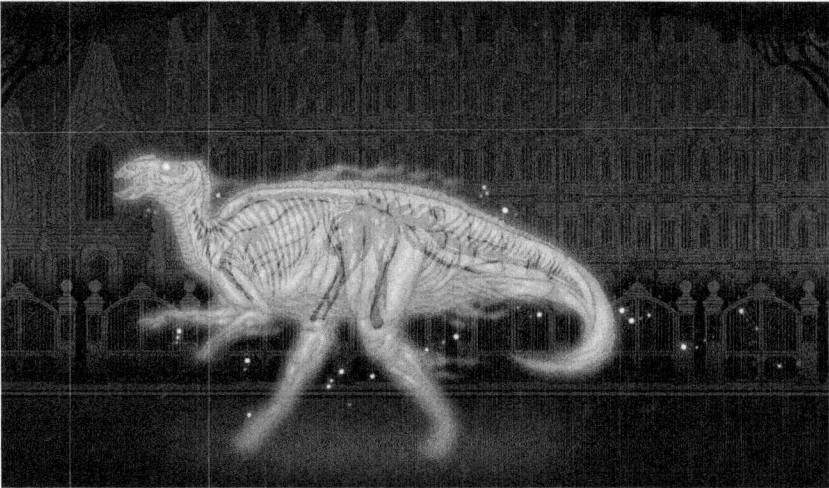

The Ghost of Haddy the Hadrosaurus (Artist: Orila Id)

It's a classic query: If ghosts are real, why don't we ever see the spirits of cavemen? At best, specters that show themselves in human form wear styles dating back only a few centuries. But there is one instance of a supposed ghost that dates back further—MUCH further, to about 80 million years

Haddy the Hadrosaurus

ago! In 1927, the revenant of one of the most famous dinosaur specimens of all time was said to have returned to haunt the New Jersey town where its remains were found, seeking its missing skull.

Hadrosaurus foulkii holds the distinction of being the first nearly complete dinosaur skeleton discovered in North America, as well as the official state dinosaur of New Jersey, an honor it achieved in 1991. Locals in Haddonfield, the discovery place of *Hadrosaurus foulkii*, have lovingly dubbed their beast "Haddy." This Late Cretaceous Period behemoth weighed about four tons ("Hadrosaurus" translating to "heavy lizard" or "bulky lizard" in Greek), spanned approximately 30 feet in length, and stood about 10 feet as it chowed down on prehistoric New Jersey's vegetation with its beak-like snout.

Hadrosaurus foulkii, in the headier times of 80 Million B.C. Restoration by Audrey.m.horn, CC BY-SA 4.0, via Wikimedia Commons.

Vertebrae from the Haddonfield Hadrosaurus were discovered during the 1830s by workers excavating a marl pit (marl being "an earthy material rich in carbonate minerals, clays, and silt") on the land of farmer John E. Hopkins. Reportedly, Hopkins initially missed the scientific value of the find and gave away some of the bones to friends as curiosities to be used as door stops and the like. It wasn't until the summer of 1858, when lawyer and amateur geologist William Parker Foulke stayed in the area and dined with Hopkins at the farmer's home, that the importance of the discovery was recognized.

Hopkins showed the unique bones to his astonished visitor and Foulke obtained full permission from the farmer to dig on his property and take away any fossils he discovered. The men searched for and relocated the overgrown marl pit, which had been dug in the bed of a narrow ravine through which a brook flowed eastwardly toward the south branch of Cooper's Creek (known as the Woodbury Formation). The geologist enlisted the help of Joseph Leidy, a renowned paleontologist from the Academy of Natural Sciences in Philadelphia, and together the pair recovered the nearly complete, fossilized skeleton of the large herbivore about 10 feet down. *Aside from its missing skull.* Leidy named the animal *Hadrosaurus foulkii* in honor of his collaborator.

Haddy the Hadrosaurus

The celebrated and scientifically important Haddonfield Hadrosaurus was the first-ever dinosaur to be mounted for exhibition. As boasted by the Haddonfield Dinosaur Sculpture Committee, "Every dinosaur skeleton mounted in every museum in the world traces its roots to Haddonfield's *Hadrosaurus foulkii*."

The specimen was unveiled at the Academy of Natural Sciences (today part of Drexel University) in 1868, where a cast remains a centerpiece of the museum's dinosaur display to this day. Benjamin Waterhouse Hawkins, who sculpted the famous life-size, concrete dinosaurs for London's Crystal Palace in 1854, volunteered to mount the Hadrosaur's bones for the Academy of Natural Sciences. With only nine teeth and a lower jaw fragment to work with, Hawkins fashioned a plaster skull that was based on and upscaled from the skull of an iguana. This modern reptile's teeth, as well as the teeth of the Hadrosaurus's Early Cretaceous relative, Iguanodon, resembled those of the Haddonfield dinosaur.

NEXT PAGE: *"Skeleton of the Great Fossil Lizard of New Jersey," circa 1876. This photograph shows the original Hadrosaurus foulkii reconstruction by Benjamin Waterhouse Hawkins on display at the Academy of Natural Sciences in Philadelphia, complete with iguana-based skull. From the collection of Richard C. Ryder.*

SKELETON OF THE GREAT FOSSIL LIZARD OF NEW JERSEY.
Hadrosaurus Foulkii Leidy.

The Academy has updated its *Hadrosaurus foulkii* skull over time as scientific understanding increased, such as an early 21st revision that correctly presented a duck-billed snout, cast from a closely related Maiasaur. Hawkin's original skull recreation has continued to be displayed separately for its historical significance.

Haddy the Hadrosaurus

The Haddonfield Hadrosaurus on display at the Academy of Natural Sciences of Drexel University in 2013, with more accurate duck-bill skull and posture. Photo by Jim, the Photographer from Springfield PA, United States of America, CC BY 2.0, via Wikimedia Commons.

But what of the Haddonfield Hadrosaur's true, original skull? Does it still lie beneath the former Hopkins farm or was it absconded during an earlier time into someone's private collection, perhaps used as a massive paperweight? Clearly, its original owner, Haddy, is none too pleased, as the following article illustrates.

The Camden, New Jersey Evening Courier published this tale of terror in its July 15, 1927 issue, complete with an artist's interpretation of the prehistoric phantom:

If That Haddonfield Monster Comes Back...

The wraith of a hydrosaur, an extinct water lizard of prehistoric days, is said to be nightly hovering over the suburban borough in search of its head which was not found when the remainder of the skeleton was unearthed in 1858. A daylight appearance of the monster on King's Highway would soon empty the street as the photo indicates.

EERIE NOISES OF NIGHT STIR STAID HADDONFIELD

Imaginative Hark Back to Pre-Historic Monster Dug From Farm

SEE SPOOKY QUEST FOR MISSING HEAD

Vies With Rumors of Nocturnal Tryout of Home-Made Airplane

Haddy the Hadrosaurus

Haddonfield ears are unusually sensitive and, because of that fact, Haddonfield nights are not what they used to be. Haddonfield's reputation as a good town in which to sleep is in grave danger.

For the darkness has for the past week become filled with strange, eerie noises that have found many explanations.

One is that some unnamed resident has constructed for himself an airplane and is giving it nightly workouts. Another report has it that a flock of strange night-flying birds has come to town, lying in seclusion during the day and going abroad from chimney hiding places in the shadows of night.

The weirdest explanation of all is that the town is haunted by the spirit of a hydrosaur, a huge prehistoric bird, whose bones were dug up and pieced together, according to historians, in the year 1859. The wraith of this creature of the dinosaur family is supposed to be seeking its head, which was missing when the remainder of the skeleton was excavated.

Cop Hears Eerie Sounds

Lieutenant William Start, of the police department, admitted last night that he had heard the almost indescribable nocturnal sounds, and that he had received reports from many residents, who told of hearing them, too.

"There seems to be the whirr of huge wings, accompanied by the clacking of bones," said Lieutenant Start. "The sound usually approaches from the north. It comes with great speed and passing over, disappears sometimes as quickly. On other occasions, it seems to be circling overhead."

With Patrolman William Hoster, Lieutenant Start told how he has stood in the open, in the wee hours of morning, trying to glimpse the cause of the disturbing sounds. Neither have been successful. Start was asked if he believed in ghosts.

"I haven't—yet," he said.

Both policemen leaned toward the airplane theory. They admitted, however, on being pressed, that the sounds were not similar to those made by any airplane they have yet seen.

The legend of the monster searching for its head is as familiar to Haddonfield as the headless Brom Bones and his chase of Ichabod Crane in Sleepy Hollow. It comes back every so often in one form or another. History backs it up to a certain extent.

The scientific books tell how in the year 1858 one William Carter [Parker—Ed.] Foulke, while watching some laborers digging marl on the John E. Hopkins farm, now part of the Birdwood tract, saw some great bones uncovered. Foulke investigated and found them to be part of the skeleton of some pre-historic animal.

Haddy the Hadrosaurus

Permission was obtained and a great crowd of naturalists and scientific men unearthed the complete skeleton of what was described by Dr. Joseph Leidy, one of the group, as a hydrosaurus, or a type of extinct mammoth lizard.

Monster Head Not Found

But though nearly all the bones were found, the head went undiscovered. Perhaps, somewhere under the town the skull still remains. Perhaps the eerie creature is taking some supernatural means of recovering it. Who knows?

The skeleton now is exhibited at the Academy of Natural Sciences, in Philadelphia. A skull was artificially made on a pattern believed at the time to have been similar to that which was not located and this graces the huge frame today. Research has now revealed the type incorrect.

A lot of people claim the skeleton and the legend that relates of its nocturnal wanderings in search of its head was the basis for the stories of the "Jersey Devil," the "Gwink," and other phenomena which left tracks in the snow and made ghastly noises in the dark at various times during the past two decades.

The revelation of some resident as an amateur aviator will cause something of a sensation. Archaeologists will murmur all over again furthermore if a flock of gigantic bat-winged birds choose to put in a daylight appearance.

But there will be something more than all that if the antediluvian monster, having finally located its head through the want-ad columns or some other medium, chooses to prance down King's Highway in the town where it used to live, long, long ago.

The details given above of the dinosaur discovery are mostly accurate, although the article calls it "hyrdosaurus" instead of Hadrosaurus. This confusion is understandable, since Leidy and scientists over the next century presumed *Hadrosaurus foulkii* to be amphibious, although today it is understood to have been terrestrial. Part of this misconception was the fact that some hadrosaurids, or duck-billed dinosaurs, had large, bony crests atop their heads that scientists once thought functioned as air reserves for traveling underwater. However, these crests are now believed to have facilitated low-frequency calls for long distance communication with other hadrosaurs. Likewise, early paleontologists thought that imprints of hadrosaur feet showed webbed toes when it was actually just the impressions left by soft tissue. Like other dinosaurs, the Hadrosaurus was thought to walk upright, dragging its tail, rather than the current model of a horizontal posture balanced by its tail. Interestingly, the 1927 article reflects the modern understanding that many dinosaurs were feathered. Alas, while evidence of feathers or fuzzy, protofeather coverings has been discovered in flying pterosaurs and a variety of dinosaurs, there currently are zero examples of this trait in long-necked sauropods or hadrosaurs.

Refreshingly, Haddy's "grave" still exists in a natural state and has not been plowed over with a parking lot. In 1994, the site was designated a National Historic Landmark. Haddonfield has dedicated Hadrosaurus Park, which is east of Grove Street at the end of Maple Avenue and adjacent to the ravine and marl pit where Haddy was uncovered. The creek that passes through has been named Hadrosaurus Run. Meanwhile, an eight-foot-tall, 18-foot-long bronze statue of Haddy stands in downtown Haddonfield. In case you were wondering, it has a head.

Does Haddy still stalk the streets and fields of Haddonfield, searching for its missing skull? It certainly wouldn't be flying around like a phantom airplane, at least in life. But in a spectral state, why the heck shouldn't Haddy soar about with the greatest of ease? Could the Ghost of the Haddonfield Hadrosaurus be the TRUE identity of the Jersey Devil? Descendants of South Jersey's Leeds family might take umbrage at the insinuation that they're related to a headless dinosaur, but anything seems possible in the wilds of the Garden State.

The preserved marl pit where the Haddonfield Hadrosaurus was discovered, pictured in 2010. Photo by Smallbones, Public domain, via Wikimedia Commons.

Wherever its bony noggin may be, Haddy has certainly enjoyed a celebrated afterlife 80 million years on as one of New Jersey's most famous denizens and a (luminous?) luminary of the paleontology world. Heads —I mean *hats*—off to Haddy!

SOURCES:

Avril, Tom. "Haddonfield's Hadrosaurus Back in Phila." *Philadelphia Inquirer*, 24 Nov. 2008, https://www.inquirer.com/philly/health/2 0081124_Dino.html. Accessed 8 Mar. 2025.

Black, Riley. "Did All Dinosaurs Have Feathers?" *Discover*, 26 Sep. 2023, https://www.discovermagazine.com/planet-earth/did-all-dinosaurs-have-feathers. Accessed 8 Mar. 2025.

Brownstein, Chase D. "Appalachia Biogeography: The Biogeography and Ecology of the Cretaceous Non-Avian Dinosaurs of Appalachia." *Palaeontologia Electronica*, 2018, https://palaeo-electronica.org/content/2018/2123-appalachia-biogeography. Accessed 8 Mar. 2025.

Coules, Victoria and Michael J. Benton. "The Curious Case of Central Park's Dinosaurs: The Destruction of Benjamin Waterhouse Hawkins' Paleozoic Museum Revisited." *Proceedings of the Geologists' Association*, 2023, vol. 134, no. 3, pp. 344-360. https://www.sciencedirect.com/science/article/pii/S0016787823000366#bb0025. Accessed 8 Mar. 2025.

"Crystal Palace Dinosaurs." *Wikipedia*, https://en.wikipedia.org/wiki/Crystal_Palace_Dinosaurs. Accessed 8 Mar. 2025.

"Eerie Noises of Night Stir Staid Haddonfield." *Evening Courier* [Camden, NJ], 15 Jul. 1927, p. 3.

"Haddonfield's Dinosaur Discovery Park." *Hadrosaurus*, http://hadrosaurus.com/hadropark.shtml. Accessed 8 Mar. 2025.

"The First Dinosaur Skeleton Ever Put on Public Display." *Hadrosaurus*, http://hadrosaurus.com/science.shtml. Accessed 8 Mar. 2025.

"Hadrosauridae." *Wikipedia*, https://en.wikipedia.org/wiki/Hadrosauridae. Accessed 8 Mar. 2025.

"Hadrosaurus." *Wikipedia*, https://en.wikipedia.org/wiki/Hadrosaurus. Accessed 8 Mar. 2025. Accessed 8 Mar. 2025.

"Hadrosaurus Foulkii ('Haddy') Information." *Borough of Haddonfield*, https://www.haddonfieldnj.org/information/about_our_town/hadrosaurus_foulkii_(_haddy_)_information/index.php. Accessed 8 Mar. 2025.

"Hadrosaurus Foulkii Leidy Site." *Wikipedia*, https://en.wikipedia.org/wiki/Hadrosaurus_Foulkii_Leidy_Site. Accessed 8 Mar. 2025.

Hawkins, B. Waterhouse. "Description of the Restored Skeleton of the Great Herbiverous Lizard, Hadrosaurus." *Twelfth Annual Report of the Board of Commissioners of the Central Park*, 1868, pp. 139-144.

Hawkins, B. Waterhouse. "Report on the Progress of the Fossil Restorations." *Twelfth Annual Report of the Board of Commissioners of the Central Park*, 1868, pp. 135-138.

"Iguanodon." *Wikipedia*, https://en.wikipedia.org/wiki/Iguanodon. Accessed 8 Mar. 2025.

"Joseph Leidy." *Wikipedia*, https://en.wikipedia.org/wiki/Joseph_Leidy. Accessed 8 Mar. 2025.

Levins, Hoag. "Hadrosaurus Site Declared National Historic Landmark, 1994." *Levins*, https://www.levins.com/parks.shtml. Accessed 8 Mar. 2025.

"A Look Back: Hadrosaurus Dinosaur at the Academy of Natural Sciences." *Courier Post* [Cherry Hill, NJ], 2 Aug. 2014, https://www.courierpostonline.com/picture-gallery/entertainment/2014/08/02/a-look-back-hadrosaurus-dinosaur-at-the-academy-of-natural-sciences/13517991/. Accessed 8 Mar. 2025.

"Marl." *Wikipedia*, https://en.wikipedia.org/wiki/Marl. Accessed 8 Mar. 2025.

"The New Jersey Hadrosaurus, 1858." *Linda Hall Library*, https://www.lindahall.org/experience/digital-exhibitions/paper-dinosaurs/08-first-north-american-fossils/10-the-new-jersey-hadrosaurus-1858/. Accessed 8 Mar. 2025.

Ostrom, John H. "A Reconsideration of the Paleoecology of Hadrosaurian Dinosaurs." *American Journal of Science*, 1964, vol. 262, no. 8, pp. 975–997. https://ajsonline.org/article/59097. Accessed 8 Mar. 2025.

Prieto-Márquez, Albert, et al. "The Dinosaur *Hadrosaurus foulkii*, from the Campanian of the East Coast of North America, with a Reevaluation of the Genus. *Acta Palaeontologica Polonica*, 2006, vol. 51, no. 1, pp. 77–98.

Ryder, Richard C. "Hawkins' Hadrosaurs: The Stereographic Record." *Mososaur: The Journal of The Delaware Valley Paleontological Society*, vol. 3, 1986, pp. 169-180.

Sarkar, Ria. "Mastodon Musings: The Story of New Jersey's State Fossil: *Hadrosaurus foulkii." Rutgers-New Brunswick School of Arts and Sciences Geology Museum*, https://geologymuseum.rutgers.edu/about-us-geology-museum/mastodon-musings/mastodon-musings/255-the-story-of-new-jersey-s-state-fossil-hadrosaurus-foulkii. Accessed 8 Mar. 2025.

"State Dinosaur." *SNJ Today*, 2 Aug. 2022, https://snjtoday.com/state-dinosaur/. Accessed 8 Mar. 2025.

"Statue of World's First Dinosaur." *Roadside America*, https://www.roadsideamerica.com/story/11155. Accessed 8 Mar. 2025.

"William Parker Foulke." *Wikipedia*, https://en.wikipedia.org/wiki/William_Parker_Foulke. Accessed 8 Mar. 2025.

The Ghost Light of Prickly Pear

Charles Tacke was killed with an axe to the skull. His body was found in a manger covered in lime. After his murderer was brought to justice, Tacke's alleged spirit returned nightly to haunt his former ranch.

The Helena Daily Herald called it "one of the most atrocious and brutal murders which ever has occurred in Montana." This was Montana *Territory*, nine years before its statehood, just outside its prosperous capital city. And this account of horrific murder, frontier justice and supernatural apparitions is a mostly forgotten yet true and sordid tale of America's Wild West.

Part I: The Savage Murder of Charles Tacke

Henry Tacke, who had been working for some time in the lower Prickly Pear Valley, arrived in town the afternoon of Monday, Sep. 4, 1880 to report that his brother was missing. No trace of Charles Tacke, an old settler and wealthy rancher, could be found and no one had seen him since the previous Tuesday. Neighbors were beginning to suspect foul play. Sheriff Chas. M. Jefferis hastened to the Tacke Ranch, located a short

The Ghost Light of Prickly Pear

The Ghost Light of Prickly Pear (Artist: Bat Sada)

distance off the main Bozeman Road, about four and a half miles outside Helena.

Soon after arriving, Jefferis entered Tacke's large, log-built stable. He noticed that nearly two barrels of lime had been emptied into one of the mangers. Perturbed, Jefferis procured a pick and knocked off one of the front boards of the manger. An appalling sight met his eyes.

There was the body of Charles Tacke, already badly decomposed by the lime with which it was covered. Careful not to disturb the remains, the sheriff returned to town and informed Coroner W. L. Steele. Summoning a coroner's jury, the group returned at a late hour to the ranch. The body of the murdered man was disinterred and found to be in terrible condition. The lime against the moist body had slacked and maintained a continual heat, causing rapid decomposition. The stench was almost unbearable. The body was dressed in sleeping clothes, suggesting a late night or early morning attack. The right side of Tacke's skull was broken in two places. The murder weapon, a bloody axe, had been buried with the body.

Suspicion was directed at Peter Pelkey, alias John O'Brien, a laborer who had recently been employed by Tacke. The man had suddenly disappeared, together with a valuable horse from the ranch. A wooden chest in which Tacke kept his money was found to have been broken open and rifled through, leaving little doubt as to a motive. Clothes that Pelkey left behind were found with lime and dark spots on them, the latter possibly blood. Once back in town, Sheriff Jefferis telegraphed in all directions a description of the alleged killer. Over the next day or two, a man fitting Pelkey's description was seen at various points on Benton Road.

At Cow Island, about 140 miles below Fort Benton, Pelkey stopped overnight at the cabin of Mike DeVall ("Duvall" in some accounts), a woodchopper who Pelkey knew previously from Minnesota. The fugitive purchased a horse from DeVall the next morning and told him before departing that he was headed for Yellowstone. Shortly afterward, parties coming down the river informed DeVall that the man to whom he had just sold a horse was a suspected murderer with a $1,000 reward on his head. DeVall and Stephen Hodgins ("Hodgman" in other accounts), his neighbor, quickly armed themselves, mounted their horses and started off in hot pursuit.

On Box Elder Creek, DeVall and Hodgins spoke with some Gros Ventre who saw Pelkey riding eastward. Near the Snowies, men from a bull train described seeing a matching horse and rider. At Reed and Bowles' ranch on Big Spring Creek, they were joined by John J. Bowles, and the trio continued the search together.

Upon hearing of the crime, Helena Under-Sheriff J. W. Hathaway tendered his resignation for his position as Marshal of the Fair—to which he had just been elected for the coming week—and set out promptly on the murderer's trail. He felt quite confident of securing his man. At Dearborn he recovered the missing horse, which had been traded to a hotel owner. With a fresh mount, Pelkey had continued his flight. A witness spotted Pelkey drinking, or pretending to drink, from a brook at Bird Tail Divide on Benton Road, careful to keep his head turned away.

James E. Stevens, the pioneering Montana printer and newspaperman who settled in Helena, claimed in 1915 that he unknowingly shared a stagecoach with Pelkey for 60 miles on the way from Helena to Fort Benton while the murderer was on the run.

Stevens said that after dinner at Rock Creek on Sept. 1, a government telegrapher, a regular soldier, told the stagecoach driver that he had been talking to Fort Benton that morning when the line suddenly went dead. The soldier rode with them to the top of Bird Tail Divide, where a pole had fallen close to the road and taken the wire with it. Upon investigation, it was found that the wire had been cut.

About 3:30 a.m. the next morning, Stevens was awoken from his slumber inside the carriage by the entry of a new passenger, "a fine appearing man about 28 years of age," at the old Sun River crossing. "He asked how far I had come, and when I told him Helena he asked what the news was there, to which I replied that there was nothing I knew of except that the new opera house was to be opened that night," wrote Stevens. [Ed. Note: This was Ming's Opera House in Helena, where Steven's friend, national theatre queen Katie Putnam, was performing a dual role in an English play called "Old Curiosity Shop."]

Ming's Opera House on Jackson Street in Helena, Montana, 1898. Image courtesy of the Montana History Portal.

The stagecoach stopped at Sun River Leavings for breakfast and a change of horses. "Before we went in to breakfast the stranger asked if I ever took a drink, and on my answer, 'Sometimes,' he invited me to 'have one,' which we did, and after breakfast we had the cigars on me," recalled Stevens. "Nothing more until we reached Twenty-eight Mile Springs for dinner, when I did the honors before meals and he reciprocated with the smokes afterwards. The stage rolled into Fort Benton about 3 o'clock that afternoon, stopping at the T. C. Power & Bro. store to unload passengers and express, and on the opposite corner to deposit the mail with Postmaster Flanagan. And that was the last I ever saw of my fellow passenger."

The next afternoon, Under-Sheriff Hathaway arrived in Fort Benton and informed Stevens that the man he had traveled with was a killer. Pelkey had departed Fort Benton by that time, but Hathaway discovered his quarry had stolen a boat that was chained to the riverbank. Pelkey had started down the Missouri River in the skiff, with Hathaway soon following on a steamboat. It was later learned that Pelkey himself had happened across the telegraph pole that had blown down and, the wire being within reach, had shrewdly cut it to head off intelligence of his crime.

DeVall, Bowles and Hodgins received news of Pelkey from time to time and eventually caught up with him at the Burrows & Allis sawmill on Robert's Creek, six miles above the Judith Gap. Pelkey had been newly employed there as a laborer, and was at the time cutting timber in the nearby woods. As dinner time rolled around, Pelkey and his co-workers returned to the camp. DeVall recognized Pelkey in the group at once. Pelkey was a French Canadian, a young man of 24. He stood five-nine, had black hair, and possessed a strong and muscular frame. His features were coarse, with Pelkey later described by the press as having "a rather stupid mien" and being a "hard-looking customer."

The wanted man was at once covered by the rifles of DeVall and Bowles. He turned to flee but DeVall placed his gun at the fugitive's head.

"You murdering son of a bitch. Throw up your hands or I'll shoot," warned DeVall.

"Yes, Mike, I am a murderer," Pelkey answered. "Shoot me through the heart."

The captors secured their man and began transporting him back to Helena. On the road, Bowles read Pelkey a newspaper account of Tacke's murder. At the conclusion of the reading, Pelkey readily admitted that he was the killer.

Pelkey told the men that on the night of the murder, he had witnessed Tacke open a trunk and place inside the money he had received that day. Pelkey glimpsed what appeared to be a small fortune within and resolved in that instant to murder the rancher.

A few moments later, Tacke headed for the stable. Pelkey ambushed him there, striking him in the forehead with the axe. After the victim fell, Pelkey struck him another deadly blow. Only when the rancher lay dead at his feet did the killer recognize the enormity of his sudden crime. He hugged and kissed the dead man, and said he would give his own life to restore him, but it was too late. He hastily placed Tacke in the manger and covered him with lime.

Pelkey returned to the trunk and examined the contents, soon realizing he had killed a man for only $240. He headed outside, mounted Tacke's horse and rode out into the darkness. But the faithful horse seemed to know he was bearing his master's killer and refused to travel, sometimes turning during the night and biting at the rider's legs. Pelkey was ultimately forced to dismount and lead the animal much of the way to Dearborn.

When captured, Pelkey carried a Henry rifle, a Smith & Wesson revolver, a slug shot and $40.

The day following his arrest, while the party was at dinner, Pelkey sprang for one of the men's repeating rifles. He placed it in his mouth and cocked and snapped it three times. But it was a Burgess gun, and Pelkey didn't know how to fill the chamber with a cartridge, so his attempt failed. After that, the group watched him more closely.

Pelkey talked freely with his captors during the rest of the journey. He was aware that his crime had no mitigating circumstances and he expected to receive the most extreme penalty of the law. Pelkey only requested a wish to be shot, as he "was a man and proposed to die like one."

At Diamond City, the trio delivered Pelkey into the custody of Meagher County Sheriff Charles T. Rader. The entire party then continued on to Helena, arriving on Tuesday, Sept. 21. Pelkey was again transferred, this time to Sheriff Jefferis. He repeated his confession and said he only desired to see a French priest, after which he was ready to die. On Sept. 22, Governor Benjamin Potts paid out the $1,000 reward to DeVall, Bowles and Hodgins, the "courageous pioneers" who brought Pelkey to justice.

Bowles wouldn't get long to enjoy his reward and newfound respect. In mid-September 1882, Bowles set the prairie on fire ("whether intentionally or not is not stated," wrote the Daily Independent) near Fort Maginnis. A group of cowboys saw the fire and commenced fighting it, while Bowles rode unconcernedly away. After putting out the fire, the enraged cowboys caught up with Bowles and hung him without further ado, a few miles from the fort. Bowles was said to have been "a hard case on general principles."

Hathaway was still on the trail in the lower country when he learned of Pelkey's capture. He returned to Helena on Sept. 23. If the Meagher County trio hadn't accomplished the task, Hathaway would still be on the camping trail, determinedly seeking out his man, noted the Daily Independent.

During his preliminary examination before Probate Judge Hedges, Pelkey went without counsel and declined to provide any defense to the murder charge against him. A few of Tacke's neighbors identified the prisoner as having been employed by the rancher at the time of his murder. Judge Hedges remanded Pelkey to custody without bail, and a trial date was set.

Part II: The Dramatic Trial of Peter Pelkey

The Lewis and Clark County Grand Jury case of the Territory vs. Peter Pelkey began on the morning of Monday, Dec. 13, 1880 before Judge J. E. Conger. Ex-District Attorney Col. J. A. Johnston appeared for the prosecution. Pelkey, who pled not guilty, was represented by attorneys Wm. H. DeWitt and I. B. Porter, who the press noted were unpaid but "guarding their client's interests as closely and zealously as if they were laboring for the most liberal fees." A large crowd of spectators filled the courtroom, closely observing all the proceedings.

The Ghost Light of Prickly Pear

At noon on Dec. 14, the prosecution completed the introduction of its testimony against Pelkey and rested. The counsel for the defense moved that the court withdraw Pelkey's prior testimony from jury consideration because the circumstances in which it was made did not constitute proper evidence. The judge overruled the motion. The defense thus began, with Pelkey testifying on his own behalf. His statement was lengthy and differed in several ways from his previous confessions.

"Charles Tacke and myself were good friends," Pelkey told the court. "He had been kind to me and I had no feeling of ill-will toward him. Every night, before going to bed, he used to take down a large bible and read a chapter from it, and explain the meaning to me."

Told in minute detail, Pelkey's new version of the killing was as follows:

He and Tacke were tending to the hogs, as some had already died of cholera and they suspected more might be infected. Pelkey recommended to Tacke they pull out any black teeth from the living hogs.

While Tacke was on his knees, trying to catch a hog, Pelkey stood over him. At that point, Pelkey slipped on an axe that was lying on the ground. He picked up the axe and swung it, intending to toss it out the door. But the axe struck an object. Turning around, he observed that the blade had hit Tacke on the head. Tacke was bleeding and staring at Pelkey. The sight of blood, the accused said, had always crazed him. Watching the red liquid trickle down the rancher's face, Pelkey felt the sudden and uncontrollable impulse to kill the man whom he had wounded take possession of him. He lifted the axe and struck Tacke on the head again, then once more with a fatal blow.

Pelkey said that under the same circumstances, he would have killed his own mother. Turning to the jurors, he said, "I would have killed either of you."

Pelkey frequently laughed during his testimony and betrayed an indifference to the atrocity of his crime, which made a deep impression on all present in the courtroom.

Pelkey then detailed how Tacke fell and mimicked the dying man's last groans and struggles. Seeing that the rancher was dead or dying, Pelkey had called to him, lamenting the deed. Then he remarked to himself that it would never do to leave Tacke lying, where the hogs would eat him. Pelkey embraced the dead man, then went out to the haystack and cleared a hole into which to place the body. But he found he could not move the corpse that far, so instead he threw it into an empty manger in the stable and covered it with lime.

PETER PELKE,

MURDERER OF CHARLES TACKE, HELENA, M. T.

Portrait of killer Peter Pelkey, published in the March 5, 1881 edition of The National Police Gazette.

At that point, it had dawned on Pelkey that he would hang for the crime. But having no money with which to make an escape, he pulled one of Tacke's legs far enough out from the lime to retrieve cash from the pockets. Unable to push the entire leg back under, he grabbed the axe again and chopped off the toes down to the lime, then sprinkled on more of the powder to stop the bleeding.

Pelkey decided at that point to end it, and searched the house unsuccessfully for rat poison. He then turned his own revolver on himself. But, he said to the jury, "As I looked at the pistol, I said to myself, 'That will hurt and I can't stand it. I will take my chances some other way.'"

Pelkey retrieved money from the wooden box, then carefully headed outside and checked that no one was approaching. In the clear, Pelkey saddled a stallion that was feeding nearby and rode off for Fort Benton.

Of course, Pelkey displayed some hint of self-preservation with this new testimony, claiming that the sight of blood had driven him insane, that his actions were unpremeditated and involuntary, and that he should not he held responsible or suffer the death penalty. Dr. Madden testified for the defense that Pelkey was indeed insane.

The next day, the prosecution began its rebuttal with the introduction of Dr. W. L. Steele, county coroner and one of Helena's leading physicians. In response to the testimony of Madden, Steele said no physician could determine a patient's sanity, the time of its inception, or its cause in just a single half-hour interview, except in well-defined cases. Under cross-examination by the defense, Steele refused to answer several questions, such as, "What is dementia?" The doctor explained that while he would willingly testify to any facts pertaining to the case, he objected to a line of questioning asked merely to test his qualifications as a physician. Steele said he had been practicing medicine for 20 years and "held his authority to practice from a source superior to the court." Judge Conger ruled that the questions were proper and must be answered. Steele repeated his refusal and was fined $50. The judge once again directed him to answer. The doctor declined and was given an additional fine of $100. Conger ordered a third time that Steele respond to the defense's questions, and once again he refused. The judge therefore found the doctor in contempt of court and ordered he be committed to the county jail. Amid much excitement from the crowd, Steele submitted himself to the custody of the sheriff and was taken away. The whole incident was viewed as regrettable. The following day, Steele provided a written statement to the court explaining that he had felt justified in his refusal to answer but had later been informed by counsel that the court had a legal right to demand his cooperation. He likewise expressed his respect for the court. Steele thereafter paid his fines and was soon released.

There were no further witnesses in the Pelkey trial. Following closing arguments, the 12-man jury retired at 6 p.m. and continued deliberating into the night. On Dec. 16, they returned a verdict that Pelkey was guilty of murder in the first degree. According to the press, Pelkey "listened to the verdict of the jury with less apparent concern than any other person in the court room."

Despite a deep covering of snow that blanketed Helena, a large crowd turned out for Pelkey's sentencing on Dec. 28. An officer escorted the manacled prisoner into the courtroom "to hear from the lips of him who represented the majesty of the law, the terrible words which should inform them more definitely than mortals ordinarily know the number of days during which they should yet sojourn among the dwellers of earth," mused the Helena Daily Independent. Pelkey stood for his sentencing and, when asked by Judge Conger if he had anything to say, politely bowed and replied, "Nothing."

Conger recounted the fair trial and the jury's decision, concluding, "With this verdict the country is content, and when judgement shall be followed by execution, your crime will be expiated, and the majesty of a broken and outraged law be restored. You will be taken from this room and kept in close confinement in the county jail of this county until the 4th of February next, and then taken to the place appointed by law, and between the hours of 11 o'clock a.m. and 3 o'clock p.m., hanged by the neck until you are dead."

Pelkey listed without apparent emotion until the conclusion of the sentence. He then made a profound bow, smiled, said, "I thank Your Honor," and took his seat. He was then removed to jail to await his execution.

Part III: The Execution of Tacke's Killer

The day before the hanging, the Daily Independent published a letter from a citizen of Helena decrying that the event would not be open to the general public. The writer learned from the sheriff that several hundred applications had been made for tickets of admission to witness the execution, but the law only permitted the judge and clerk of the court, the prosecuting attorney, two physicians, a preacher, two relatives or friends of the prisoner, such peace officers the sheriff deemed proper, and 12 other persons styled by the law as "reputable citizens." The writer urged that the Helena Legislative Assembly should loosen the law to allow more viewers. "Capital punishment is partly intended as an awful example to evil-doers, but the effect of the example is in a great measure lost, if only a few persons—selected on account of their good repute—are permitted to witness executions. The purposes for which capital punishment is inflicted would, I think, be best subserved by public executions," wrote the unnamed citizen.

On Feb. 3, a reporter from the Helena Daily Independent visited the jail and somewhat facetiously asked if Pelkey was in. A deputy replied that he was and could be interviewed, if desired. The reporter found Pelkey standing at the grates of his cell, smoking his pipe. "He is a constant smoker, and evidently enjoys it," wrote the reporter. "As from time to time he puffs out huge volumes of curling smoke, he looks more like a philosopher perfectly contented with his lot than a doomed criminal about to be executed."

The walls of the cell were elaborately decorated with wood cuts taken from illustrated papers and fashion plates. Upon a stand lay a Bible and several other religious books. Pelkey joked with other prisoners who passed by. J. H. Kennedy, a fellow prisoner, had been reading the Bible daily to Pelkey, who could not read English.

"The wildness in his eye, formerly apparent, has passed away, and he meets your gaze with apparent resignation. He said he was perfectly reconciled to die," wrote the reporter. "He felt that his sentence was just, and that he ought to suffer death. He still insists that his crime was unpremeditated, and that a moment before it was committed he had no thought of it, and that he shed tears over his victim a moment after the deed was done."

The Ghost Light of Prickly Pear

Pelkey said that at an early age, he had left home and gone to Maine, where he was employed in a lumber camp. He afterward worked at lumber camps in New Hampshire and Minnesota, and came to Montana 18 months prior. His parents still resided in Canada, but he had not communicated with them and hoped they never learned of his fate. He acknowledged that he had been in prison before, once for nine days and once for 10 days, but only for fighting. "I am very strong," said Pelkey, "and when I found it out I used to love to fight."

The condemned said he did not fear death, and would have been content to have confessed in court and been hung immediately. He had spent much of his imprisonment in prayer and believed God had forgiven him. "I will at least get out of this dungeon," he said. "A grave can be no worse than this for my body, and my soul will be free."

For anyone unable to attend Pelkey's execution on Friday, Feb. 4, 1881, the Helena Daily Independent and Helena Daily Herald provided lengthy, meticulous accounts of the proceedings. Up until his last night on Earth, Pelkey had enjoyed excellent health, slept well and partaken heartily in his meals. Perhaps due to the admission of several petty offenders to the jail and perhaps due to meditating on his fate, Pelkey's final night was restless. He had no appetite for anything more than a few crackers for his final meal the following morning. Still, the condemned appeared cheerful and prided himself on having "sand in his gizzard." When asked about his fate, Pelkey repeated that his trial had been fair and the verdict just. He said he merited his sentence and wanted to die. He felt nothing but profound gratitude toward Sheriff Jefferis and Peter Tone, his jailer, for the uniform kindness they had shown him.

Catholic Rev. L. B. Palladino visited Pelkey's cell at 10 a.m. and prayed with him. At 11:45 a.m., the sheriff asked the priest when they would be ready. "We are ready any time," responded the clergyman.

A crowd had begun to assemble outside the jail before 11 a.m., with boisterous spectators filling all available footholds on neighboring roofs, sheds, and other elevated places from which they could view the hanging inside the jail's courtyard. The press noted that even a few women were present. The sheds adjoining the jail yard were so densely packed with spectators that the roofs of three went down with a crash, a few people narrowly escaping injury.

Sheriff Jefferis read Pelkey his death warrant, the prisoner listening attentively to every word. At the conclusion, he bowed his head low and said with a pleasant smile, "That is all right." Pelkey was dressed for his execution in a new alpaca coat, well-worn, light pantaloons and new sandals. Led by the sheriff and accompanied by the priest, the prisoner was conveyed into the jail yard. The cheerful audience suddenly hushed.

Unflinching, Pelkey looked up at the scaffold and perhaps caught a glimpse of his coffin waiting beneath the platform. He ascended the steps and knelt down on the trap door for a few moments in prayer. The officers thereafter pinioned his waist, arms, wrists, knees and ankles with leather straps. Just before his arms were secured, Pelkey shook Jefferis' hand and said, "Goodbye." Pelkey stayed calm and even moved his head around to assist the lawmen in securing the noose around his neck. His face was covered with a black cap and, at one minute past 12, the signal was given. The under-sheriff unloosened a small cord and the trap door blew back with a startling crash. Pelkey shot down through the open space like lightning for a distance of about five feet and stopped with a dull thud. As the Daily Independent put it, Pelkey hung motionless for a few seconds and then quivered in "that struggle for separation of body and soul, which we call death." Over the next several minutes, Doctors Morris and Madden monitored Pelkey's pause as its slowed, until it ceased altogether at 14 minutes. The "majesty of the law" vindicated, Pelkey's body, its neck broken, was placed inside its coffin and delivered to the county undertaker.

It was the third ever legal execution by hanging in Montana's state capital. But as we shall soon see, death was only the beginning of the story.

Part IV: The Ghost Light of Prickly Pear

Charles Tacke, 50 at his death, was a bachelor described as eccentric, living a mostly secluded life and seldom associating with his neighbors. He was born in the town of Helen on the banks of the Weiser River in the Dukedom of Brunswick, Germany. Tacke arrived in America in 1853, joining his brother in St. Joseph, Missouri. Though a shoemaker by trade, he engaged in teaming until 1864, when he came to Alder Gulch and worked in the placers. Tacke moved to Helena in 1866 and for several years was involved in the freight business. He purchased a ranch in the Prickly Pear Valley in 1870, and a year later bought the ranch on which he last resided from Fred Reese. Tacke lived on the land in an ancient, one-story log cabin. Altogether, the rancher owned 320 acres and was regarded as a thrifty, prosperous man.

Not long after Tacke was brutally murdered with an axe by Peter Pelkey, farmers who lived on adjoining ranches began seeing mysterious lights floating and "moving of their own accord" over their deceased neighbor's farm fields, house and outbuildings. For a while, Helena residents ignored talk of the illuminated farm. But so many people reported seeing strange lights while passing the Tacke Ranch at night that citizens were abuzz and the press began to investigate.

One "stolid German farmer," who lived near Tacke's place, told the Helena Weekly Herald that the phenomenon looked like the light thrown from a red glass lantern at first, but had since been growing paler and lighter in color. He had seen from one to four of the lights moving in different directions about the ranch, some going up as high as 20 feet. Sometimes they settled on the corners of the fence, then began traveling to the house, barn, corrals, etc. before finally sinking down in an instant, leaving darkness behind. He couldn't think of an explanation.

Another farmer said he first noticed the mystery lights early the previous fall when he was late one night returning from business in town. He described them as clear, bright lights moving slowly about the open fields. Sometimes they rose to a considerable height, going over and around the house and barn, and visiting the pig pens, chicken houses and corrals. They either disappeared suddenly or rose up and sailed slowly across the valley until lost from view. The Helena Weekly Herald expressed skepticism of this particular unnamed witness, claiming he took "a good deal too much stimulus" and that his imagination played tricks on him. "Yet he is truthful and believes what he says," the paper added.

On March 15, 1881, a group of "sober-minded, reliable" Helena citizens rode out to the Tacke Ranch at night in order to witness the phenomenon for themselves. Belated on account of bad roads, they arrived at the Tacke Ranch around 10 p.m. Two of the party turned onto the road which passed the farm and traveled along the fence. All of a sudden, a large, bright light moved over the open field, somewhere from 10 to 40 feet above the ground. The object was four to six inches in diameter and about 18 to 24 inches in height. The body of the light was orange, occasionally flashing off rays of a greenish or sometimes blueish tinge to a distance of 40 or 50 feet. It moved up and down and over the fields slowly, then gradually sunk down and vanished. The pair also saw two other lights moving around, which resembled lamp lights surrounded by porcelain globes. While the witnesses couldn't discern as many details, these lights were white, mild and distinct. Another man said he only saw lights which might have been singular, or lights in the windows of farm houses, but he wasn't sure.

"We have heard of no rational attempt to account for the singular lights seen," wrote the newspaper. "Some believe they are connected with the end of the world, which [English soothsayer] Mother Shipton prophesized will take place this year.

Others say they are electric lights that have escaped from Edison's or Brush's laboratories, but they cannot see why they hang around one place so persistently. Others are sure they are sent out from hell by the murderer to find the place where the murdered man had buried his money." The Helena Scientific Club was planning to take up the investigation.

On the evening of March 30, the (unnamed) editor of the Independent and a few other residents went out to investigate the lights. They arrived at the home of Tom Darrington, which adjoined the Tacke premises, at about 8 p.m. and found several neighbors already assembled.

"Come to see the lights?" Darrington accosted the newcomers, who acknowledged that was their purpose. "I don't keep hotel," said Darrington, "or I might do a lively business entertaining the sightseers." Darrington's house was within a few hundred yards of Tacke's cabin.

The Independent learned that the lights had been more audacious than usual the prior night. One of the lights approached within about 60 yards of an old neighbor who had not enjoyed an amiable relationship with the deceased, appearing hellbent on getting closer. In self-defense, the man raised his gun and fired at the light, which promptly disappeared.

"It was amusing to hear the assembled neighbors all speak of the strange light as 'Charley Tacke' or 'him,'" wrote the editor. "They seemed to entertain no doubt as to the identity of the mysterious visitant."

According to a statement by neighbors, the strange light first appeared just before Christmas 1880, when the ground was covered with snow. It was red and brilliant, more so than at present, and resembled the head of a locomotive both in appearance and size. It wandered around the Tacke farm, sometimes passing over the top of the house but usually gliding a few feet above the ground. At times, as many as three lights were seen in close proximity to one another. They were usually visible for a few moments at a time, sometimes a half hour, but always vanished abruptly. Often their appearance was like a sudden blaze, expiring almost instantly. At first the lights visited every tenth night, but recently they were appearing every evening between 8 and 10 p.m.

Darrington and his fellow neighbors theorized that since Tacke's murder happened so suddenly, he didn't yet know that he was dead. They supposed that his disembodied spirit had returned, perfectly absorbed in his business as a rancher and intent upon preparations for the cropping season.

The Ghost Light of Prickly Pear

Accompanied by Darrington, the group proceeded to the murdered man's deserted residence. "Grim and dark, the outlines of the house and barn arose against the background of the starry sky," wrote the editor. "We entered the barn and were pointed out the stall where the murdered man was hidden under the lime. There, by the light of a match, we saw stains of blood still upon the posts of the stall. The boots of the victim still lie in the same position in which they were left some eight months ago, and a portion of the lime that covered his remains is still visible."

More curiosity seekers from Helena arrived, the party growing to 14. Soon there arose a cry from the barn. "There he is! There is Charley!" Sure enough, the Independent editor saw a glimmering light, much like a lantern, gliding about 400 yards from where the party stood. Faint and flickering, the gleam showed for a moment, then disappeared and reappeared. "That's Charley," said Darrington solemnly. A man holding a double-barreled shotgun proposed to shoot the light once it came into range but the target didn't immediately return.

The group decided to seek out the light and walked briskly toward its last location. They halted at about 300 yards, when suddenly a bright light arose like an extraordinarily intense candle flame within 100 yards of their position. It moved up and down in a zigzag way for an instant and then disappeared once again. Everyone in the party saw it distinctly. Then, another flame materialized about 200 yards off, moving rapidly along the ground like a man running with a lighted torch. It sped toward the group, then receded and circled around. "Watch it," said Darrington, "that's Charley's light." But soon it was gone.

The Independent editor suggested an experiment in which one person would step away 100 yards, light a match and wave it around to contrast the light. Just as this was done, a different sort of light flamed up an equal distance from the group. They yelled out to whomever might be behind the mystery light but no one answered. Once again, it blinked off before the gunman could take aim.

At various intervals, the gliding light could be seen glimmering along the horizon at assorted positions, but always within a few-hundred-yard radius of Tacke's cabin. The neighbors, many who had lived there for 12 years, said no such lights had been witnessed before the previous winter. They had investigated spots where the lights appeared while snow was on the ground but never found human footprints or indications that "a mortal agency" had created the odd display.

Some of the more superstitious folks were certain of Tacke's ghostly return. "You know, gentleman," said one neighbor, "that the ancients had a tradition that until a body was decently interred, the discontented ghost was unable to cross the Styx and continued to wander around among the habitations of men. Wash away the blood stains and remove Tacke's boots from the stable— perhaps that will allay the troubled spirit." On the other hand, some thought that the money-saving rancher had buried treasure on the property and that a search should be instituted at once.

There were more skeptical opinions, as well, such as the effect being phosphorescent light. Others argued that the surrounding ground was high and dry, and it was unlikely for there to be phosphorescence over snowy ground when it was 30 degrees below zero. Mischievous hoaxers were another hypothesis, although anyone doing so risked life and limb when there were men armed with rifles and shotguns blazing away at the mysterious visitant. The group finally dispersed without reaching a conclusion.

Henry Tacke stopped by the office of the Helena Daily Independent on the morning of April 2 and expressed his constant annoyance at the number of people entering the ranch at night to see the lights. More than 100 gawkers had stopped by the previous evening, he complained. They were tramping all over the grounds, liable to set fire to the straw with their lighted cigars and pipes and burn down the stables and corrals. He had no objection to people stopping by in the daylight. Tacke said he had seen none of the Ghost Lights which had been reported. As administrator of his brother's estate, Tacke was planning to sell its stock in the near future, but the ranch itself was not for sale. On June 6, Tacke completed the estate sale on his brother's ranch via Curtis & Booker, Auctioneers. Sixty-five horses sold, from yearlings up to aged adults, for an average of $41 each. Wagons, harnesses, plows and other farm implements were among the auctioned items.

Vaudeville performer Otis Shattuck, in residence at Ming's Opera House in Helena, announced that he had written and would perform "The Tacke Ranch Mystery" on April 18 and 19, the last production before his departure to San Francisco. Shattuck boasted that he had secured a personal interview with the ghost and learned all the particulars and modus operandi of its nightly visitations. "The Tacke Ranch Mystery" was described as a farcical comedy in four scenes in which Shattuck would appear as, erm, "his wonderful Chinese character."

While the ghost excitement abated within Helena as spring took hold, Darrington maintained that the mysterious lights continued to appear nightly at the Tacke ranch, "notwithstanding the ridicule that has been made in the matter."

Rev. Robert S. Clark proposed a grounded solution to the Tacke mystery, which had become generally known as "Charlie's Light," in a letter published in the Daily Independent on May 19, 1881. Clark had himself witnessed the lights while traveling home past the ranch on a stormy evening two weeks earlier. He wrote:

I found the light to be of two kinds—red and white. The former, upon investigation, proved to be sparks that came from a stove in Charlie's house, and on that occasion ascended until they flashed out upon the face of a cloud that lay beyond. It will be remembered that sparks from stove pipes or flues receive their color all the way from a pale white to a deep red, from the degree of heat and the quality of wood from which they are produced, and that they also ascend or descend or move at angles or in horizontal relation to the earth, as the state of the air with which they have to do may determine. And there is another thing in the degree at least, that is true of these sparks that I have not noticed of them in other countries, but have on several occasions witnessed here, and that is, that whatever may be their line of movement, though it may embrace any or all of the points of the compass, their passage may be partially or entirely concealed through the more dense body of air that may surround the pipe or flue from which they come. But upon reaching rarified currents, that abound in our Montana atmosphere, they flash into brilliancy and immediately go out. These flashes will be intensely brilliant if there should be a dense strata of air near it, beyond, to catch and reflect its kindled rays. A few miles makes but little if any appreciable difference in their appearance, especially in relation to distance, for in this I find that they are quite deceptive. I have seen them seven miles away, and yet the distance as represented by them was inconsiderable.

The white light that stood still, moved near the earth's surface, kindled up and went out at intervals, I found to be a light in a residence in the valley beyond the swamp, miles away, the rays of which, in their passage through the varied conditions of the atmosphere that intervened were made to assume all of the phases that are known to characterize "Charlie's light."

Clark described recently seeing a mirage on the road ahead of him that fluctuated between looking like a woman walking with two children to a horse and rider leading another horse.

Now if, as in this case, the rays of light were so distorted by the state of the air through which they passed to me as to present images so radically different, so false to the objects which they represented, may not the rays from lights at night, in their passage to the eye, across creeks, bogs or spring heads, be bent to the right or left, thrown up or down, appear suddenly near, and as suddenly disappear, as the different conditions of the air through which they passed might determine, especially that of their concentration and reflection upon the more smooth parts of the surface of the jets of steam that arise from streams and damp localities, such as are on the Tacke place, presenting the light from which they come, though miles away, at that point where they had become collected upon planes that are ever and anon formed for their reception by the irregular and constant movement of the vaporized current of air, and as these planes are constantly changing into rugged mountains, the rays are suddenly distracted, and the light suddenly disappears behind the rising jet of humid air as if blown out, to appear again when new planes are formed for their reception. I found that when viewed from a window upstairs in Darrington's home the display was much improved. Indeed, I found that when I went down to where the light seemed to be, that it stood still in the distance. This was because the vaporized air had collected and become sufficiently dense to collect and disperse its rays, but being upstairs in the house I was above the theatre of their action, and hence their display.

This theory accounts for the facts connected with "Charlie's Lights." First, its appearance in the winter as well as in the spring. Second, that it could be seen in the evening about the time that lights were kindled in through the valley, and that it disappeared about the time that these lights were extinguished. And last, that it could not be seen on bright moon-light nights.

The Helena Daily Herald was satisfied with Rev. Clark's lengthy explanation and wrote, "It is quite learned, and we trust so satisfactory that people will not be alarmed by seeing these lights hereafter."

Perhaps the reverend's theory did suffice, as the Daily Independent noted on Oct. 23, "The Tacke ranch ghost has almost been forgotten by the Helena public, but nevertheless is it still said to be making itself at home down at its old roving ground in the valley." The source was Darrington, seemingly intent on keeping the tale alive. He averred that the Ghost Light was still frequently witnessed at night, hovering about in the vicinity of the stable in which Tacke was murdered. Two or three weeks prior, the German who had been farming the Tacke ranch was visiting Darrington's house one night. Darrington glanced out his window and noticed a light burning brightly in the window of Tacke's house, which was about a half mile away. [Ed. Note: This conflicts with an earlier report that the houses were only a few hundred yards apart.] Darrington asked the German if he had left a lamp burning in the house, and he said he had not. The men watched as the light burned steadily for a few moments, then flickered and went out. Upon returning to Tacke's old house, where the German had been living for the past six months, the new resident found everything as he had left it. He had frequently seen the fitful gleams of the ghostly visitant at night, but it never disturbed him and he paid the light no mind.

On Jan. 13, 1882, the Daily Helena Independent claimed that a persistent reporter on its staff had finally "ferreted out" the cause of the ghostly manifestations on the Tacke ranch. It apparently stemmed from none other than Darrington and a dispute he once had with his now deceased neighbor. Tacke had sourced his ranch's water from Darrington's property via a ditch that the latter had several times threatened to plow over. The previous summer, shortly before the first appearance of the mystery lights, Darrington had finally made good on his threat to shut off the water supply. Of course, Tacke was no longer around to object. The shifting lights debuted the next night and continued to appear on an almost daily basis. The Ghost Lights always materialized where the ditch had once been and traveled along its course to Darrington's house, where they hovered all night, floating outside his window and disturbing his sleep. Several nights earlier, Darrington finally had enough and called out from his bed, "That will do, Charley; I will open the ditch in the spring." At that proclamation, the light immediately vanished and had not been seen since. Darrington said he intended to keep his promise.

The Tacke mystery was remembered, as a point of comparison, when a brand-new ghost story emerged from the Prickly Pear Valley in July 1882. As reported in the local press, two young duck hunters from Helena, Al Oldham and Norrie Travis, stayed overnight at an old, deserted ranch house after the first day of their excursion. They barely drifted off to sleep when they heard disembodied footsteps scurrying up and down the stairs. Further commotion erupted beneath the floor. The young men began communicating with the entity, successfully requesting it rap on the floor, ceiling and walls and invisibly move objects around the house. They began asking it simple questions (two knocks for yes and three for no) and ascertained that the presence belonged to a murdered man, whose identity they determined, letter by letter, as an individual who had disappeared 11 years earlier. Spooked long enough, the hunters spent the remainder of the might camping on the prairie.

Newspaperman James E. Stevens, in his 1915 account of encountering Pelkey during the criminal's flight, also shared his memories of the Prickly Pear Ghost Light:

After the capture and execution of the murderer, Helena was treated to a mild sensation by the report that the spirit of the murdered man was haunting the old Tacke home. People declared they had seen lights flitting about the empty house every night, and many a party was organized to try to capture the "spooks," but they never did, though it was afterwards believed the lights and the stories had been the work of someone who sought to frighten others out of the way of investing in the property, perhaps thinking to purchase it themselves. The excitement, however, soon died out.

Via administrator T. H. Kleinschmidt, the 320-acre Tacke estate finally changed hands for $3,600 in a probate court sale on April 15, 1882. While details of who purchased the property appear scarce in public records, Henry Tacke's 1905 obituary referenced his brother having been murdered on the Galen Ranch in Prickly Pear Valley. Hugh F. Galen was one of Montana's pioneers, operating stage lines from Helena to Bozeman in the south and Fort Benton in the north, and investing fruitfully in Helena real estate. He owned ranchland among his many properties, including 420 acres of farming land in Lewis and Clark County at the time of his death in 1899.

If there was any truth to Stevens' assertion that someone invented the Ghost Lights to thwart others from purchasing Tacke's ranch, one ponders if the most likely suspect wouldn't have been Darrington, the neighbor who was so insistent on keeping the story of the Spook Lights alive. Interest in the phenomenon seems to have extinguished after the ranch sold. Of course, maybe it all came down to that water ditch!

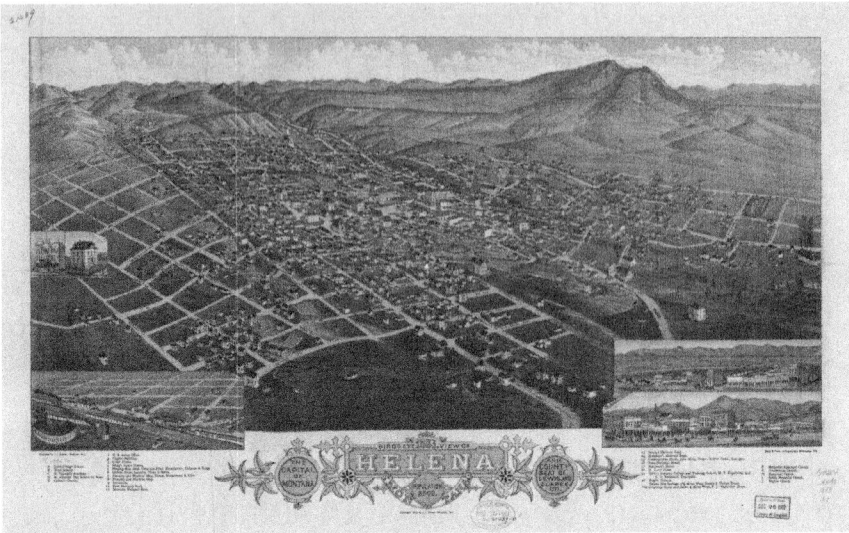

Bird's eye view of Helena, Montana Territory, 1883.

Part V: American Spook Lights

Ghost or "Spook" Lights have long been a phenomenon reported in various parts of the United States, becoming deeply enmeshed in local folklore. They parallel European tales of Will O' the Wisp or Jack O' Lantern lights said to be spirits luring travelers into dangerous territory or pointing out where to dig for buried treasure, depending on the nature of the phantom. However, the enlightened age revealed many of these luminous specters to be simply iridescent marsh gas (yes, swamp gas), per author Frank Smyth.

Over the years, Skeptical Inquirer has investigated a number of the American Spook Light cases, revealing more pedestrian explanations:

The Ghost Light of Prickly Pear

- Residents of the once bustling mining community of Silver Cliff, Colorado reported seeing dancing blue spheres and white points that receded when approached among the graves of the old cemetery, located about a mile from town on a dirt road. Investigators Kyle J. Bunch and Michael K. White determined in 1988 that these Spook Lights were caused by the moon, stars and electric lights of Silver Cliff reflecting off the polished marble headstones. The twinkling was caused by temperature fluctuations as the ground cooled in the evening following the day's heat, along with unconscious motions of the eye when all visual references disappeared at night in the dark graveyard.

- In 1992, Herbert Lindee of the Houston Association for Scientific Thinking examined two Spook Light locations in Texas, at Saratoga in the eastern part of the state and Marfa in the west. Lindee determined the cause of the Saratoga Lights to be headlights from distant, northbound cars on Highway 787 as they approached Bragg Road, an arrow-straight, seven-mile stretch of former railroad bed lined with trees and thicket. As a car rounded a slight rise in Highway 787, its headlights would appear first as a glow as they pointed into the sky, then burst dramatically into view as a singular bright spot in the middle of this "tunnel of vegetation." Lindee described this effect as startling and eerie. He also noticed that the light was stronger in winter, perhaps due to summer foliage and humidity. He surmised that residents knew the true explanation for the lights but avoided speaking about it because they benefited from the tourism it brought to the area. Similarly, Lindee concluded that the Marfa Lights were headlights from cars traveling north from Presidio to Marfa along Highway 67. The viewing site on Highway 90, located nine miles east of Marfa, offered an expansive, 30-mile view of the basin to the mountains. The headlights from distant cars did not appear to move, only blinking in and out of existence as the cars went behind cuts in the roadway and into valleys.

- Investigator Joe Nickell explored the Brown Mountain Lights of Morgantown, North Carolina and wrote about his findings in 2016. Nickell shared the evolving legends associated with the lights, such as them being Cherokee women searching for their beloved warriors who died on the mountain during a battle with the Catawba in 1200; the lantern of an old slave who became lost and is eternally searching for his master's home; and UFOs coming and going from an underground base. Descriptions of the lights vary, although they are generally seen as different-colored orbs that dart around the mountain. Nickell concluded that there is no single phenomenon at Brown Mountain, a flat-topped, "plateaulike" formation standing 2,600 feet. Instead, Nickell (and previous scientific evaluations he cited) argued that it was a collection of lights from automobiles, trains and airplanes, campfires and distant town illumination. Unstable atmospheric conditions in the basin-like area surrounded by mountains, coupled with dust particles and mist, causes refraction that distorts these everyday sources of light, presenting something that merely looks mysterious to some viewers.

- In 2017, Benjamin Radford examined the Paulding Light, said to be visible from a lonely road in Michigan's Upper Peninsula. Local lore attributes the light to a swaying lantern carried by the ghost of a railroad brakeman who was crushed by an oncoming train, or even to the light of a ghost train itself. Citing research from Michigan Tech, Radford wrote that the Pauling Light appears to in actuality be the headlights of distant cars, distorted by heat rising off the pavement. An inversion layer may also create stable air that increases the visibility of headlights across the 4.5-mile stretch between US-45 and the viewing area, shared Radford.

What's key here, I think, is that many Spook Light cases turn out not to be just tall tales or hoaxes but real phenomena, seen by numerous witnesses over a period of decades, even centuries. The only real difference lies within the interpretation and explanation of the lights.

Nickell, intentionally or not, closed his report on the Brown Mountain Lights with the dismissive tone that is common to a number of modern skeptics and so irritates believers and lovers of lore. "As with UFOs, some lights will remain unidentified—not because they are inherently mysterious but because they are just eyewitness reports or snapshots with so many variable factors. But to claim that something unknown (negative evidence) is therefore paranormal is to engage in the logical fallacy of arguing from ignorance: drawing a conclusion from a lack of knowledge. Consider this the next time Brown Mountain 'researchers' engage in their mystifications," he wrote.

Compare Nickell's viewpoint to how Lindee concluded his paper on the Saratoga and Marfa lights: "A reminder that caution must be taken. Because what we saw for four nights in Saratoga and three nights in Marfa did not go out of the bounds of the ordinary does not mean that the extraordinary has never occurred in either place. I think we sometimes forget that skepticism must be open-ended. I do not think that anyone will ever see at Marfa or at Saratoga anything not explainable by natural or man-made causes, but too many skeptics think the door is shut when it should always be slightly ajar."

Lindee displayed a scientific curiosity coupled with a respect for the local folklore and the possibility that, just maybe, his brief time examining the phenomena did not produce ALL the answers. What the scientific perspective often ignores or superiorly degrades as simple-minded superstition persists in spite of their findings because it has *meaning*. It is part of human nature to seek out and relish stories that suggest an unfathomable order and even joy inherent in a universe that offers such an unending stream of horror and chaos. Humanity is complicated, and there's no reason we can't accept and live with disparate explanations that stimulate both the mind and soul.

Charles Tacke's murder was a random, horrid, and brutal act of violence. Peter Pelkey grimly accepted his greedy, homicidal nature, an impulse he felt unable to control. Knowing immediately that he had ended both his victim's life and his own in that one awful moment, he displayed an uncommon resignation to his fate. Overall, the entire situation was a tragic episode in Wild West history. Maybe the Ghost Light of Prickly Pear was just a mirage or the spark from a stove pipe, as Rev. Clark suggested. Perhaps it was a scheme by a prospective bidder who wanted to get a better deal on the ranch, like a plot from "Scooby-Doo." But if Charlie Tacke's neighbors wanted to believe the murdered man had returned as a bright orb to tend his farm, so be it. Consider that it might be a subconscious coping mechanism to process the fact that anyone's lights can be flicked off permanently by an unexpected act of ruthless inhumanity. At the end of the day, a good story has more mileage and meaning, and the ethereal nature of Spook Lights offers an open canvas for the imagination.

With so many witnesses and an abundance of press coverage, it appears highly unlikely that the Prickly Pear Ghost Light was just a fabrication. Compared to some of the other cases of American Spook Lights, the Ghost Lights of Prickly Pear were reportedly seen at fairly close range. They moved about the ranch, seemingly with intelligence, and are reminiscent of the glowing, color-changing orbs sometimes associated with UFO cases, particularly involving crop circles. Spook Lights have been around a long time, but the explanations have varied with changes in human culture. As for the strange lights encountered in 1880's Montana, at this point it's up to you to decide what you think they might have been.

SOURCES:

"Administrator's Sale." *Daily Helena Independent* [Helena, M.T.], 24 Mar. 1882, p. 2.

"Administrator's Sale." *Daily Independent* [Helena, M.T.], 15 May 1881, p. 3.

"Arrest of a Murderer." *Daily Independent* [Helena, M.T.], 22 Sep. 1880, p. 3.

"At a Ripe Old Age." *Daily Independent* [Helena, M.T.], 31 May 1899, p. 5.

"Auction Sale." *Helena Daily Herald* [Helena, M.T.], 5 Jun. 1883, p. 3.

"A Bloody Tragedy." *Helena Daily Herald* [Helena, M.T.], 6 Sep. 1880, p. 3.

"Brief Items." *Daily Independent* [Helena, M.T.], 12 Dec. 1880, p. 3.

"Brief Items." *Daily Independent* [Helena, M.T.], 17 Dec. 1880, p. 3.

"Brief Items." *Daily Independent* [Helena, M.T.], 15 Apr. 1881, p. 3.

Bunch, Kyle J. and Michael K. White. "The Riddle of the Colorado Ghost Lights." *Skeptical Inquirer*, vol. 12, no. 3, Spring 1988, pp. 306-309.

"Capital Punishment." *Daily Independent* [Helena, M.T.], 3 Feb. 1881, p. 3.

"Captured and Caged." *Helena Daily Herald* [Helena, M.T.], 22 Sep. 1880, p. 3.

Clark, Robert S. "The Tacke Mystery." *Daily Independent* [Helena, M.T.], 19 May 1881, p. 3.

"Committed Without Bail." *Daily Independent* [Helena, M.T.], 23 Sep. 1880, p. 3.

"District Court." *Daily Independent* [Helena, M.T.], 17 Dec. 1880, p. 3.

"Estate of Charles Tacke, Deceased." *Daily Independent* [Helena, M.T.], 26 Sep. 1880, p. 3.

"Executions at Helena." *Helena Daily Herald* [Helena, M.T.], 16 Feb. 1888, p. 3.

"Funeral of Pioneer." *Montana Daily Record* [Helena, MT], 27 Jan. 1905, p. 4.

"The Ghost Story." *Daily Helena Independent* [Helena, M.T.], 19 Jul. 1882, p. 3.

"Ghostly Visitations!" *Helena Weekly Herald* [Helena, M.T.], 17 Mar. 1881, p. 7.

"Hugh F. Galen's Will." *Helena Weekly Independent* [Helena, MT], 22 Jun. 1899, p. 12.

"An 'Independent' Sensation.'" *Helena Daily Herald* [Helena, M.T.], 17 Jul. 1882, p. 3.

"Launched into Eternity!" *Helena Daily Herald* [Helena, M.T.], 4 Feb. 1881, p. 3.

"The Law Vindicated." *Daily Independent* [Helena, M.T.], 5 Feb. 1881, p. 3.

"The Lights Again." *Helena Daily Herald* [Helena, M.T.], 2 Apr. 1881, p. 3.

Lindee, Herbert. "Ghost Lights of Texas." *Skeptical Inquirer*, vol. 16, no. 4, Summer 1992, pp. 400-406.

"Lynched by Cowboys." *Daily Helena Independent* [Helena, M.T.], 22 Sep. 1882, p. 3.

"The Magic Lights." *Daily Independent* [Helena, M.T.], 1 Apr. 1881, p. 3.

"Ming's Opera House." *Daily Independent* [Helena, M.T.], 12 Apr. 1881, p. 2.

"Ming's Opera House (1865-1901)." *Montana Cowboy Hall of Fame*, Aug. 2010, https://montanacowboyfame.org/inductees/2010/8/ming-s-opera-house. accessed 8 Jul. 2025.

"Mirage." *Wikipedia*, https://en.wikipedia.org/wiki/Mirage. Accessed 8 Jul. 2025.

"Mother Shipton." *Wikipedia*, https://en.wikipedia.org/wiki/Mother_Shipton. Accessed 5 Jul. 2025.

"Murdered." *Daily Independent* [Helena, M.T.], 5 Sep. 1880, p. 3.

"Mystery Explained." *Helena Daily Herald* [Helena, M.T.], 19 May 1881, p. 3.

Nickell, Joe. "The Brown Mountain Lights: Solved! (Again!)." *Skeptical Inquirer*, vol. 40, no. 1, Jan./Feb. 2016, https://skepticalinquirer.org/2016/04/the-brown-mountain-lights-solved-again/. Accessed 7 Jul 2025.

"Our Ghost." *Daily Independent* [Helena, M.T.], 23 Oct. 1881, p. 3.

"Personal." *Daily Independent* [Helena, M.T.], 24 Sep. 1880, p. 3.

"Peter Pelkey." *Daily Independent* [Helena, M.T.], 4 Feb. 1881, p. 3.

"Pioneer Montana Newspaperman Is Claimed by Death." *Daily Missoulian* [Missoula, MT], 22 Oct. 1931, p. 6.

Radford, Benjamin. "Mystery of the Paulding Light." *Skeptical Inquirer*, vol. 41, no. 2, Mar./Apr. 2017, https://skepticalinquirer.org/2017/03/mystery-of-the-paulding-light/. Accessed 7 Jul 2025.

"The Reward Paid." *Daily Independent* [Helena, M.T.], 23 Sep. 1880, p. 3.

Silva, Freddy. "The Crop Circles Are Not Hoaxes." *Mysterious Places: Fact or Fiction?*, edited by Tom Head, Greenhaven Press, 2004.

Smyth, Frank. "Spook Lights Over America." *Unexplained*, vol. 4, No. 46, 1981, pp. 906-909.

Stevens, Jas. E. "How 'Steve' Overlooked Chance to Land Murderer." *Daily Missoulian* [Missoula, MT], 18 Apr. 1915, p. 14.

"The Tacke Ranche Mystery." Daily Independent [Helena, M.T.], 5 Apr. 1881, p. 3.

"The Tacke Sale." *Helena Daily Herald* [Helena, M.T.], 7 June. 1881, p. 3.

"Territory vs. Peter Pelkey." Daily Independent [Helena, M.T.], 15 Dec. 1880, p. 3.

"Territory vs. Peter Pelkey." *Daily Independent* [Helena, M.T.], 16 Dec. 1880, p. 3.

"That Ghost." *Daily Helena Independent* [Helena, M.T.], 13 Jan. 1882, p. 3.

"Town Talk." *Helena Daily Herald* [Helena, M.T.], 12 May 1881, p. 3.

"Town Talk." *Helena Daily Herald* [Helena, M.T.], 15 Apr. 1882, p. 3.

United States, Air Materiel Command. *Unidentified Aerial Objects: Project "Sign"*. Technical Intelligence Division, Feb. 1949.

"Until You Are Dead." *Daily Independent* [Helena, M.T.], 28 Dec. 1880, p. 3.

The Actor and the Hydroplanic Sea Serpent of the White Star Line

Less than a year before the Titanic sunk, another ocean liner from the same fleet encountered a dragon-like sea beast that seemed to emerge from ancient myth. The primary witness was a famous Broadway stage actor.

Austin H. Clark, zoologist and marine biologist at the Smithsonian's National Museum of Natural History in Washington, D.C., declared in 1930 that modern steamships had destroyed the fables about sea serpents residing in American waters and beyond. It might be true that humankind's conquering of the oceans dispelled the old fears of ancient mariners who were tossed about the sea in rickety wooden boats. By the dawn of the 20th century, thousands of passengers were riding high on steel behemoths that could cross the Atlantic Ocean in mere days. But accounts of sea serpents still trickled out into the press during this era. In fact, a spectacular sighting occurred in 1911 aboard one of the world's largest ocean liners, operated by the White Star Line—the same company whose hubris would be tragically tempered by the loss of its "unsinkable" Titanic less than a year later. And the primary witness was one of the most famous actors of his day.

Victorian matinee idol Robert Hilliard, "the handsomest man on the American stage"— essentially the George Clooney of the 1870s—was known for his sartorial appearance and performance in "he man" roles during his Broadway heyday. Hilliard was celebrated for his immaculate dress. A striking figure on Manhattan streets, he wore a white carnation in his lapel that matched the silver whiteness of his hair in later years.

Robert Hilliard, 1912

Hilliard's greatest success was his starring role in "A Fool There Was," described contemporarily as "a daring and realistic play that startled New Yorkers from their Lenten lethargy like a sudden explosion of dramatic dynamite." Hilliard began his run with the play at the Liberty Theatre on Broadway in March 1909 and continued to tour with the show for several years. Hilliard played the titular fool, who loses both his family and successful career as a Wall Street lawyer/diplomat when he succumbs to his lust for the (non-undead) "vampire woman," a femme fatale who enjoys using her charms to seduce men and ruin their lives. American playwright Porter Emerson Browne based "A Fool There Was" on Rudyard Kipling's poem "The Vampire," which was in turn based on a well-known 1897 painting, "The Vampire," by Kipling's cousin, artist Sir Philip Burne-Jones. "In making the vampire woman of 'A Fool There Was' a brunette, we followed Burne-Jones' painting exactly," Hilliard once mused. "As a matter of fact blondes—the real ones, not the peroxides—are the most dangerous type of womankind. There is ample scientific authority for this conclusion." Theda Bara portrayed the vamp in the 1915 movie version of "A Fool There Was," one of the popular starlet's few surviving films, opposite Edward José as the fool.

Hilliard traveled to London with the express purpose of attending a production of "A Fool There Was" in the spring of 1911. No sooner did he step foot on land than he learned that the British production had been shut down for good the previous night. Severely disappointed, Hillard headed for Liverpool and boarded the RMS Celtic for the trip back across the Atlantic Ocean toward New York City.

The Actor and the Sea Serpent

A black and white reproduction of "The Vampire" (1897) by Philip Burne-Jones. The original painting is lost.

The massive ocean liner RMS Celtic was launched in 1901 by the White Star Line, the same company that would debut the doomed RMS Titanic in

1912. Celtic exceeded 20,000 tons and could accommodate nearly 3,000 passengers, eschewing speed in preference for luxury and size. Averaging 17 knots, Celtic traversed its assigned 3,000-mile route across the Atlantic Ocean between Liverpool and New York in about eight days. Built by the Harland & Wolff shipyard in Belfast, Ireland, as was Titanic, Celtic was briefly the largest the ship in the world until White Star launched RMS Cedric in 1902.

CELTIC IS NOW BIGGEST STEAMSHIP IN THE WORLD

After Making Successful Trial Trip Immense Boat Goes to Liverpool for Regular Service

The Largest Ship in the World: The New White Star Liner, "Celtic," 20,880 Gross Tonnage, Launched at Belfast on April 4, 1901. The Gross Tonnage of the "Celtic" is 1965 Tons More Than That of the "Great Eastern."

The RMS Celtic was briefly the largest steamship in the world. From the July 13, 1901 Philadelphia Inquirer.

The Actor and the Sea Serpent

The Celtic, carrying the deflated Hilliard on his return trip, pulled into port at New York on Sunday, June 4, 1911. That afternoon, reporters from the city's "ultramarine" press, including the Times and Sun, boarded at the ship's quarantine and headed for the smoking room to learn the latest gossip and news from the journey. It was here that a steward revealed the Celtic's surprising encounter with a "monoplanic" sea serpent at dawn Saturday morning, which Hilliard corroborated "under duress." The actor begged that his statements not be printed since he disliked notoriety, a wish we only know about since The New York Times gleefully reported it.

The early-rising steward saw the strange sight off the Celtic's starboard bow and, instead of carrying the news to the bridge, ran to the rooms under his care and begged those within to come on deck and see it. This included Hilliard, who, in the actor's own words, per the Sun, had requested to be awoken "if anything unusual occurred on shipboard or out in the illimitable ocean." Hilliard drew on his pajamas and went out on deck to join a mixture of fellow passengers and crew, where the supposed sea serpent was pointed out to him "as the first great streaks of dawn appeared far off on the ocean's misty brim," said Hilliard.

"The sea serpent—witnesses differ as to its length—was sighted holding a bewhiskered, calf-like head ten feet above water. Behind, where the ears ought to have been, were two wings extending outward about ten feet, thus giving the saurian monster the appearance of an aeroplane skimming over the sea. The steward, in fact, described it as a monoplane sea serpent," wrote The New York Times. The serpent, according to Hilliard and the steward, was either pursuing a school of whales or keeping company with them. The steward claimed that the sea serpent turned a pair of "large, mournful green eyes" toward the spectators on the Celtic's deck. "Then it passed on its monoplanic way, dipping up and down, just like that, but otherwise holding its head erect. Behind it appeared at intervals a dark-green body, moving through the water with a wiggly motion," according to the Times. Captain A. E. S. Hambleton did not enter the incident in the Celtic's log, unsurprisingly.

The New York Sun's article on the incident, written in a glaringly more absurd fashion, described the sea serpent as having a white beard that reminded Hilliard of King Lear. The monster was at least 200 feet long, with 20 "convolutions" showing above the ocean's surface, and rising from its back were two wings that were at least 100 feet from tip to tip, according to the Sun. An amateur aviator onboard remarked that the serpent reminded him of a hydroplane. As the Sun article also contained the jest that a four-masted "Swiss Navy" schooner had been dragged down to its demise when the leviathan dove, it is best to take their report with an ocean's worth of salt. Nevertheless, the Sun softened its outlandish claims, writing, "The purser denied the story, declaring that the Celtic had not been chartered as a seeing-the-serpent yacht, but he admitted that there had been an unusually large Sunday school of whales noted off the starboard bow, or inshore, toward Amagansett [on Long Island—Ed.] early yesterday morning before anyone who had gone to bed was up. He could not account for the visions of those who had not gone to bed and who might have been holding royal flushes made up of marine monsters before the lights in the smoking room were extinguished."

Samuel A. Wood, a veteran reporter for the Sun and "dean of the ultramarines," told his counterpart from the Times that, "Sea serpent stories are rare at this port nowadays, but in the old days the men on sailing vessels saw many of them. Forty years ago, I wrote many of those stories, but as steam has replaced sail and romance departed from the seas, the sea serpents have evidently moved away from the steamship tracks." Wood's tenure might have been exaggerated here, as in 1906 the Times wrote that he had been "recording the coming and going of the ships from New York for 20 years." That March, between 50 and 60 ship news reporters, past and present, had gathered to celebrate the

50-year-old Wood for his professional accomplishments. L. A. Southworth of The World preceded the presentation of a loving cup to the senior reporter by "hazarding the guess that if Mr. Wood had not seen the Half Moon sail up the Hudson, he certainly had been at the launching of the old Peruvian bark Calisaya, with her renowned cargo of knotholes."

The ultramarine team gleaned some additional news tidbits from Hilliard in addition to the sea serpent sighting: Actress Grace Carlyle, a fellow passenger, had gone to London to study the play "Passers-By" by C. Haddon Chambers and would be the leading woman in the Broadway production, despite Carlyle keeping mum on the subject to reporters. (For the record, "Passers-By" ran at the Criterion Theatre on Broadway for 124 performances between September and December 1911, but it does not appear Carlyle was in the cast, with Louise Rutter as the female lead.) Also, Carlyle had been compelled to pay a $75 duty for bringing her Pomeranian dog onto the Celtic, and was "rather pleased to be the first person taxed under the new tariff on all American animals brought back to America."

In addition, Hilliard had won about $300 during the voyage betting against fellow passengers on the English Derby, accurately picking both the first and second horse. (This was some time before the sea serpent became visible.) Not content with

Grace Carlyle. 1917

those spoils, Hilliard won an additional $50 in
wagers thanks to his quick thinking and
ingenuity. The actor had worn his trademark
boutonnière on his lapel every day of the trip until
the last, when a flower could not be obtained. The

passengers joked about it, and Hilliard bet he would have one on by four o'clock. Hilliard wired ahead to a valet to bring a fresh flower to the pier. The valet rushed onboard the newly arrived vessel and Hilliard placed the boutonnière in his lapel a minute before the clock struck four, winning the bet.

Sea serpents were once enough of a going concern that when breaking the somber news of the Titanic's sinking on April 15, 1912, some newspapers clarified that the creatures were not the cause of the disaster. "It is clear enough that the accident which has overtaken the 'Titanic' was due to an iceberg, either submerged or floating above water. When fifty or so years ago large vessels failed to reach their destination, it was quite common to attribute their loss to the machination of 'sea serpents'—more or less mythical creatures of enormous size. There are plenty of people even today who believe in the existence of these fabulous animals," wrote the Manchester Courier. In pondering the myriad ways that ocean liners like the Titanic become lost at sea, an article in Tulsa World stated, "The secrets of the sea have been investigated so well that no destructive agent is likely to exist which is not known to science. Collision with a whale would not damage a liner, though it would be bad for the whale. The sea serpent may be dismissed without comment."

The Actor and the Sea Serpent

THE GREAT SEA SERPENT AGAIN

PREVIOUS PAGE: *THE GREAT SEA SERPENT AGAIN.—Captain J.F. Cox, master of the British ship "Privateer," which arrived at Delaware on September 9 from London, says:—"On August 5, 100 miles west of Brest (France), weather fine and clear, at 5 p.m., as I was walking the quarter-deck, looking to windward, I saw something black rise out of the water about twenty feet, in shape like an immense snake of 3 feet diameter. It was about 300 yards from the ship, coming towards us; it turned its head partly from us and went down with a great splash, after staying up about five seconds, but rose again three times at intervals of ten seconds, until it had turned completely from us, and was going from us with a great speed, and making the water boil all round it. I could see its eyes and shape perfectly. It was like a great eel or snake, but as black as coal tar, and appeared to be making great exertions to get away from the ship. I have seen many kinds of fish in five different oceans, but was never favoured with a sight of the great sea snake before."—The Illustrated Police News, Oct. 4, 1879*

As an interesting aside, you might wonder what became of the White Star Line following the tragic loss of the RMS Titanic and several other vessels. Did it go out of business? Nope; it merged with its chief rival, the Cunard Line, in 1934, and Cunard was absorbed into the Carnival cruise line in 2005. The company that launched liners such as

The Actor and the Sea Serpent

Titanic, Olympic, Oceanic, Britannic and Celtic lives on in the "White Star Service" that Carnival offers its passengers in the present day.

As bizarre and mismatched as a "transmedium" sea serpent with wings might sound, there were scattered reports of them following the 1911 encounter on the Celtic:

- In February 1912, Miss Gertrude Green, a Maryland girl who won a trip to Bermuda in a publicity contest, returned on the Bermuda-Atlantic steamship Oceana with an amazing story. She and the four other Maryland girls who accompanied her on the voyage witnessed a weird creature rise up from the sea when the ship was about five miles out from Hamilton, Bermuda's capital city. The girls were so startled that they had trouble describing what they had seen to the Bermuda-Atlantic press agent, but all agreed that the monster of the deep had white wings and green eyes.

- In September 1922, a dispatch from Constantinople stated that the Greek government had ordered an armed fleet to the Sea of Marmora to pursue a winged sea monster which had appeared off the Princes' Isles. The creature was first sighted in the Aegean Sea off the island of Negroponte (aka Euboea), where it frightened fishermen before passing unseen through the Dardanelles. Witnesses declared that the monster measured 40 feet "and that its flappers alone would smash a ferry-boat." The passengers and crew of the Siri Sefain saw the serpent halfway between Pendik and Cartal, a station of the Anatolian railway in Turkey. There was a violent commotion on the surface of the otherwise tranquil sea, followed by the appearance of the vague form of an enormous winged monster. First the head and then the tail were seen. The Siri Sefain danced about in the disturbed waters "like a toy ship" until the monster dived and disappeared toward the islands. Naturalists, of course, believed the monster to be a whale.

- A sea serpent with "a set of large wings resembling those on an airplane" was spotted on July 26, 1938 on Jefferies Bank, 35 miles northeast of Cape Ann, Massachusetts. The crew of the small fishing boat Giuseppe reported that a strange-looking black creature, 50 to 60 feet long with a head like a horse, broke the surface of the water several times that day within one-quarter of a mile from where they were fishing. Each time the serpent emerged, it opened its huge mouth wide, striking terror into the hearts of the fishermen. It also

The Actor and the Sea Serpent

frightened the large whales that were swimming in the vicinity, sending them scattering in all directions. The crew of the Giuseppe postulated that the monster was feeding on the shrimp that were abundant in the area. The sailors were unable to offer a more complete description of the winged serpent, as they weren't particularly interested in getting too near it.

Theda Bara in the 1915 film "A Fool There Was"

The White Star Line had a storied and tumultuous history, but who would have thought an encounter with a winged sea serpent was among those chapters? As for Hilliard, he is a reminder that even the most cherished celebrities can be forgotten in the passage of generations and time. But sea serpent legends are immortal, and the actor's brush with one—even if it was the result of bleary eyes and a long night playing cards—brings him back to top of mind for today's lovers of the strange.

SOURCES:

"Actress Pays Duty on Pomeranian Dog." *San Francisco Chronicle*, 5 Jun. 1911, p. 1.

"Aeroplanic Serpent Visible After Dawn." *New York Times*, 5 Jun. 1911, p. 20.

"Austin Hobart Clark." *Wikipedia*, https://en.wikipedia.org/wiki/Austin_Hobart_Clark. Accessed 29 Nov. 2024.

"Big Four (White Star Line)." *Wikipedia*, https://en.wikipedia.org/wiki/Big_Four_(White_Star_Line). Accessed 28 Nov. 2024.

"Celtic Is Now Biggest Steamship in the World." *Philadelphia Inquirer*, 13 Jul. 1901, p. 9.

"Concilio Et Labore." *Manchester Courier* [Manchester, England], 17 Apr. 1912, p. 6.

"Flower in Lapel Wins Actor $50." *Spokesman-Review* [Spokane, WA], 10 Jun. 1911, p. 11.

"Flying Sea Monster." *Evening Sun* [Baltimore], 21 Feb. 1912, p. 6.

"A Fool There Was (1915 Film)." *Wikipedia*, https://en.wikipedia.org/wiki/A _Fool_There_Was_(1915_film). Accessed 27 Nov. 2024.

"Good Enough Sea Serpent" *Sun* [New York], 5 Jun. 1911, p. 3.

"Hilliard Services Tomorrow Morning." *Brooklyn Daily Eagle* [New York], 8 Jun. 1927, p. 3.

"How Ocean Liners Become Lost at Sea and Are Never Heard From." *Tulsa Daily World* [Tulsa, OK], 17 Apr. 1912, pp. 3-4.

"Largest Ship Afloat." *Bridgeton Pioneer* [Bridgeton, NJ], 15 Aug. 1901, p. 7.

"Passers-By." *IBDB*, https://www.ibdb.com/broadway-production/passers-by-7338#OpeningNightCast. Accessed 29 Nov. 2024.

"Philip Burne-Jones." *Wikipedia*, https://en.wikipedia.org/wiki/ Philip_Burne-Jones. Accessed 27 Nov. 2024.

"Rialto Comment." *Cincinnati Enquirer*, 11 Jun. 1911, p. 47.

"Robert C. Hilliard, Dead at 70, Began as Boro Society Idol." *Brooklyn Daily Times* [New York], 8 Jun. 1927, p. 20.

"Robert Hilliard, Famed Actor, Dies." *Oakland Tribune* [Oakland, CA] 7 Jun. 1927, p. 1.

"Samuel A. Wood Honored." *New York Times*, 30 Mar. 1906, p. 4.

"Sea Serpent Season Soon." *Gothenburg Times* [Gothenburg, NE], 2 Apr. 1930, p. 7.

"Sea Serpent with Wings." *Green Bay Press-Gazette* [Green Bay, WI], 8 Sep. 1922, p. 6.

"Six New Plays Invite First-Nighters." *New York Times*, 10 Sep. 1911, part 7, p. 6.

"Streamlined Winged Sea Serpent Seen by Fishermen 35 Miles Out." *Boston Globe*, 27 Jul. 1938, p. 3.

"Titanic." *Wikipedia*, https://en.wikipedia.org/wiki/Titanic. Accessed 28 Nov. 2024.

"The Vampire Woman." *Brooklyn Times* [New York], 18 Oct. 1911, p. 3.

"Was Titanic Unsinkable: Why Did People Think It Was?" *History on the Net*, https://www.historyonthenet.com/the-titanic-why-did-people-believe-titanic-was-unsinkable. Accessed 29 Nov. 2024.

"White Star Line." *Wikipedia*, https://en.wikipedia.org/wiki/White_Star_Line. Accessed 28 Nov. 2024.

The Flaming Skull from Space and Lost Cosmonauts

In 1926, a California gem miner claimed to have found a recently fallen meteorite that was the skull of an alien being. His story brings to mind tales of Soviet astronauts who were lost during the Space Race, their corpses doomed to forever orbit the Earth.

I've previously covered the saga of the "Flaming Hand," a meteorite which fell near Atlantic City, New Jersey in 1916 and looked like a petrified alien hand with elongated fingers, broken off at the wrist. It was viewed as an omen yet gained fame as a Boardwalk attraction. A decade later, another meteoric "body part" crashed down in northcentral California, this one resembling a "Flaming Skull." One ponders imaginatively if this skull and hand belonged to the same "body."

Charles E. Grant, the gem miner who discovered the Flaming Skull, indeed thought that what he recovered wasn't any ordinary meteorite but the skeletal remains of some unfortunate alien traveler. "If the body can only be found, it will convince the most skeptical person that other planets are inhabited as well as this," said Grant.

According to Grant, the skull fell "in a flash of fire" near his mountain cabin in Cherokee, Butte County, on May 20, 1926. Its descent was witnessed by a "reputable well-to-do" California man who was camped in his car near Grant's cabin. The witness alerted Grant the following morning, prompting the miner's successful search and retrieval of the fallen star.

Grant described the eye sockets of the skull as appearing Asian in shape. "The largest ear hole on the right side is depressed and the left is about normal. The skull circles around in a layer above the eyes, a slight crack between eyes going up to the left of the forehead in place of a nose. The chin is broken, as if it had been severed with a knife, taking the whole neck off right to the skull," said Grant.

Ben G. Cline, a reporter for the Consolidated Press Association, wrote that Grant had sent him a photograph of the meteorite, but this image was frustratingly omitted from his syndicated article about the find. But Cline agreed that the object discovered in Butte County had "the shape of a human skull, with depressions suggesting facial organs. The writer's first-hand knowledge of races inhabiting planets other than mother earth is limited, and he hesitates, therefore, from the picture, definitely to place the Butte County visitor in the nebular scheme of things."

A writer from the Daily Argus-Leader in Sioux Falls, South Dakota complained, "It's dangerous enough to walk down the street now, in this day of aviators, careless window cleaners and thoughtless suicides, without having people dropping on us from another world."

On June 8, a Mr. Harrington and a Mr. Walker were staying at the Park Hotel in Chico, about 20 miles northeast of Cherokee, when they saw another meteor fall in the nearby foothills. This news excited Grant, who thought it "would be a great help to scientific people of the world" to find what was likely the "meteorite body" in order to match it up again with the "meteorite skull" in his possession.

"Now, gentlemen," the gem miner postulated, "it is quite likely that the two meteors are one and the same as they were traveling in the same course, namely in a northerly course, and fell only a few miles apart, the skull being severed from the body, being the smallest and retaining the less gas when getting near this planet, would be likely to come through the air a lot faster than the body. I intend to keep the skull in my possession until the body is found, with all due respect to government and science."

By June 24, a crowd of ranchers and miners were combing the hills near Chico in search of the second meteorite. If they ever succeeded, the news does not appear to have been reported. It seems Grant was never able to confirm his hypothesis that petrified alien body parts were dropping down from outer space.

The Flaming Skull and hand (and possibly torso) generate strange visions of a doomed extraterrestrial visitor, his craft somehow obliterated on a scouting mission to Earth, his corpse left to orbit the planet for millennia like some ghastly moon. In that way, it is not dissimilar from an equally morbid conspiracy theory that arose during the early years of humanity's own Space Race—that of the Lost Cosmonauts.

The United States and the Soviet Union wrestled for dominance of the cosmos in the mid-20th century, with every advance in spaceflight a prideful step forward for either nation. On the flip side, every setback was a reason to celebrate for the opposing country. Within that context, it's easy to understand how even the flimsiest rumors about Soviet failures gained traction in the American press.

Among the most pervasive whispers about the Space Race was that Yuri Gagarin was not actually the first human being to be rocketed into space, where he completed one orbit of the Earth on April 12, 1961. Only a few weeks before Gagarin's successful flight, the Associated Press reported that the USSR had supposedly lost seven cosmonauts before him at different stages of their respective missions, starting as early as 1957. Among the most unsettling of these rumors were two cosmonauts who supposedly made it into space and then were doomed to float there for eternity when their equipment failed.

"Washington Merry-Go-Round" columnist Drew Pearson wrote, "The first Columbus of the cosmos reportedly was a World War II pilot named Alexis Ledovsky, who zoomed in a rocket to an altitude of 200 miles, then disappeared forever. Another launching was attempted a few months later, in early 1958. This time Terenty Shirborin went up and never came back. The two losses forced the Russians to postpone their manned rocket flights for a year." According to the AP, "Czech sources" were the origin of these claims.

Per James Oberg, the "Dean of Space Historians," the credited source for this clandestine information about dead cosmonauts was an unnamed, high-ranking Czech communist that had shared the stories with a contact in Prague. The story was first reported by the Italian news agency Continentale in December 1959. According to Oberg, this was not the first time that Continentale had reported exclusive news about the Soviet space program which remained unconfirmed by any other sources. The news agency thus gained a reputation as a "rumor factory."

Thomas Ellis, writing in 2017 for the National Air and Space Museum, said, "The Lost Cosmonaut rumors have been persuasively debunked as far back as the mid-1960s. It is now known that the Soviets did cover up disasters and accidents within the space program, but there is no evidence to suggest they ever covered up any deaths in orbit."

Of course, Grant could not have anticipated tall tales of dead human beings adrift in space, even if

Martians or other cosmic visitors were on his mind. Grant, 75 at the time he found the Flaming Skull, was popularly known to Butte County residents and tourists as "the gem man." In his younger years, Grant had left his home in Bangor, Maine and "sailed the seven seas," developing his mining skills in Australia. He settled in California in the early 1900s and moved to Cherokee in 1920, drawn to dig in the foothills for diamonds and semi-precious stones. The lapidarist cut and polished the gems he found at his cabin workshop, fashioning them into jewelry that he sold to visitors. An institution of Butte County, Grant died aged 84 on Feb. 3, 1935. The present-day location of the Flaming Skull, or any other meteoric, potentially alien body part, is currently a mystery.

SOURCES:

"California Farmer Sees Flaming Skull Falling from Skies." *Oregon Daily Journal* [Portland, OR], 19 Jun. 1926, p. 9.

"Charles E. Grant, United States Census, 1930." *FamilySearch*, https://www.familysearch.org/ark:/61903/1:1:XCXP-FHG. Accessed 31 Dec. 2024.

Ellis, Thomas. "Ivan Ivanovich and the Persistent Lost Cosmonaut Conspiracy." *National Air and Space Museum*, 23 Mar. 2017, https://airandspace.si.edu/stories/editorial

/lost-cosmonaut-conspiracy. Accessed 20 Dec. 2024.

"Gem Man' of Cherokee, Dies." *Oroville Mercury Register* [Oroville, CA], 4 Feb. 1935, p. 1.

"Inter-planetary Jaunts." *Daily Argus-Leader* [Sioux Falls, SD], 28 Jun. 1926, p. 6.

"Lost Cosmonauts." *Wikipedia,* https://en.wikipedia.org/wiki/Lost_Cosmonauts. Accessed 20 Dec. 2024.

"Meteoric Skull Falls at Cherokee." *Sacramento Bee* [Sacramento, CA], 18 Jun. 1926, p. 8.

"Meteorite 'Skull' Stirs Californians." *Evening Sun* [Baltimore], 24 Jun. 1926, p. 31.

Oberg, James. "Phantoms of Space." *Oberg Corner,* 1996, http://www.astronautix.com/p/phantomsofspace.html. Accessed 20 Dec. 2024.

Pearson, Drew. "Drew Pearson's Washington Merry-Go-Round." *Star-Ledger* [Newark, NJ], 21 Apr. 1961, p. 10.

"Seven Have Died in Red Space Tries Parade Says." *Honolulu Star-Bulletin,* 25 Mar. 1961, p. 1.

"Skull Starts Hunt for Body in California." *Casper Daily Tribune* [Casper, WY], 25 Jun. 1916, p. 2.

Sarah Whitcher, the Lost Little Girl Protected by a Bear

Did a friendly black bear watch over a three-year-old child who went missing in a New Hampshire forest for several days in 1783?

When three-year-old Sarah Whitcher wandered off into the extensive forests of Warren, a hamlet nestled among the White Mountains of New Hampshire, she was awed by the brand-new world in which she found herself. The ancient trees seemed to reach into the heavens as strange birds sang their harmonious calls. Squirrels chattered and scolded one another. Sarah gleefully picked a handful of deep red wild peony and continued her jaunt along the forest path.

It was a balmy Sabbath in June 1783. The mills had ceased their chatter, carts paused their rumbling down stony village paths, and ploughs and axes stood still in their sheds. As mellow sunbeams and a gentle breeze caressed the landscape, all nature seemed to join in worship. Sarah's parents, taking advantage of the day, had decided to enjoy a pleasant stroll through the woods on their way to visit a relative who lived an hour distant up the mountain summit.

Not content to remain at their cabin with her siblings as instructed, Sarah had snuck away in pursuit of her parents. As the day wore on, Sarah kept moving, flowers still grasped in her hand, driven by the constant hope that her mother and father would be just around the next bend in the trail. An eagle screeched past Sarah, and a wildcat sprang across her path. Sarah's bare feet were bleeding, scratched up by the underbrush. As the sun fizzled out and raindrops began to pour, the young girl sank down onto a thick patch of moss, despairing and exhausted. That's when Sarah heard a crackle in the underbrush, and a large, black form emerged from the darkness...

John and the elder Sarah Whitcher arrived home that night to the realization that no parent wants to endure—their youngest was missing and possibly alone in the untamed New Hampshire wilderness. They sounded the alarm and neighbors gathered to find the lost girl, shouting her name and building large fires to light their way through the night. As word spread, residents from surrounding communities hurried to join the search effort.

The Whitchers agonized as the week wore on. Tuesday night came the unsettling news that a child's footprints had been found in the sand and mud along Berry Brook, alongside the tracks of a bear. "She is torn in pieces! She is eaten up!" people cried.

By Thursday, searchers resigned themselves to the fact that if Sarah was not recovered by sundown, it would be apropos to quit and accept the girl's sad fate. Around noon, a Mr. Heath, who had walked the long distance from Plymouth, arrived at the Whitcher's cabin. "Give me some dinner," he requested of a pair of local women who were cooking a bushel of beans for hungry searchers, "then show me the bridle-path to the north, and I will find the child." Bemused but hopeful, the ladies listened to Heath as he ate and described a dream that had come to him three times the previous night. In each dream, Heath had found young Sarah "lying under a great pine top, a few rods to the southeast of the spot where the path crossed Berry Brook, guarded by a bear." Heath finished his lunch and set off with another neighbor, Joseph Patch, to find the girl. Patch held the distinction of being the first white settler in Warren, arriving in 1767.

*THE OLD BARN AT THE HOMANS PLACE, BUILT BY JOSEPH PATCH ABOUT 1768.

The first framed dwelling in Warren, New Hampshire was built by Joseph Patch, the first white settler who had arrived there in 1767, by the roadside on the northerly bank of Patch Brook. Illustration from "The History of Warren; A Mountain Hamlet, Located Along the White Hills of New Hampshire" by William Little, 1870.

Sarah Whitcher and the Bear

As nightfall began to overcome the community, multiple gunshots echoed out across the countryside. It thankfully signaled a happy moment. Sarah had been found exactly where Heath's dreams had predicted, although no bear was in sight.

"Carry me to mother," the groggy and famished child had pleaded to Patch, who swept her up in his arms. When asked if she had seen anyone during her ordeal, Sarah said that "a great black dog" had stayed with her every night. Patch carried the girl back to her family's cabin, searchers hurrahing and waving their hats. Upon seeing her daughter, Mrs. Whitcher fainted. Mr. Whitcher smoked his pipe as hard as he could, attempting to tamp down his surge of emotion. For the rest of his days, Heath was revered for his prophetic dream.

Historian William Little included testimony from residents who were present for Sarah's ordeal in his book, "The History of Warren; A Mountain Hamlet, Located Along the White Hills of New Hampshire," published in 1870.

Sarah herself told the story of her harrowing week during her adult years. That first night, as she sat in the darkness with tears rolling down her cheeks, a "great shaggy black bear" had approached her. It sniffed her face and hands and licked the blood from her feet. Sarah was no more afraid of him than of her own large dog at home. She dared to stroke the bear's long, brown nose, and rested an arm across his neck. The bear lay down beside her, and Sarah placed her head upon his shoulder. Snuggled up in the inky night amongst the dense woods, the unlikely pair quickly drifted off to sleep. Townspeople would later suggest that the bear had guided Sarah to the path Heath had dreamed about, where she was soon after located.

Sarah grew up and married Richardson "Dick" French on Oct. 16, 1800. The couple settled on French's farm on Brier Hill in nearby Haverhill, near the pond which would later bear his name. Dick was a famed trapper and hunter who, in a terrible irony, did much to rid Haverhill and the surrounding countryside of bears. Dick and Sarah French had 11 children, and Sarah passed away Apr. 5, 1858, at age 78.

Children's fiction author and New Hampshire resident Elizabeth Yates immortalized the tale with the publication of her 1971 book, "Sarah Whitcher's Story," a classic still popular with young readers. In 2022, the New Hampshire Division of Historical Resources installed a highway marker in honor of "Sarah Whitcher and the Bear" at the intersection of N.H. Route 25 and Swain Hill Road in Warren. The marker was proposed by Holly Christensen's class of first and second grade students at Dublin Christian

Academy, who had read "Sarah Whitcher's Story" and then gathered the required signatures for a highway marker application.

Black bears were historically abundant in Grafton County, which contains Warren, so it is not unlikely that little Sarah encountered one during her nature trek in the post-Colonial era. But could a black bear have befriended and cared for her, or was that just a heartwarming tall tale?

Though capable of killing humans, black bears are typically timid and more likely to run away than attack. A 1924 survey of black bears by the New Hampshire Fish and Game Department noted the animals as "the most sly and retiring," and that they had never been known to attack a man unless in defense of their young. Black bears are primarily vegetarian aside from such prey as insects, fish and young or sickly deer, so humans are not on the menu. Perhaps Sarah's black bear didn't see her as a threat or as prey, but as a friendly companion and source of bodily warmth during cool nights in the forest? It would be easier to assign the bear as a figment of the frightened girl's imagination, conjured to comfort her, if searchers hadn't found their footprints side by side along the creek.

"Feral children" who become lost in the wilderness only to be rescued and raised by wolves, apes or bears is a common motif in myth and folklore.

There have been documented cases of feral children raised by animals throughout history, although most of them have turned out to be hoaxes. Reports exist of feral children being discovered in the vicinity of wild animals, but there is an absence of credible witness reports of these animals actually caring for lost children.

However, an incident from as recently as 2019 closely mirrors Sarah's story from 236 years earlier. Three-year-old Casey Hathaway was playing with two friends in his grandmother's backyard in Ernul, North Carolina on a frigid Tuesday in January. When he didn't come inside with the other kids, the adults began to panic. Casey was nowhere to be found and was not dressed for the frozen conditions, with temperatures plunging into the 20s Fahrenheit. Hundreds of volunteers combed the woods for the next two days, aided by helicopters, drones, K-9 units and divers. On Thursday night, the wind and rain became so powerful that searchers were warned to halt their efforts. Just in time, rescuers heard Casey's cries and waded through waist-high water to reach the boy, who was tangled up in thorn bushes. Uninjured aside from some scrapes, Casey just wanted water and his mother. Once safe, the boy made a remarkable claim—that he was helped by a friendly black bear who remained with him and protected him the whole time.

Sarah Whitcher and the Bear

Chris Lasher, a North Carolina wildlife expert, told Inside Edition it was certainly possible that Casey saw a black bear, endemic to the state. But he doubted that a bear, while nurturing to its own species, would have recognized a human child in distress as something it needed to assist. Nevertheless, Casey's family took the boy at his word that a black bear was his savior during his trial in the frozen forest.

There is one fascinating inconsistency in Sarah's story, in that when first recovered the girl didn't claim it was a bear that had cared for her but "a great black dog." The most plausible explanation is that at only three years old, Sarah wasn't as yet that familiar with bears and associated the creature with her family's pet dog. By the time she grew into an adult, Sarah would have correctly understood that the animal she encountered was a bear.

However, this was the late 18th century and there is a disquieting fact that might shock modern residents of New Hampshire—wolves were an enormous presence during this era. The predators were prevalent throughout New England when Europeans first arrived, and continued to be a factor at the time Sarah was lost in the woods. Wolfpacks roamed throughout the region, great numbers of the animals storming New Hampshire in 1744, 1764 and 1784. During the Revolutionary War, with most men away fighting, women and children in Plymouth were often frightened by wolves howling throughout the night. In neighboring Warren, wolves prowled outside houses in the dark, standing with their paws against windows to peer inside. Many towns issued hefty bounties on wolves, and they were extirpated in the state by about 1880. Dick French, Sarah's husband and apparently the Big Game Terminator, gained local fame as a wolf hunter. The wolves that were endemic to New Hampshire displayed diverse coloring, including black fur, with the latter pelts being highly valued by the area's indigenous people.

So, could it be that the "great black dog" which protected Sarah was not a bear at all but a black wolf? While it may be hard to believe that a carnivorous wolf would see a small child as a helpless being to be nurtured and not devoured, it fits a tradition going all the way back to Romulus and Remus in ancient Rome.

Or perhaps this was some ursine variation of the third man factor, the phenomenon in which people enduring mortal peril, like stranded mountaineers and shipwrecked sailors, report an unseen presence that comforts and supports them. Notably, the rescuers of Sarah and Casey never saw the bear that the children said was with them constantly, although it is probable that the animal fled upon hearing the approach of adult humans. Still, one ponders if the invisible "guardian angel" reported in third man cases could be visualized as a warm, friendly bear in the naturally imaginative minds of children who are undergoing traumatic experiences.

The story of Sarah Whitcher and the bear has timeless appeal. It suggests that even in the savage recesses of the natural world, there is room for empathy and caring, especially when it comes to the most vulnerable members of our society. And let's be honest, who deep down in their desires doesn't want to snuggle with a bear?

SOURCES:

"American Black Bear." *Wikipedia*, https://en.wikipedia.org/wiki/American_black_bear. Accessed 23 Nov. 2024.

"Did a Bear Really Take Care of a Missing North Carolina Boy?" *Inside Edition*, 12 Feb. 2019, https://www.insideedition.com/did-bear-really-take-care-missing-north-carolina-boy-50698. Accessed 23 Nov. 2024.

Dombrowski, Stefan C., et al. "Feral Children. (Abstract)" *Assessing and Treating Low Incidence/High Severity Psychological Disorders of Childhood*. Springer, 2011, https://link.springer.com/chapter/10.1007/978-1-4419-9970-2_5. Accessed 23 Nov. 2024.

"Dublin Schoolchildren Driving Force Behind Newest NH Historical Highway Marker." *New*

Hampshire Department of Natural & Cultural Resources, 8 Jun. 2022. https://www.dncr.nh.gov/news-and-media/dublin-schoolchildren-driving-force-behind-newest-nh-historical-highway-marker. Press release.

Little, William. *The History of Warren; A Mountain Hamlet, Located Along the White Hills of New Hampshire. Manchester, N.H.*, William E. Moore, 1870.

Radford, Benjamin. "Feral Children: Lore of the Wild Child." *Live Science*, 27 Nov. 2013, https://www.livescience.com/41590-feral-children.html. Accessed 23 Nov. 2024.

Silver, Helenette. *A History of New Hampshire Game and Furbearers.* New Hampshire Fish and Game Department, 1957.

"Third Man Factor." *Wikipedia*, https://en.wikipedia.org/wiki/Third_man_factor. Accessed 23 Nov. 2024.

"Three-Year-Old Boy Missing in Woods for Two Days Says Friendly Bear Kept Him Safe." *Guardian*, 28 Jan. 2019, https://www.theguardian.com/us-news/2019/jan/28/three-year-old-boy-missing-in-woods-for-two-days-says-friendly-bear-kept-him-safe?. Accessed 23 Nov. 2024.

Sarah Whitcher and the Bear

Whitcher, William F. *History of the Town of Haverhill, New Hampshire.* 1919.

Yates, Elizabeth. *Sarah Whitcher's Story.* Bob Jones University Press, 1994.

The Haunting History of Gown Man and the Hugging Mollies

Nefarious, disguised muggers prowled the American South during the early decades of the 20th century, straddling a murky line between real-life criminal and folklore.

The Gown Man (Artist: Bat Sada)

Gown Man and Hugging Mollies

While investigating the strange case of the Monster of Marmotte Street (aka the Mary Shelley-inaccurate "Frankenstein" of Fisher's Alley), I came across another strange character that once prowled the same streets in North Mobile, Alabama. One newspaper compared the hysteria surrounding the Marmotte Street Monster of January/February 1938 to the "Gown Man" who once stalked Davis Avenue, draped in white and terrifying pedestrians. *Who was this Gown Man?* I needed to find out and was surprised to uncover that he was a presence who haunted the Mobile area, not just once but multiple times throughout several decades. And it went beyond Mobile... I soon learned that the Gown Man was a specter deeply entwined with the entirety of the American South, ever present in the shadowy subconsciousness of its residents.

Before we continue, I want to touch on a conundrum that sparks a continual wrestling match within my brain. One challenge in writing about these events in North Mobile is the fact that early 20th-century news articles aren't exactly known for their racial sensitivity. As North Mobile was a predominately Black community, the articles about the Gown Man and Monster of Marmotte Street routinely underlined that fact. Many articles were written neutrally, although they used now-outdated nomenclature. But some articles dripped with ugly and obvious racism, and it's rather shocking to see today. It is also blatant that some of these stories were painting Black residents as superstitious and excitable. Of course, that scene plays out throughout time in news stories about mass hysteria surrounding various mysterious fiends, no matter the town or its demographics. As a writer who obsessively cites his sources, I struggle with even stating the headlines of some of these old news articles. Should I present the citations as they were, or strike out offending words (as I currently have done)? Within the body of my text, I try to avoid references to more objectionable content unless absolutely necessary to convey the correct historical context. That is hard to ignore in presenting this topic, which explores a possibly folkloric phenomenon documented in Black communities throughout the American South during the late 1800s and early 20th century. In any case, it's just a reminder that history isn't very pretty but you disparage truth if you ignore it.

During the winter panic over the Frankenstein of Fisher's Alley in 1938, the Pensacola Journal stated on Jan. 29 that "not since the notorious 'Gown Man' of Davis Avenue had there been such a scare" in the primarily Black neighborhood of North Mobile. The menace had appeared "clad in white" and "frightened the wits out of his victims." This particular Gown Man was likely a reference to John Coleman, an African-American man who terrorized hundreds of residents along Davis Avenue several years earlier before his capture and arrest. The Pensacola Journal stated that the Gown Man was a thief who had been sentenced to a stint in the penitentiary, although this could have been a blurred memory of an earlier Gown Man, Willie Taylor, who was a purse snatcher given hard labor for his crimes. Coleman was more of a prankster, whose modus operandi during both of his two tenures as the Gown Man was to accost pedestrians, raise his overcoat over his head, make faces, and shout, "Boo!" The cops preferred a vagrancy charge for Coleman, who paid a $10 fine for the offense in police court. But this was just the latest adventure of Mobile's Gown Man.

Historical Note: Davis Avenue, which has been renamed to Dr. Martin Luther King Jr. Avenue, is celebrated in the present day for its role during the 1940s-1970s as Mobile's "'Black Main Street'– a hub of black-owned businesses and venues, [and] a walkable and tight-knit community with dense activity," according to the Alabama Contemporary Art Center.

To learn more about the Gown Man, we need to travel further back in time, starting on Dec. 10, 1927. Per a report in the New Orleans States, Mobile's police force was on the hunt for the Gown Man, a "mysterious night prowler who has terrorized residents in the northern part of the city and shifted to a different locality." Passing motorists and a resident of the St. Charles apartments spotted the "apparition" and alerted police, putting them on the trail early that morning. Police ultimately admitted failure after "the curious figure of the much-wanted intruder disappeared in the darkness just as pursuing officers reached the spot where he was last reported."

Turning the clock back further, we learn that the Gown Man was especially active in Whistler, an Alabama community about seven miles northwest of Mobile. An article published in the Sept. 29, 1921 Wiregrass Farmer offered a detailed description of the Gown Man, or at least one version of him, and his notoriety:

"GOWN MAN" APPEARS AGAIN

Whistler's "gown man," the mysterious figure which has appeared for four consecutive years in Mobile's suburb, has come back again. The heavily robed figure appeared for the first time this year last Friday, when several Whistler residents saw him go into a pine thicket near the Turnerville road. The figure was covered by a flowing gown and wore a high hat coming to a point.

The stories as told about the "gown man" as it is known over the section brand it as a rather harmless specter, but the mystery which surrounds it comes from the fact that it has never been seen at close range. Every time a "materialization" is made, a crowd is organized to catch it, but after hundreds of these chases the "gown man" is still free. Every year he appears about the same time and is glimpsed practically every night until late in the winter.

The gown man makes a specialty of frightening children, though no record has been made of any harm being done. He seems to take especial delight in appearing suddenly to youths after dark, and the bona fide nature of many a wild chase is attested to by the leading residents of Whistler.

Organized effort was made to get the wanderer last year, and on several occasions it seemed to [be] cornered, but always escaped. One night during last winter the figure was seen to leap into an empty freight car on a railroad track, but when the pursuers came up to the car it was empty. There was only one door to the car.

Since the re-appearance of the "gown man" Friday, Whistler residents have begun a movement to catch the person, and finally get at the bottom of the mystery. Meanwhile the children in Whistler are keeping pretty close to their homes until the capture is made.

Looking back, it's hard not to notice the unsettling similarity between the Whistler Gown Man's "flowing gown" and "high hat coming to a point" and the traditional attire of the Ku Klux Klan. According to the Anti-Defamation League (ADL), the original KKK that formed in the wake of the U.S. Civil War wore masks or hoods and sometimes robes but it was the second version of the hate group, started in 1915, that firmly established the well-known look of the hooded and robed Klansmember. The organization formed in Alabama following the Civil War to oppose the extension of citizenship and voting rights to former slaves as well as ending Republican control of the state government, per the Encyclopedia of Alabama. The KKK disbanded during the early 1870s but returned in 1915, establishing a Birmingham chapter the following year and expanding statewide throughout the early 1920s. This timing eerily correlates with the emergence of Whistler's Gown Man. Were residents seeing local Klansmen on their way to meetings deep in the woods, or was it just a coincidence? Overall, could the Gown Man phenomenon have reflected fears in the African-American community of a very tangible threat that was lurking in the underbelly of the South? Perhaps, but the Gown Man as described in 1921 was a more benign boogeyman, possibly even a non-human phantom. Also, when various Gown Men were unmasked, they were most frequently Black, revealing that the culprit was preying on their own community. The various Gown Men also wore a variety of robes and women's clothing of different colors, and their activity ranged from pesky to nefarious. As you will see, the Gown Man might represent folklore developed specifically within African-American communities in the South during the late 1800s and first few decades of the 20th century.

In 1920, we come across the very human Gown Man who seems to be at the root of the long-lasting phenomenon. On July 24, Willie Taylor was paraded before Mobile police court wearing the blue gown, black bonnet and mask in which he had been captured. North Mobile residents testified that Taylor was indeed the figure who had been terrifying the residents of Davis Avenue for several weeks. Taylor's specialty was purse snatching, and he had been arrested on the complaint of such by one of his recent victims, Irene Hawkins. Even worse, Taylor had allegedly frightened and robbed children who had been sent to local stores on errands. Taylor was convicted of his crimes and given a year of hard labor.

Was Taylor the original Gown Man, whose exploits became urban legend around Mobile and fueled stories of more evasive robed strangers in subsequent years? Perhaps he inspired later Gown Men like John Coleman? Possibly, but Taylor's arrest was just a bump in the road for the Gown Man, whose history in Mobile stretched back decades.

On Nov. 2, 1900, Mobile police were looking for a man in a "Mother Hubbard" dress (a long, wide, loose-fitting gown with long sleeves and a high neck), who had "disturbed the peace and serenity of the western portion of the city and prevented many from staying out late for fear of coming in contact with the mysterious individual," wrote the New Orleans Times-Democrat. Police planned to redouble their efforts to discover and make known this individual's identity, "as well as the object he could have in masquerading out of season." Mobile police provided an update six days later, which also might be the first time the ominous character was referred to as "gown man." As reported in the Times-Democrat: "Chief Soost, believing that the 'gown man' is being used as a subterfuge for disorderly persons to carry guns, has issued some orders on the subject. He states that his detectives have investigated the subject, and found the 'gown man' to be a myth, and there is more danger from the gangs hunting the 'gown man' than from the imaginary gentleman." The reference to a mob searching for the Gown Man reflects the posse of armed vigilantes that patrolled North Mobile looking for the Monster of Marmotte Street in 1938 and had to be dispersed by police lest someone get shot.

Even if the original Gown Man was a myth, there is evidence that he permeated local popular culture. Mobile held its Mardi Gras festivities on Feb. 19, 1901. During the parade, the "Commic Cowboys" presented eight humorous floats portraying local events, themed "Mobile's

Expansion." These floats were titled: Return of Our
Mystics, Mrs. Nation and the City Ordinances, The
Mobile Press Baseball Club to the Rescue, Mobile
New Year's Caller, Public Library, Alabama's
Motto, New Union Depot, and The Gown Man.

*Matira Bambridge wearing a Mother Hubbard
dress, mid-1800s.*

Newspapers outside of Mobile reported on the Gown Man, and he would appear in cities throughout the South in the coming years. Did these news articles implant the idea in the head of readers in other states? Or could it mean that the Gown Man was a wider phenomenon? As you will see, the answer is that there were multiple other Gown Men operating throughout the American South, and under a variety of nicknames.

The Strange Menace of the Hugging Mollies

Before the Gown Man, there were the "Hugging Mollies." Their reign of terror lasted for over a decade in Macon, Georgia and ultimately spread outward.

"Macon, Ga., is worried by a class of criminals new to this climate," stated a February 1875 news report. These mysterious men in women's apparel were said to halt people on the street during late-night hours. When an unsuspecting pedestrian stopped to see what the supposed woman needed, they would be seized and robbed of all their valuables. Several of the Hugging Mollies were eventually caught and severely punished by Macon authorities, ending the trouble.

But on the night of July 13, 1883, a Collinsville man named Holliday "attempted to revive the old order," per the Macon Telegraph and Messenger. Holliday dressed in female attire and prowled the highway, where he jumped upon a woman, Nancy Boon, and "abused her outrageously." Boon, a well-known woman who sold roots, herbs, barks, etc., recognized Holliday's voice and reported him to the police. This Hugging Molly was arrested and fined $10, but defaulted on payment and was sent to the chain gang.

Yet another Hugging Molly surfaced in Macon during August 1885, assaulting people near a synagogue. He was seen loitering near the gate of a house on Pine Street, near Second, on the night of Aug. 13. The homeowner came out and attacked the Hugging Molly, who fled. Police assumed it was the same perpetrator who had attempted to burglarize a house a few nights earlier and escaped when the resident discovered him.

On Sept. 1, Macon Bailiff W. W. Henderson sold off a trunk belonging to one of the city's Hugging Mollies for $15. The buyer, C. Perryman, opened the trunk to find it contained "a quantity of fine underclothing, probably stolen from one of the Hugging Molly's numerous victims."

On the night of Sept. 2, one of the Hugging Mollies grabbed a woman at the Hawkinsville depot in Georgia, about 40 straight miles southeast of Macon. The woman struggled to escape and a scuffle ensued, during which the Hugging Molly bit off the victim's left forefinger.

A rare female Hugging Molly named Josephine Slater was arrested by Macon police for various robberies and sent to a chain gang. (Georgia indeed sentenced female prisoners to hard labor in the late 1800s.) On Nov. 20, 1885, Slater was reported to have been transported to a hospital, as she was dangerously ill with consumption and had little prospect for recovery.

Black residents in the western part of Macon were said to be extremely cautious of a new Hugging Molly seen on Ross Street, between Hawthorne and Oglethorpe, in March 1888. This masquerader was said, uniquely, to carry with him a small child as he walked and hid throughout the neighborhood each night starting at 8 p.m. The Macon Telegraph wrote that residents were still on edge about the Hugging Mollies who had menaced the area in past years.

Much like the Gown Man, the Hugging Mollies and their victims were said to be primarily African-

Gown Man and Hugging Mollies

American. They were reported throughout the southern United States following their long tenure in Macon.

A gang of Hugging Mollies invaded Columbia, South Carolina in July 1884, generating "wild reports of men in women's clothing suddenly seizing pedestrians on the back streets at night and relieving them of their valuables." One of the victims was a penitentiary employee, who on July 23 was captured by four of the night prowlers in the pines north of his workplace. The quartet of highwaymen detained the man as a prisoner for several hours and stole his gold watch and chain. Meanwhile, a group of boys armed with guns, baseball bats, sticks and stones paraded through half the city's back streets in search of the Hugging Mollies, who they alleged had attacked two of their peers the previous night. Authorities dispersed the mob. Four or five of the Hugging Mollies were eventually arrested, according to the Atlanta Constitution.

The Hugging Mollies emerged in another Columbus, the city in Georgia, in September 1885. A Georgia newspaper defined a Hugging Mollie as "a female who inhabits the back alleys in cities, and when she sees a gentleman pedestrian approaching, she electrifies him by gently throwing her arms about him and relieving him of all his cash and other valuables."

For several years in the early 1890s, Baton Rouge was afflicted by a strange, white-robed man who was known as "Hugging Molly." He would hide in the bushes on North Boulevard, waiting for a woman to walk by, then would rush out and crush the terrified lady in a passionate embrace. His intent in wearing a sheet was evidently to appear as a woman to the casual observer. Baton Rouge trembled in fear, with its Black populace alarmed by the resemblance of Hugging Molly's drapery to the robes of the Ku Klux Klan—dormant at that time but not forgotten. Years later, the man under the sheet—whose name has been lost to time—passed away and the old Hugging Molly disguise was discovered in his dingy, one-room loft apartment. He was said to be a mentally unbalanced individual who had not committed any crimes other than his "amorous squeezings."

George Apostle and Chas. Gordon, "two widely-known white boys," appeared in Pensacola, Florida police court on Sept. 16, 1901. The young men pled guilty to masquerading as "Hugging Mollies" in female attire to scare some other boys. They were each sentenced to 30 days in the city jail and were given a lecture by the mayor. The boys had been captured by Chas. Johnson and City Clerk Jones near the Christ Church after a long-distance chase. "Mr. Johnson said Mr. Jones was about frightened to death, while the latter says the same thing of Mr. Johnson," wrote the Pensacola News.

Another Hugging Molly, this one an African-American man with a passion for embracing passing women, appeared in Pensacola around the turn of the year from 1907 to 1908. He spread fear throughout the city, until the hugging fiend finally came across a woman he couldn't intimidate. She was a trained nurse well-known in Pensacola as "Sister Nellie," and she was hurrying to the bedside of one of her charges. Hugging Molly jumped out in front of Sister Nellie, only to be surprised when the nurse swung her strong right arm and administered a knock-out blow. The costumed man crashed down to the pavement, stretched out and unconscious. He awoke to Sister Nellie shaking him vigorously back to his senses.

Pratt City, a neighborhood of Birmingham, Alabama, was in a furor over a Hugging Molly in September 1912. The fiend was known to spring upon each unsuspecting victim from a dark corner, hugging and squeezing them strenuously. A local man was charged with carrying a concealed pistol and testified in police court that he was "toting" the gun to defend himself against Hugging Molly. After terrorizing nearby Ensley's African-American population "with her bear-like proclivities," a Black woman named Sylvester McCarter was arrested Sept. 13 for being Hugging Molly. "It is said she has been an inmate of an asylum and there seems no doubt that she is crazy now," the Birmingham News sensitively reported. McCarter had crashed a children's birthday party at the home of Thomas Long, hosted by Miss Sallie Long in honor of her two little cousins. "Then 'Hugging Molly' came into the yard and grabbed Miss Willie Long [a white girl] in a tight embrace. She screamed for help." Three men pulled McCarter off the young lady and turned the hugger over to police. "She caused some trouble at the jail last night," reported the Birmingham News, "several husky policemen being required to incarcerate her."

The "Mother Hubbard Man," a personality similar to Hugging Molly, walked the streets of Alexandria, Louisiana for several weeks in August 1919. Clothed in a loose, black robe, he was witnessed nightly by several people in the African-American part of town known as the Sonio Oil Mill quarters. Although the Mother Hubbard Man frightened residents, he did not commit any crimes and vanished as abruptly as he first appeared. This account, considered in aggregate with the various tales collected here, illustrates what seems to be a relationship between and possibly evolution from Hugging Molly to Mother Hubbard Man to Gown Man.

Residents of Macon, seemingly the birthplace of Hugging Molly, did not forget their fearsome fiend. By 1951, Hugging Molly had mutated into a monstrous form somewhat reminiscent of the antagonist in Stephen King's "IT."

"Wild rumor has created in Macon a hairy monster with arms six feet long who stalks about at night in search of victims to cut or stab," wrote Bill Ott in the Jul. 20 Macon Telegraph. "An amazing portion of the city's population has heard fantastic descriptions of this creature, which, for some unknown reason, the more terror-stricken have named Hugging Molly." Ott might not have been aware of Macon's long-festering association with Hugging Molly. As before, the entity primarily stalked Macon's African-American community.

Law enforcement officers throughout the city and county of Macon fielded "wild, unfounded" reports of Hugging Molly sightings. One caller described Hugging Molly as having arms "clammy enough to chill and so slick they feel like an eel." Some housewives learned of Hugging Molly's exploits from their cooks and promptly determined to board up their windows to protect their families.

Most of the accounts appeared to derive from the mysterious slashing of an expectant mother several days earlier, wrote Ott. The woman had been sleeping in her home when a prowler stepped through a window and stabbed her in the abdomen. A neighbor heard the woman scream and then saw a man walk down a nearby alley and wash his hands at a fire hydrant.

Ott discerned that an incident near Hazel Street School, in which someone supposedly witnessed *a hand reaching out of a sewer*, caused the legend to grow to "alarming proportions." Police were called and arrived to find a large, armed crowd ready to deal with the creature. While the public continued to insist that Hugging Molly prowled the streets and had cut several victims, police marveled at their gullibility. Authorities laughed at the rumors but also took serious note of their consequences.

Macon's mass hysteria over Hugging Molly grew dangerous, as reported in the Macon News. On the night of Jul. 18, Helen Temple decided to show her sister, Catherine Glover, what she would do "if Hugging Molly came to her home." She pulled a double-barrel shotgun out of her closet and fired it twice. The charges accidentally struck and wounded Glover's daughters and Temple's nieces, nine-year-old Jeanette and eight-year-old Marilyn. While Marilyn was not seriously hurt, Jeanette was hit in the back with nearly the full load of shot. The older girl was taken to Macon Hospital in serious condition, and thankfully pulled through. Temple regretted her reckless actions and cooperated with police, who said that both women had been drinking when the shooting occurred. Temple was charged with assault with attempt to murder, but pled guilty to shooting at another, and was sentenced to two to five years.

The Abbeville Herald in Alabama noted in 1976 that most communities have their own "private local legend" which is passed down through generations, and that "Abbeville is no exception."

The article stated that "possibly the most outstanding of several legends known today is one of several stories which are still being told about Abbeville's exclusive character called 'Hugging Molly' and another or, maybe the same personality, known as 'The Woman in Black.' We are advised by a prominent citizen that both female characters were men." (We will further explore the connection between Hugging Molly, the Woman in Black and the Gown Man later in this chapter.)

The Herald shared a Woman in Black tale related by Elbert Tiller, dating back to 1922. According to Tiller, the dark lady first appeared on the road from Haleburg to Abbeville, then several times in town. She only came out at night, especially when it was exceedingly dark and hard for anyone to view her in detail. The Woman in Black was caught several times and always managed to escape. One night, the Lady in Black was seen entering an old grammar school near a graveyard. Police and 20 men armed with guns and lanterns surrounded the building. When they entered, ordered to either capture or shoot the stranger, she had disappeared like a ghost. Another night, the Woman in Black emerged from an old barn and stopped an elderly man named Levin who was passing by. The startled pedestrian pulled out a knife. "Levin, don't cut me," the Woman in Black pleaded. "Don't you know who I am?" Levin was shocked to realize the Woman in Black was actually an old friend, and a man on whose family farm he had worked decades earlier. While Levin didn't give up the Woman in Black's identity, Abbeville residents developed their own hypothesis. They believed he was a young man from a prominent local family who, back in the 1800s, had murdered his rival for the heart of a woman, waiting in ambush and shooting the man dead as he rode by on his buggy. The murderer fled to Texas and lived there 60 years before deciding to return home to live out the remainder of his days. He stayed in a barn on Old Columbia Road during the daytime, hidden by family, and only emerged at night wearing a long, black coat that looked very much like a dress.

The Herald sourced the local historical society for another tale about Hugging Molly, who was said to be about seven feet tall and "as big around as a bale of cotton, and lives in a dark gulley down behind the schoolhouse." Late at night, Molly would creep "out of her eerie nest" and sweep "her skirts through the streets of Abbeville." This Hugging Molly was said not to be that worrisome, content to give her victims a mighty bear hug and scream in their ear.

Meanwhile, Tiller shared a very different tale about Hugging Molly's origin, dating back to a time when Abbeville was barely settled and still surrounded by thick forest. There was a little kindergarten schoolhouse about a mile from town, and the students would often stay until late afternoon. One day, as the shadows grew thick and evening approached, a little girl named Molly collected her books and headed for the door. Knowing that Molly had a long walk home through a dangerous patch of woods, the teacher offered to accompany her. Molly, wanting to appear brave, declined and set off for home. Halfway through the woods, a huge bear attacked Molly and dragged her a long way down the road. A group of men cutting firewood heard Molly's screams and ran to help her, scaring off the bear. But they looked down in horror to see that the animal had bitten off one of Molly's arms at the elbow. The men placed Molly in a buggy and raced several miles away to the nearest doctor, who was actually a horse veterinarian. He was able to save the girl's life but couldn't do much aside from cord her stump and bandage it. He did have a golden arm and gave this to Molly as a prosthetic. Even after she recovered, Molly was ashamed of the golden arm and always held it close to her body, "hugging" it. Molly apparently lived to be 85 or 86 and was buried in the cemetery behind Abbeville's First Baptist Church.

These old legends persist in Abbeville today, so much so that "Huggin' Molly" has been adopted as the city's mascot and appears on its welcome sign. There is even a 1950's-themed restaurant downtown named Huggin' Molly's. "Anybody who grew up in Abbeville grew up knowing the legend of Huggin' Molly," proprietor Jimmy Rane said on the eatery's website. "If your mother or dad didn't want you to be out after dark, they'd tell you Huggin' Molly would get you. And you believed it, too."

Welcome to Abbeville, Home of Huggin' Molly. Map data ©2025 Google.

Rane is an Abbeville native and wealthy businessman who has taken great strides to revitalize his hometown and preserve its history. Per the restaurant's account of the legend, Rane was fascinated by the tales he heard in his youth of the seven-foot-tall, black-clad ghost, sweeping her skirt along Abbeville's streets and chasing down wandering souls to forcefully hug them and scream in their ears.

Gown Man and Hugging Mollies

The Gown Man and the Lady in Black

Whether a flesh-and-blood prowler or a spectral nightmare, the Gown Man haunted the American South for half a century, his notoriety spreading further as the years went by. The Gown Man appears to have been a cousin to the Woman in Black of northern states, who we previously met in Chapter 6.

In mid-July 1920, a Gown Man frequented the neighborhood of Bradford Street, between Reynoir and Lameuse streets, in Biloxi, Mississippi. On dark nights, he roamed the local Jewish cemetery and the larger cemetery north of Reynoir Street. There had been a similar specter spotted months earlier near Crawford Street and then Lee Street, but it was unclear if this was the same Gown Man. Residents chased this latest Gown Man and were unable to catch him. Biloxi Chief of Police Bills learned of the matter and tasked Officer Michel to search for the costumed interloper.

The Gown Man was spotted the night of Aug. 6 in a yard on East Washington Street. Residents, armed with pistols and shotguns, started out in search of the alleged man dressed in women's clothing. When the posse finally crossed paths with the Gown Man, they fired at least 15 shots. When the smoke cleared, the stranger was gone. The next morning, the searchers returned but found only the sheered tops of small pine trees and bushes they had blasted away with their bullets. Chief Bills soon after said he believed that imagination had much to do with the sightings of the Gown Man in various sections of Biloxi, terror spreading in whichever area he suddenly appeared. Police responded to a reported Gown Man sighting near Lee Street on Aug. 17, but found it was just a harmless old woman. She was dressed in a dark shirt with a white waist and an apron that made it appear she was wearing trousers under her dress. A similar report of a Gown Man during April 1914 in Tampa, Florida turned out to be an elderly man in a hospital gown who had escaped a local hospital.

On Feb. 11, 1921, Baton Rouge Police Captain Comeaux and Frank Schoonmaker completed a thorough search of South Baton Rouge for the Gown Man who was reported to be holding up Black residents on the lower end of town and committing various robberies. The thief wore a white bonnet and a long, flowing white gown. He was said to creep stealthily through South Baton Rouge, sticking up victims in dark alleys. "Captain Comeaux states that the reports have been very much exaggerated," wrote the Baton Rogue State Times Advocate. "After a three-day search and after questioning practically everybody in the neighborhood where the 'gown man' operates, it was found that no one has been held up, [and] no one knows of anyone else who has been robbed by the mysterious man." This Gown Man, concluded the police, was merely a rumor fueled by excitement. Despite this conclusion, the Gown Man would return to Baton Rouge.

Around 1930, a character known as the "Domino Man" struck the sparsely inhabited Gentilly suburb of New Orleans. Development had barely begun, so there were numerous empty lots that were thickly wooded and overgrown with tall weeds. The Domino Man, dressed in a white robe and hood, waited in the trees and dropped down into the lanes to chase little girls who were on their way to school, gesticulating wildly. After frightening the children, he would leap back into the trees with "the agility of a monkey" and vanish. Since the kids were always too frantic afterward to be certain of his size, a theory emerged that the Domino Man was actually a monkey that someone had dressed up as a practical joke. All witnesses swore the Domino Man never attacked or followed the children very far, content to depart once they screamed and ran. Armed men had pursued the Domino Man and fired directly at him, certain their bullets had hit their target, only for the troublemaker to reappear the next day, unharmed. Some locals concluded that since most of the kids were Catholics, the Domino Man might be a Ku Klux Klan member. The KKK rode a nativist wave of Anti-Catholicism during the 1920s, holding that Catholicism conflicted with democracy. They also believed that parochial schools encouraged separatism, which kept young Catholics from growing into loyal Americans. So, apparently their way to solve that issue was by leaping at children from trees?

In July 1934, the Gown Man targeted and robbed several African-American citizens on the southern outskirts of Baton Rouge. The Morning Advocate described him as "a very real bogey man" who dressed in "an appallingly long black gown" underneath which he carried a big pistol.

Gown Man and Hugging Mollies

Witnesses described the Gown Man as "tall and fierce." He robbed a pedestrian of his cash on July 10, then went on a spree the next night, stealing five cents from one victim and $4.85 from another before frightening an elderly man "almost into fits." A woman named Annabelle, a cook at a local boarding house, said she had been asking her employer to leave work early before it got dark. This followed an incident in which the Gown Man beat a man who didn't have any money nearly to death. A number of residents were barring their doors and remaining in their homes once evening fell. The Gown Man, however, met his match in a man named McCuir. The mugger cornered McCuir in a blind alley, pistol raised. But McCuir gave in to his instinct to run and plowed right through the Gown Man, knocking the criminal down and tromping him as he fled. Police and deputies, vowing to catch and unveil the disguised predator, responded to a call on July 17 but the Gown Man had vanished by the time they arrived.

The Baton Rouge Morning Advocate boldly declared on Aug. 5 that, "While the 'Gown-Man' has grown to be a spectral figure of terror, still there isn't such a person." Police had unraveled the sinister trail of the hooded "hi-jacking terror" and "found there only a maze of hood-winking with a bit of supernatural fear thrown in." Anxiety over the Gown Man persisted in Baton Rouge, with some young men courting serious legal trouble by carrying around guns for personal protection during their evening perambulations.

When the Gown Man first appeared in Baton Rouge, garbed in either women's pajamas or a short robe, some residents feared he might be Gabriel Talley, who was wanted years earlier in Iberville Parish for the brutal murder of a woman with a cane-knife. Son Talley, Gabriel's brother, was tried and sentenced to prison in Baton Rouge for a different killing. While on the lam, Gabriel had frequently visited relatives in Baton Rouge dressed as a woman to conceal his identity. Locals spotted him but were afraid to report his presence to police. But as more stories began to circulate and the stature of the robed desperado grew, he was said to be the ghost of a Baton Rouge police officer. "Finally, he became just the 'Gown-Man'— the symbol of fear," wrote the Morning Advocate.

According to Deputy Sheriff Ed Whitney, who beat the streets of South Baton Rouge seeking an answer to the mystery, there was an actual basis to the now pervasive tales of the Gown Man. It had started with the mugger who had been trampled by one of his intended victims (McCuir) the previous month. Dressed in a short robe or raincoat with a dark hat pulled low over his eyes, this particular Gown Man had successfully robbed three local Black residents. But the man, who was also Black, had been arrested after robbing a white man and was by then confined to jail at

Edgard, so he couldn't be the Gown Man still bedeviling Baton Rouge.

Whitney said it was possible that there had been additional hold-ups performed by other men dressed as the Gown Man. There was also a "veritable maze" of practical jokes. In one instance, a local resident hung a hat and old cloak on a coat hanger, attached it to a string, and ran the string over a telegraph pole and then to some bushes. When a group approached, the practical joker yanked on the string and the spectral figure arose, jostling around and startling the pedestrians before vanishing when the operator released the string. "Those who saw the flapping figure told a harrowing story of fierce pursuit and narrow escape," it was reported.

The Big Easy also had its own Gown Man, who aroused curiosity and fear during the last couple months of 1934. Walter Fervas was accosted while walking alone in downtown New Orleans around midnight. On the vague edge of light cast by infrequent lampposts, Fervas saw against a dark wall the form of a darker figure, tall but shapeless, its head a monstrous, angular shadow. It called out to Fervas, not in a ghostly croak but in a low, truculent voice. Fervas whirled around and ran, looking back to see the dark figure flapping in pursuit. The chased man careened across vacant lots, following a shortcut to his home on Touro Street, between Hope and Duels streets. Hearing the Gown Man curse behind him, Fervas plunged into his house, slammed the door shut and bolted it. "Gownman," he told his frightened wife between panting, "chased me all the way home."

"He was a tall man, well over six feet," Fervas recalled. "He was dressed in a long black gown that touched his feet, and he had on a black sunbonnet that shaded his face so you couldn't see it at all." Fervas and his neighbors began observing 9 p.m. curfew on a long stretch centering about Annette Street, back of town and in town, and between Claiborne and Broad streets, as far in as Bourbon Street.

Some New Orleans residents said that Fervas got off easy, as they knew others who had been caught, robbed and beaten by the Gown Man. The fiend was said to lurk in the branches of sycamore trees that hung over a block of Bourbon Street near Dorgenois, diving down onto passersby "like a snakebird dives under water," pinning his victim to the sidewalk. Neighbors recalled that the Gown Man had robbed a boy of $3.50 and then beat up another young man who didn't have any money. They said the Gown Man was not new to the neighborhood, having been seen for the previous two or three years, but only in winter. "People run too fast when they are not tied up in overcoats," one resident suggested.

Gown Man and Hugging Mollies

The Gown Man was so prolific that New Orleans citizens assumed there must be more than one. He had been sighted in and outside town, in the Treme on Orleans Street, farther out than Broad, almost at the river, even uptown. Among the suspected Gown Men was "Chicken Charley," a violent neighborhood criminal, although police had no recent record of him. A "notorious brigand" nicknamed "Stack of Dollars" was another suspect. The Gown Men were thought to inhabit and change their regalia in a vacant building on Prieur Street, a former grocery.

Marcel Fortune, who lived near the abandoned grocery, was walking past it at about 1:30 a.m. when he heard a voice call, "Fortune!" He looked down the dark alley next to the deserted building and saw a Black man standing there in the shadows. "Where are you going?" the stranger inquired. "To work," answered Fortune. "No, you're not," the stranger retorted. "You're going to spend the night here with me." Fortune noticed a rolled-up bundle of black cloth at the stranger's side, and the mystery man smiled evilly. "I know you, but you don't know who I am," he said. "You didn't know I was a gownman, did you? And there are three more in the alley." Fortune then heard additional voices emanating from said alley. Just then, an older man came walking down the opposite sidewalk. Fortune called to him and ran across, the Gown Man shouting curses behind him but not following. Fortune decided not to report the incident to police out of fear that the Gown Men might retaliate. His older brother and a friend escorted him to his job at the Van Geffen Bakery moving forward.

A 1934 illustration of the New Orleans Gown Man, published in the New Orleans Item-Tribune. Included here on a Fair Use, educational basis.

Gown Man and Hugging Mollies

As real a threat as the Gown Man, or men, were to New Orleans residents, to police it was just a vague rumor that the African-American community had developed amongst itself. Citizens began discussing going out armed and in groups to bring an end to the Gown Man's terror.

A marauder nicknamed "The Black Phantom," "The Skirt Man" and "Huggy Molly" spread fear throughout the residential section of Montgomery, Alabama bordering the State Normal School (today Alabama State University) in August 1943. Police authenticated two attacks on young women in their rooms. The Black Phantom entered the home of a teacher and slapped his daughter before fleeing. He then did the same to the daughter of Rufus Williams, manager of the Nu Deal Taxi Company. Descriptions of the phantom varied, other than him being a Black man who was focusing his mischief on members of the African-American community.

Huggy Molly eluded police and citizens for some time but by Aug. 11 had failed to appear for several days. Police suspected that a pursuing mob might have finally caught up to the Black Phantom and beaten him so severely that he was unable to continue his depredations. "It was admitted, however, that however elusive the phantom might be, the excitement and fear engendered by his two known acts were still present and very real," reported the Montgomery

Advertiser. On the night of Aug. 22, two men were trailing a masked man who suddenly turned around at the corner of Morgan and Stone streets and fired a pistol at them. Police, who scoured the neighborhood for several hours afterward unsuccessfully, did not believe their quarry was the much talked about Skirt Man.

The Gown Man was still active in New Orleans in 1945, at least within the rich traditions of the city's African-American denizens recorded by the Louisiana Writers Project. "The Gown Man is tall and slim and wears a black cap and long black gown that reaches to the ground," said Olivia Collins, who resided at Camp Street near the levee of the Mississippi River. "He has a long black automobile, I done seen it, parked down at the bottom of the levee." Collins said that the Gown Man would approach women, but not if a man was around. She was uncertain of his race. "I know one thing," Collins concluded. "He's a real man, and not no ghost!" Other residents, however., were certain that the Gown Man was a phantom, driving his long, shiny car around the neighborhood of the levee. When he showed up in other sections of the city, he would drop out of the trees and send women "fleeing and screaming for their lives and virtues."

The Gown Man bears a striking resemblance to the Woman in Black, another wraith of the witching hour that prowled city streets across the

Gown Man and Hugging Mollies

United States during the same era. While these wispy-thin ladies dressed head-to-toe in black mourning clothes were mostly spectral in nature, gliding along at inhuman speeds and dispersing suddenly into thin air—there was also a subset described as flesh-and-blood men in drag who accosted pedestrians.

One such example was the Greenville Ghost (explored further in Chapter 6), who bred hysteria throughout Jersey City, New Jersey in the winter of 1901-02. This ghost was more accurately described as a six-foot-tall, muscular man dressed in deep black women's clothing with a hat and heavy veil. He grabbed and sometimes hugged lone women, and on some occasions was reported to rough them up. Any man who tried to interfere found themselves knocked senseless by the Black Ghost. Armed groups of citizens, including children, patrolled the streets looking for the prowler. Police finally revealed that they had identified the ghost as a local man, who happened to be Black, and had a penchant for practical jokes. He was warned to cease his moonlight activities or face punishment. However, other reporting contradicted this identification, with police suggesting the whole story was either an exaggeration or a tall tale. I rehash this story to demonstrate how similar some of the Lady in Black stories were to the contemporaneous Gown Man.

The Woman in Black appears to have frequently been a northeastern and midwestern U.S. phenomenon, occurring in communities that ranged greatly from diverse urban cities to rural coal-mining towns. It is possible that the Gown Man might represent a unique southern variation of the same theme, one which arose predominately in African-American communities. It appears that Hugging Molly as a name for this entity evolved into the Gown Man, as they occupied the same region and presented similar dress and behaviors.

An 1894 article in the Daily Enquirer of Columbus, Georgia underlined the connection between the Woman in Black and Hugging Molly, writing, "Have you seen the Lady in Black? She is a ghost-like apparition on the 'Hugging Molly' order, which flits around at night, but seems intangible. A mortal dread has fallen upon the community and many people are afraid to poke their heads outdoors after night. Who or what is the Lady in Black?" If you will recall, Abbeville, Alabama folklore also drew a connection between Hugging Molly and the Woman in Black.

In an early report dating back to October 1867, the gender of the Woman in Black was already in question. Citizens of Milan, Ohio proposed that the witching-hour phantom stalking their streets and evading capture—a six-foot-tall, heavily built figure garbed in a black dress—might in actuality be a man.

As pointed out by author and folklorist Chris Woodyard in his excellent articles about the

Woman in Black, these stories appear to reflect societal norms of the era which viewed cross-dressing as an aberration that was not to be trusted. It didn't seem to matter whether the Woman in Black was a thief masquerading in disguise or an innocent man who wished to express his sexual identity by appearing in public dressed in women's clothing, albeit safely obscured by a veil. Starting in the mid-1800s, more than 40 cities across the U.S. passed laws criminalizing cross-dressing. Gender inappropriateness or variance was viewed as an amoral sickness and a public offense.

Although this intolerant attitude is infrequently stated directly in stories about the Woman in Black, Hugging Molly and the Gown Man, it clearly underpins the fear of these boogeymen that links the various cases. Aspersions, however, are coded in the use of the term "Hugging Molly" to refer to cross-dressing prowlers and muggers. In 18th century London, "Molly" was a slur used for effeminate, gay men, with "Molly Houses" describing "the clubs, taverns, inns, or coffee houses where they met up in secret," according to the British Newspaper Archive. Homosexuality was punishable by law, with sentences ranging from standing in the pillory, to jail time, up to execution for sodomy, depending on the individual case and evidence. So, these venues offered a safe and private place for men to openly express their sexual identities and find acceptance, even though the "Molly Houses" were at constant risk of being raided by police. Interestingly, a member of the Folklore and Mythology subreddit named LeanBean512 recalled hearing the term "Huggin' Molly" used colloquially in Mississippi "as a put down to describe a pathetic man, like a pervert or a flasher," so a pejorative use of the term appears to persist in the present day, possibly connected to the Hugging Molly legend.

Unlike the Woman in Black, the Gown Man was infrequently ascribed a supernatural nature. A corporeal man, sometimes an entire gang, was assumed to be masquerading in clothing of the opposite gender. The Gown Man was often feared as a robber, but like Hugging Molly before him, just as often engaged in mischief designed to scare, prank and stupefy his victims. Whatever his crimes, the Gown Man was viewed as a legitimate threat and a reason to dread walking alone at night. Residents reacted with outrage, and police appear to have taken the reports seriously, at least at first. While some of the news articles might contain journalistic sensationalism, they seem to have documented a mix of truth and mass hysteria, likely perpetuating the latter. Some of the Gown Men were arrested, named and tried. Others just vanished into the void from which they came. Perhaps some criminals and pranksters were inspired by stories of Gown Men and dressed the part, or just took advantage of a concealing, obfuscating disguise, blending into the overall legend.

Another Woman in Black of an earthly nature forlornly wandered the streets of Louisville, Kentucky in October 1868, ringing doorbells late at night and then failing to acknowledge in any way the confused residents who answered. While not suggested to be a disguised man, the Louisville Courier-Journal wrote, "She is very large, weighing two hundred pounds perhaps, which precludes the idea that she is a ghost or spirit. She is clad in black from head to foot; a black bonnet covering up her face in the ancient style; a black veil hanging over the bonnet; a black shawl; a black dress. At a distance she looks like a small-sized hearse."

New Orleans did have its own Woman in Black for at least six months in 1869, somberly dressed as she strolled along the "almost solitary desert" of the levee from Luggars' Bay to the Morgan Steamship Landing. She promenaded like clockwork each night, appearing with the first shade of evening and vanishing before the first streak of daylight, even in inclement weather. The lady was tangible, distrustful police having arrested and brought her to the station at least a dozen times. She always gave police a different name, such as Virginia, Mary or just Madame. The woman was thought to be perennially vigilant for a friend she expected to arrive on a ship, one which was unfortunately destined never to reach port. The Woman in Black offered no objection when other pedestrians chose to accompany her through the labyrinth of boxes and bales along the pier, and responded to queries with education, intelligence and dignity. But at the first indication of day, she hastened off like a scared ghost. It is interesting to note that the New Orleans Woman in

Black, like the Gown Man, was a strange living character rather than an outright phantasm.

Maybe it is just coincidence, but these masked and costumed nocturnal marauders like the Gown Man share some commonalities with fictional superheroes like The Shadow and Batman that became popular during the first half of the 20th century. While standing on the opposite side of justice, and preferring capes over dresses, such superheroes similarly catered to a public fascination with masked mystery men lurking on our city streets.

But a more apt comparison is probably Candyman (memorably portrayed by Tony Todd), the serial killer of urban legend created by Clive Barker for the titular film series that began in 1992. In the films, Candyman emerges as a Bloody-Mary like specter of fear in the primarily African-American public housing project of Cabrini-Green Homes in Chicago. The Candyman myth is presented throughout the films as a community reaction to generations of racial injustice and the murders of innocent Black men. This includes Candyman himself, an African-American artist and son of a slave who was lynched in the late 1800s over his relationship with a white woman. Despite his origin, the feared Candyman kills residents of Cabrini-Green when needed to keep his legend alive. Although the Gown Man was a much less lethal character, could he have developed in a similar way to the fictional Candyman within African-American communities across the American South?

Enigmatic phantom assailants have materialized throughout the centuries to frighten communities for a period of time and then vanish back into the shadows, a phenomenon explored by Robert E. Bartholomew and Paul Weatherhead in their excellent 2024 book, "Social Panics & Phantom Attackers." Fearsome fiends of this order have included Spring-Heeled Jack in 1830's England, phantom Zeppelins in 1909 New Zealand, the Mad Gasser of Mattoon, Illinois in 1944, and the 2001 Monkey Man scare in New Delhi, India. "These sagas are powerful human creations that reflect prominent fears in society at any given time," wrote Bartholomew and Weatherhead. The authors argue that these outbreaks do not derive from any external bogeyman, but from human imagination fueled by our prevailing anxieties and deepest terrors. For example, the Mad Gasser coincided with widespread press speculation that the failing German military might resort to chemical weapon attacks on American cities during the waning months of World War 2. This existential fright was transposed into a local threat in which an unseen marauder was indiscriminately spraying poison gas into household windows across Mattoon. These mysterious assailants can evolve into urban myth and serve as cautionary tales, such as emphasizing the dangers to young women which lurk in a city's dark alleys at night.

Although each social panic has a unique context and the form of the aggressor varies, there is a discernible pattern that plays out across time and the world. According to Bartholomew and Weatherhead, a community will unconsciously create a scapegoat for their problems in the form of evil-doers, which unites them against a common enemy. Often, vigilante groups will form and patrol the streets, at times accusing innocent parties of being the mystery assailant. Residents, suddenly hyper-aware of their surroundings, begin seeing sinister threats all around them. Many people stay inside their homes, which impacts the local economy during the scare. Initially, authorities and the press add oxygen to the claims, investigating reports and taking them seriously. Due to the prevalence of incidents, they might assume there are multiple assailants operating in different areas. But after failing to find any supporting evidence, and encountering misidentifications and hoaxes, authorities and the same media that gave the claims credence begin to shed doubt on the whole phenomenon, even ridiculing sightings as flights of imagination. Further witnesses become hesitant to come forward, and the entire threat withers.

Phantom assailants are not the territory of the weak-minded; everyone is susceptible to self-deception, our perception and memory highly prone to influence by external pressures. It is just part of the human condition. "Our eyes do not simply reflect what is in our environment; our brains have a major influence on how we perceive the world and prime people to see what they expect to see," wrote Bartholomew and Weatherhead. As is evident in reviewing the multitude of cases explored in this chapter, the Gown Man, Hugging Molly and Woman in Black closely fit the patterns these authors identify in phantom assailants.

Hugging Molly and the Gown Man first appeared in the decades following emancipation, and the timing closely parallels the rise of the KKK. Did fear of the hate group and its disguised members (not to mention everyday racism) blend with similar tropes of ghostly ladies and enshrouded thieves from elsewhere in the country? If so, why were so many of the Gown Men unmasked to reveal they were Black men preying on their own communities? It suggests ever-present anxieties couched in the familiar, a menace that is close to home, material and frightening, yet also less dangerous, more vague and more controllable than an outside threat. The Woman in Black, Hugging Molly and the Gown Man all symbolize a general fear and warning of walking alone in the dark through urbanized areas. Yet the latter two entities appear to uniquely reflect the trauma of African-Americans who were establishing themselves as freed individuals in a South that had within living memory completely oppressed them.

POSTSCRIPT: I am writing this article as a 21st century white man and amateur folklorist who lives in the northeastern U.S. I am certainly open to hearing differing opinions and expertise from those with a more educated perspective on race relations in late 19th century/early 20th century America. I began writing this lengthy essay after stumbling upon a reference to the mysterious "Gown Man" in an article about the Monster of Marmotte Street. Once I realized it was a prolific character who appeared in news and lore from the American South over the course of several decades, I decided it was worth documenting and compiling an article on the phenomenon. My topmost goal is the preservation of American history and folklore that has mostly been forgotten, and to hopefully provide some valuable context about the era and place from which it originated. It would have been dishonest to ignore the fact that these stories center mostly on African-American communities in the American South during a time fraught with racial tension in the decades following the Civil War. Perhaps I am wrong about a visceral connection between the

Gown Man and Hugging Mollies

Gown Man and the KKK, although some contemporary articles also drew that comparison. In my opinion, the Gown Man/Hugging Molly is a unique piece of Southern folklore, likely connected to some real incidents, that is best remembered, understood and even celebrated for its uniqueness in the present day. I hope you agree!

SOURCES:

"Abbeville's Ghost Legends." *Abbeville Herald* [Abbeville, AL], 1 Jul. 1976, p. 11.

"Alabama State University." *Wikipedia*, https://en.wikipedia.org/wiki/Alabama_State_University. Accessed 22 Jan. 2025.

"Alias Gown Man in Biloxi." *Daily Herald* [Gulfport and Biloxi, MS], 16 Jul. 1920, p. 3.

"Annette Street Mystery." *New Orleans Item*, 30 Nov. 1934, p. 1.

"Anti-Catholicism in the United States." *Wikipedia*, https://en.wikipedia.org/wiki/Anti-Catholicism_in_the_United_States. Accessed 18 Jan. 2025.

"Arresting Dress: A Timeline of Anti-Cross-Dressing Laws in the United States." *PBS*, https://www.pbs.org/newshour/nation/arresting-dress-timeline-anti-cross-dressing-laws-u-s. Accessed 24 Jan. 2025.

Bartholomew, Robert E. and Paul Weatherhead. *Social Panics & Phantom Attackers.* Palgrave Macmillan, 2024.

"Biloxi Gown Man Again Shows Up." *Daily Herald* [Gulfport and Biloxi, MS], 7 Aug. 1920, p. 6.

"Black Gown-Man Spreads Terror with -----Town Robbery Series." *Morning Advocate* [Baton Rouge, LA], 13 Jul. 1934, p. 8.

"'Black Phantom' Frightens -------." *Montgomery Advertiser* [Montgomery, AL], 11 Aug. 1943, p. 7.

"Brief Mention." *Constitution* [Atlanta], 22 Nov. 1885, p. 2.

"Brief Mentions." *Newberry Herald* [Newberry, SC]. 24 Feb. 1875, p. 2.

"Cabrini–Green Homes." *Wikipedia*, https://en.wikipedia.org/wiki/Cabrini%E2%80%93Green_Homes. Accessed 24 Jan. 2025.

"Candyman (Character)." *Wikipedia*, https://en.wikipedia.org/wiki/Candyman_(character). Accessed 24 Jan. 2025.

"City Items." *Telegraph and Messenger* [Macon, GA], 18 Jul. 1883, p. 4.

Dawson Journal [Dawson, GA], 17 Sep. 1885, p. 2.

Dumenil, Lynn. "The Tribal Twenties: 'Assimilated Catholics' Response to Anti-Catholicism in the 1920s." *Journal of American Ethnic History*, Vol. 11, No. 1, 1991, pp. 21-49.

"Formal Charges Are Filed in Wounding of Two Children." *Macon Telegraph* [Macon, GA], 31 Jul. 1951, p. 5.

"Georgia and Florida." *Savannah Morning News* [Savannah, GA], 6 Sep. 1885, p. 5.

"Girard." *Daily Enquirer-Sun* [Columbus, GA], 28 Oct. 1894, p. 7.

"'Gown Man' Again Terrorizes -------." *Pensacola Journal* [Pensacola, FL], 17 Nov. 1936, p. 2.

"'Gown Man' Appears Again." *Wiregrass Farmer* [Headland, AL], 29 Sep. 1921, p. 5.

"'Gown Man' Who Snatched Purses Sent Up for Year." *New Orleans States*, 25 Jul. 1920, p. 2.

"'Gown-Man Is Reported Seen Again." *Morning Advocate* [Baton Rouge, LA], 18 Jul. 1934, p. 2.

"Gown 'Woman' Caught Last Night." *Daily Herald* [Gulfport and Biloxi, MS], 18 Aug. 1920, p. 4.

Guhl, Kevin J. "Terror of the Black Ghost." *ThunderbirdPhoto*, 23 Oct. 2024, https://thunderbirdphoto.com/f/terror-of-the-black-ghost. Accessed 23 Jan. 2025.

Hébert, Keith S. "Ku Klux Klan in Alabama from 1915-1930." *Encyclopedia of Alabama*, 22 Feb. 2012, https://encyclopediaofalabama.org/article/ku-klux-klan-in-alabama-from-1915-1930/. Accessed 11 Jan. 2025.

"A Hugging Mollie." *Macon Daily Telegraph* [Macon, GA], 20 Mar. 1888, p. 7.

"The Hugging Mollies." *Atlanta Constitution*, 29 Jul. 1884, p. 1.

"Hugging Mollies." *Morning News* [Savannah, GA], 19 Sep. 1901, p. 8.

"Hugging Molly Gets the Blame for Gun Blasts." *Macon News* [Macon, GA], 20 Jul. 1951, p. 14.

"'Hugging Molly' Is Put Under Arrest." *Birmingham News* [Birmingham, AL], 14 Sep. 1912, p. 4.

"The Hugging Molly Again." *Constitution* [Atlanta], 8 Oct. 1885, p. 2.

"'Hugging Molly' Terror to Blacks." *Birmingham News* [Birmingham, AL], 12 Sep. 1912, p. 4.

"The Hugging Molly's Trunk." *Constitution* [Atlanta], 2 Sep. 1885, p. 2.

"Is It an Apparition?" *Courier-Journal* [Louisville, KY], 30 Oct. 1868, p. 4.

"Ku Klux Klan Robes." *ADL*, https://www.adl.org/resources/hate

-symbol/ku-klux-klan-robes. Accessed 11 Jan. 2025.

LeanBean512. *Reddit*, 10 Feb. 2025, https://www.reddit.com/r/FolkloreAndMyt hology/comments/1im8em9/comment/mc13bbg/ . Accessed 11 Feb. 2025.

Le Breton, Edmond. "Ghostly 'Gownman' Spreads Terror Among City's --------." *Item-Tribune* [New Orleans], 2 Dec. 1934, p. 28.

"The Legend of Huggin' Molly." *Huggin' Molly's*, https://www.hugginmollys.com/legend. Accessed 4 Feb. 2025.

"Local News Notes." *Daily News* [Pensacola, FL], 16 Sep. 1901, p. 5.

Mandy, Charles H. "A Strangle Hold and a Break-Away." *Age Herald* [Birmingham, AL], 18 Sep. 1912, p. 5.

"Masked ----- On Prowl; Police Trail." *Montgomery Advertiser* [Montgomery, AL], 23 Aug. 1943, p. 2.

McKee, Mary. "18th Century Molly Houses – London's Gay Subculture." *British Newspaper Archive*, 19 Jun. 2020, https://blog.britishnewspaperarchive.co.uk /2020/06/19/18th-century-molly-houses-londons-gay-subculture/. Accessed 11 Feb. 2025.

"Mobile Mardi Gras." *Montgomery Advertiser* [Montgomery, AL], 20 Feb. 1901, p. 3.

"Mobile's 'Gown Man' Is Real Phantom, Report." *New Orleans States*, 11 Dec. 1927, p. 6.

"Mother Hubbard Dress." *Wikipedia*, https://en.wikipedia.org/wiki/Mother_Hubbard_dress. Accessed 11 Jan. 2025.

"----- Section Terrorized by Night Stalking Monster." *Pensacola Journal* [Pensacola, FL], 29 Jan. 1938, p. 10.

"A New Orleans Mystery—The Woman in Black." *Cincinnati Daily Enquirer*, 5 Nov. 1869, p. 3.

"News of the Gulf City." *Times-Democrat* [New Orleans], 3 Nov. 1900, p. 9.

"News of the Gulf City." *Times-Democrat* [New Orleans], 9 Nov. 1900, p. 9.

"Night Gown Clad Man Walks in West Tampa." *Tampa Morning Tribune* [Tampa, FL], 23 Apr. 1914, p. 5.

"Officers Unravel Trail of Elusive 'Gown-Man.'" *Morning Advocate* [Baton Rouge, LA], 5 Aug. 1934, pp. 1-2.

Ott, Bill. "Monster Stalks at Night: Wild Rumors Create Ogre with Six Arms Six Feet Long." *Macon Telegraph* [Macon, GA], 20 Jul. 1951, p. 1.

"Police Are Unable to Find 'Gown Man.'" *State Times Advocate* [Baton Rouge, LA], 11 Feb. 1921, p. 1.

"Police Hope Scare Rumor to Fade Out." *Macon News* [Macon, GA], 21 Jul. 1951, p. 11.

"Remembering the Avenue." *Alabama Contemporary Art Center*, https://www.alabamacontemporary.org/events/the-avenue/. Accessed 24 Jan. 2025.

"Revival of 'Hugging Mollies.'" *Telegraph and Messenger* [Macon, GA], 15 Aug. 1885, p. 5.

Ryan, Hugh. "How Dressing in Drag Was Labeled a Crime in the 20th Century." *History*, 14 Sep. 2023, https://www.history.com/news/stonewall-riots-lgbtq-drag-three-article-rule. Accessed 24 Jan. 2025.

Saxon, Lyle, et al. *Gumbo Ya-Ya: A Collection of Louisiana Folk Tales*. Louisiana Writers Project, 1945.

"They Believe It." *Pensacola Journal* [Pensacola, FL], 2 Jan. 1908, p. 4.

"Thompson Does Not Enter Plea." *Macon Telegraph* [Macon, GA], 15 Nov. 1951, p. 2.

"Two Youngsters Shot by Aunt." *Macon News* [Macon, GA], 19 Jul. 1951, p. 1.

"A Veritable 'Jost.'" *Cleveland Daily Leader*, 29 Oct. 1867, p. 4.

"Women in Convict Camps." *Georgia Exhibits*, https://georgia-exhibits.galileo.usg.edu/spotlight/convict-labor/feature/women-in-convict-camps. accessed 20 Jan. 2025.

Woodyard, Chris. "The Woman in Black – Victorian Mourning as Criminal Disguise." *Haunted Ohio*, 25 Mar. 2017, http://hauntedohiobooks.com/news/the-woman-in-black-victorian-mourning-as-criminal-disguise-10250/. Accessed 23 Jan. 2025.

Teddy the Cat, Celebrity Scourge of Omaha's Dogs and Golfers

A rambunctious feline claimed a Nebraska park and golf course as his own in 1926, and everyone loved him for it.

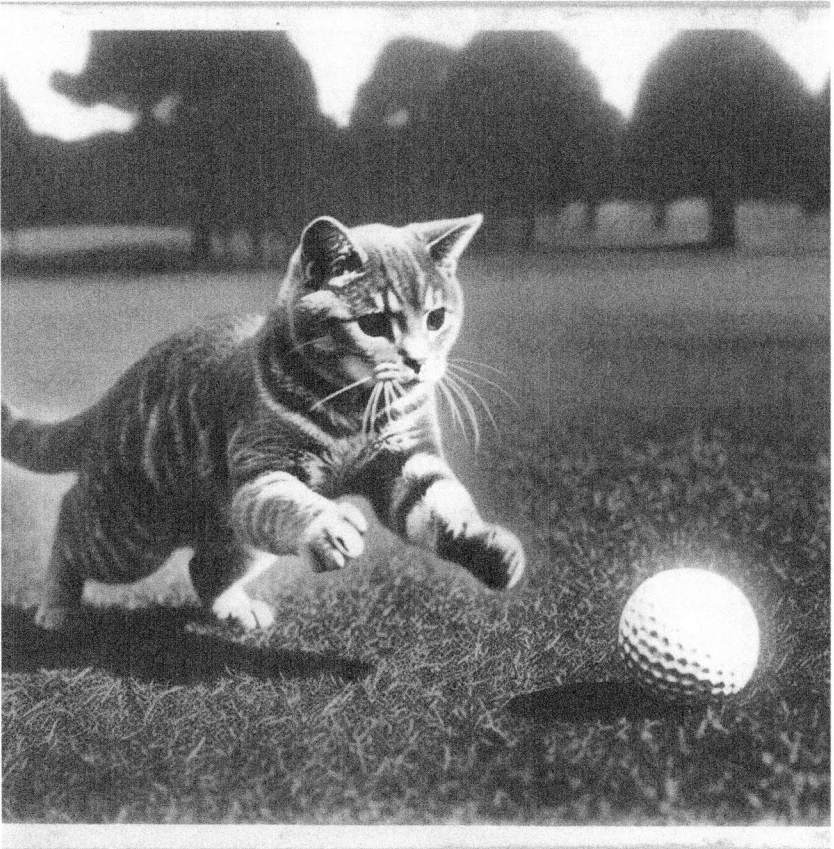

"'Teddy' is a golf cat. This tiger-like Tom is owned by Bernice and Beryl Melvin, 15, twin daughters of Mr. and Mrs. Alex Melvin, caretakers of the Miller Park pavilion. But 'Teddy' seldom heeds his mistresses. He does as he darn well pleases. And usually that is a game of hide-and-seek - around tee No. 1 of the Miller Park golf course."—Omaha Sunday News, July 4, 1926.

Omaha, Nebraska is home to many famous animals. There was the Necktie Goat, who hung around a once-vacant lot on 25th Avenue and Dodge. He didn't earn his name because he wore a necktie, sadly. Rather, any unwary businessman who stopped to pet him might suddenly find their tie bitten half-off and swallowed. Then there was Jackie the Squirrel, who lived in an old icebox at a restaurant on North Street and quite enjoyed consuming coffee and pie. But neither was as notable as Teddy, feline overlord of North Omaha's 79-acre Miller Park and golf course.

Teddy's antics were elegantly explained in this article from the June 24, 1926 edition of Omaha's Morning World Herald:

'Teddy' Has Catty Ways

Enforces Miller Park Edict Against Dogs; Makes Life Miserable for Golfers.

Teddy the Cat

Teddy, in a Quiet Moment.

"S-s-fitz!" A yelp. A dog streaking down the fairway. A flash of grey in pursuit. "Teddy," the terror of Miller Park, is in action.

"Teddy" is a large, tiger-type tomcat, jointly owned but not controlled by Bernice and Beryl Melvin, 15-year-old twin daughters of Mr. and Mrs. Alex Melvin, caretakers of the Miller Park pavilion.

Born on Saint Patrick's Day in the morning, he has developed a natural fighting instinct to a remarkable degree of efficiency, in the one short, eventful year it has been his joy to live.

And dogs, it seems, are "Teddy's" particular "meat." It is not known that "Teddy" can read. But he does his part in carrying out the orders which are printed on signs here and there in the park. "No dogs allowed." Few tarry, nor linger long when "Teddy" is around. He has "made 'Christians' out of all the pups on the place," as one of the youngsters at the pavilion put it.

"Teddy" is playful, too. And golf is his favorite sport. He likes to hide in waiting near the first tee, and many a good drive has been temporarily upset by his meteor-like appearance. At the critical moment, he loves to dash forth and "slap" the ball with his paw. If the golfer shouts a protest, "Teddy" humps his back, gives vent to a "Felix" grin, and is away.

"Teddy" has his quiet moments, however. Salmon has a soothing effect, as has raw hamburger and ice cream. But the park, with its numerous attractive possibilities, calls to him, and during the day and sometimes during the night, it is to be regretted, "Teddy" runs rampant. He's a great favorite nevertheless.

The Omaha Sunday News of July 4, 1926 declared that Teddy the golf cat and his fellow "semi-wild pets," Jackie the Squirrel and the Necktie Goat, were "better known than some humans." Indeed, another adventure of the "grey, oversized rowdy tom-cat" was reported just four days later in the Evening World-Herald.

Teddy cartoon from the Omaha Sunday News, July 4, 1926.

"Teddy has taken up water sports," the article announced. "Several mornings ago, a park policeman and the park golf starter, walking along the edge of the lake, saw a drenched, blinking cat standing in the water up to his chin. They fished him out and found him to be Teddy. One carefully wiped the water from his eyes while the other consoled 'Poor Teddy' with soft words and kind strokes. After a moment of this molly-coddling, however, Teddy rebelled. A small fish jumped from the water a few feet from shore, and Teddy, seeing an opening, leaped from the arms of his Samaritan into the lake, emerging with a succulent carp, and scampered to safety."

Established in 1891, Miller Park with its Swiss chalet-style pavilion, golf course and lagoon remains a treasured landmark of North Omaha. Let's hope one of Teddy's descendants still prowls the area, running off roving dogs and treating golf balls like toy mice.

5452. Pavilion, Miller Park, Omaha, Nebr.

Miller Park Pavilion, approx. 1912.

SOURCES:

"After 'Rescue' from Lake, Cat Jumps in Again, Catches Fish." *Evening World-Herald* [Omaha, NE], 8 Jul. 1926, p. 5.

"Alexander Melvin, United States Census, 1930." *FamilySearch,* https://www.familysearch.o

rg/ark:/61903/1:1:XQK4-RX3. Accessed 29 Dec. 2024.

"Famous Omaha Animals." *Omaha Sunday News* [Omaha, NE], 4 Jul. 1926, Metropolitan Page.

Fletcher Sasse, Adam. "A History of North Omaha's Miller Park." *North Omaha History*, https://northomahahistory.com/2024/11/28/a-history-of-the-miller-park-in-north-omaha/. Accessed 29 Dec. 2024.

Fletcher Sasse, Adam. "Miller Park Pavilion." *North Omaha History*, https://northomahahistory.com/2024/11/28/a-history-of-the-miller-park-in-north-omaha/miller-park-pavilion/. Accessed 29 Dec. 2024.

"Miller Park (North Omaha)." *Wikipedia*, https://en.wikipedia.org/wiki/Miller_Park_(North_Omaha). Accessed 29 Dec. 2024.

"Miller Park Pavilion." *Darland*, https://www.darland.com/miller-park-pavilion. Accessed 29 Dec. 2024.

"'Teddy' Has Catty Ways." *Morning World Herald* [Omaha, NE], 24 Jun. 1926, p. 6.

Bigfoot vs. The Jersey Devil

A gorilla-like Wild Man and The Jersey Devil competed for headlines as they terrorized southern New Jersey in the summer of 1927.

Bigfoot vs. The Jersey Devil (Artist: Robert Jacob Woodard)

Bigfoot vs. The Jersey Devil

For centuries, residents of southern New Jersey were accustomed to periodic visits from the abominable Jersey Devil. "It often appears during August," wrote the Atlantic City Daily Press during that very sweltering month in the summer of 1927. "It has cloven hoofs, a long tail, and eyewitnesses claim, it makes 'an uncanny noise' as it leaps over the pumpkin vines." But that year, another monster arrived to steal headlines away from Mother Leeds' little boy—a tall and hairy, Bigfoot-like "Wild Man" who had a strange proclivity for snatching and defacing vehicle tires.

The Wild Gorilla Man

"Gloucester County may have its 'Jersey Devil,' but Salem County has its own 'wild man of the woods,'" wrote the Camden Evening Courier on Aug. 27. "The 'wild man,' said to be a big, tall brute, hairy, but otherwise unclad, is being sought by numerous searching parties throughout this section. Residents in the vicinity of Quinton and Sharptown are especially active, inasmuch as he has been reported in both sections more often than anywhere else. According to the breathless tales of those who say they have seen this mysterious individual, he is said to be ferocious of countenance but very shy. They say he has the speed of an antelope and, with just one exception accredited to him, has done nothing to prove he's a wild man."

The "one exception" involved Thomas Smith, a 15-year-old boy who lived on Quinton Road. Smith was riding his bicycle about two miles north of Salem when he spotted someone peering out at him from the woods. Suddenly, what Smith described as a "big, hairy man without any clothes" jumped out from the trees, slashed the tires of his bicycle and then chased the boy along a cornfield. Smith escaped back home to his father, and they reported the incident to Sheriff J. Emmor Robinson. The sheriff launched a manhunt at once, accompanied by several local officers, a group of state troopers, and about 25 citizens.

The posse scoured the woods and fields, searching for "a long-haired, bearded individual" who they suspected might have escaped from a lunatic asylum. But the elusive Wild Man left nary a trace, no footprints nor any other clues.

However, four men, frightened and breathless, dashed into the farmhouse of Edward Jones, near Sharptown, and told him they had seen the Wild Man near a deserted schoolhouse. Jones and another farmer, Cooper Wilson, followed the men back and also encountered the Wild Man. He fled and the men gave chase, but the Wild Man's speed was so great that he easily eluded them. The group returned and summoned Chief of Police Floyd Pennel, of Woodstown, and Walter Crispin, undersheriff. But despite scouring the area, the lawmen failed to locate the Wild Man. Jones and Wilson described the Wild Man as a "'Borneo' specimen"—a reference to the orangutan, which was also referred to during that era as a "Wild Man of the Woods."

For a time, old residents of the area were inclined to regard the Wild Man as "just that old Jersey Devil poking its nose around again." But as furor over this new and different antagonist grew, the Atlantic City Daily Press was prompt to express its disdain over any comparison to the beloved Leeds Devil.

"A short time ago we were bold enough to write that we believed unqualifiedly in August freaks, but that was before the alleged appearance of a 'wild man of the woods' on the outskirts of Salem, New Jersey," the Daily Press indignantly wrote on Aug. 29. "We rise quickly to say that we are willing to believe in any other kind of freak, but in a South Jersey 'wild man'—never. We trust that all other good Jerseymen will join us. Too long have we placed our faith in the regular seasonal appearance of that strange dun-coated hybrid, the 'Jersey Devil,' to allow ourselves to be carried away by Salem's flimsy makeshift, which is entirely too human and runs every time one looks at it." In past decades, the famed Jersey Devil had traditionally appeared in winter, leaving hoof-like marks in the snow. The rivalry was on.

On Aug. 28, the Wild Man defied his earlier daylight appearances in Salem's woodlands and swamps with a nocturnal visit to one of the city's cemeteries. One Salem man glimpsed him skulking in and out amongst the tombstones. It was a drizzly and dark night, and the witness was unable to discern if the Wild Man wore any clothing, as he told authorities. An investigation at the graveyard failed to reveal any trace of the strange visitor.

Near midnight on Aug. 30, a taxi driver parked his vehicle at the Half Way House gas station, midway between Salem and Bridgeton, filled up the tank and headed inside to pay. When he stepped back outside, he saw the passengers in the back of his cab peering out the windows like something had startled them. Gazing from one side of the cab to the other, the driver was able to distinguish an indistinct form on the far side. Hastily moving around in front of the taxi, he was just in time to see a figure turn and slink away into the darkness. Despite only getting a glimpse, the driver described the man as being more than six feet tall and weighing more than 200 pounds. The Wild Man retreated into the woods near the gasoline station, waving his arms and emitting guttural sounds. As the taxicab departed and rolled slowly down the highway, the occupants could hear the man moving rapidly within the trees, crashing through the underbrush and against branches. "He must have had good eyesight," said the driver, "for he seemed to stay up, despite the things in his way." The taxi driver and passengers watched for the Wild Man to come out of the trees into the roadway again, but instead heard his movements grow less and less distinct as he headed deeper into the woods. Authorities were notified and a hunt was again started for the elusive Wild Man, who they suspected was "living like an animal in the woods."

The next sighting of the Wild Man happened in Shirley, about six miles from the gas station at 10 p.m. on Sept. 4. George Masknell, a farmer from Shirley, finished weighing his truck on the local scales and parked several yards away in the semi-darkness. He awaited the arrival of his neighbor in another truck carrying tomatoes, so the two could head together to the nearby cannery. With a longer wait than expected, Masknell dozed off, only to awaken with a start when he heard a basket of tomatoes crash from his truck to the roadway. Peering out from the cab, he saw the basket on the ground with two or three of the tomatoes spilled out. Unable to account for it being there, he watched the spot for several minutes. Just as Masknell was preparing to get down from the cab to replace the basket on the truck, a long, hairy arm reached out from the rear, snatched up the container, hoisted it under its left arm, and bounded off down the road. Dazed at the sight, Masknell was unable to tell whether the man wore clothes or not. But the farmer was impressed by the thief's size and strength, evident by the ease with which he carried away the heavy basket of tomatoes. When he had collected himself, Masknell hastily summoned several residents in the vicinity. They tracked the man, following his huge footprints some distance up the road to a cornfield, where the trail was lost. In any case, it's good to see the Wild Man appreciated the state's greatly renowned Jersey Tomatoes!

The Camden Morning Post recounted the Wild Man's next adventure on Sept. 10:

Salem's 'Gorilla Man' Steals Automobile Tire.

Pennsylvania Motorist Leaves Jack and Flat Shoe on Road and Drives Away in Fright on Rim

Salem. Sept. 9.—Does Salem County's wild man own an automobile? If not, why should he steal an automobile rim and tire?

These questions are puzzling those who have seen the "gorilla man" appear on the Salem-Bridgeton Road and other lonely places throughout the county.

A Pennsylvania motorist reports the loss of a spare tire from the front of his automobile as he was preparing to change a flat this morning at 3 o'clock.

Bigfoot vs. The Jersey Devil

A gorilla-like man or animal grabbed the tire and rim under his arm and sped off into the darkness.

The Pennsylvanian, too frightened at the appearance of the visitor to give chase, hastily climbed into his machine, left his jack on the road and hurried into Salem on the rim.

The automobilist told his story to several taxi drivers in Salem on his arrival. He said that he had a blowout about two miles from the Half Way House, midway between this city and Bridgeton. It was near this point that the "wild man" made an appearance two weeks ago.

Stopping his machine along the road, the Pennsylvanian removed the spare tire from the rear and took it to the front of the car in order to place it on a front wheel. His wife and two children remained in their seats, partially asleep.

As he jacked up the wheel, he felt the car rolling forward and backward. When he stood erect to place something under the tires to keep the car from shaking, he said he was startled by a pair of long, hairy arms pulling on the lamp.

Almost as soon as he looked, he said, the man or animal realized that he was being watched. Hastily grabbing up the spare tire with an arm that seemed to reach almost to the ground, the thing turned and was off into the darkness before the man realized what was taking place.

Not even hesitating long enough to gather up his jack and the flat tire, the motorist jumped into his machine and sped down the road. He failed to see any signs of his unwelcome visitor in the trip to Salem, fourteen miles distant.

Still showing signs of the fright, the motorist stopped only long enough here to tell his story to taxi men at the courthouse and to inquire the shortest route to Philadelphia.

During the past three weeks, several appearances of some strange, wild creature have been reported as seen in three or four sections of the county. Except in the first case, at Sharptown, those who report the cases are able to catch but a glimpse of him. All the descriptions have him as a huge, heavy man, probably more than six feet tall and weighing more than two hundred pounds.

At Sharptown he was said to have lacked all clothing, while at other places it was impossible to distinguish in the darkness whether he was wearing anything or not. He moves rapidly, appears to have great strength, and so far has failed to say anything on being discovered.

The Jersey Devil

The perennial Jersey Devil was not about to be outshone by this hairy, tire-and-tomato-thieving newcomer, and put in several appearances of its own in South Jersey during the summer of 1927.

Bigfoot vs. The Jersey Devil

On Aug. 4, Huckleberry pickers toiling in the cedar swamps a few miles from Swedesboro (near Bridgeport in Gloucester County) reported the appearance, at a distance, of a feathered quadruped about the size of a fox, with a cry that was "half bark, half hoot." The berry pickers reported that they had startled the animal, which "uttered angry hoots when they pursued it and showed such speed that it easily escaped them." Its feathers were compared to those of a chicken.

This news excited the Shoot and Miss Gun Club. While some members began devising plans to capture the Devil, club president J. Franklin Rider rejected the ideas and seemed more intent on hunting the beast. Members Mickey Groff an "Al" Sheets, both expert marksmen, announced their intent to spend one of their vacation days searching for the animal.

On Aug. 8, the Woodbury Daily Times reported that "one of the 1927 editions of the Jersey Devil" had been spotted nearby in Paulsboro. The description of the animal, a dog-like shape with feathers, was exactly like the one spotted in the Cedar Swamp the previous week. Driven to action, Shoot and Miss Gun Club President Rider and Secretary Pete Lock armed themselves and headed up a blackberry-picking party which sailed up Raccoon Creek on the evening of Aug. 9 aboard the S. S. Kangaroo. The pickers found a bounty of fruitful bushes in the wild and soon all their buckets were filled with fine, large berries. Rider and Lock kept a sharp lookout during the outing, a large double-barreled shotgun loaded with special shot at the ready. However, no trace of the Jersey Devil was seen. By Aug. 25, Sheets and Groff announced their intent to capture the beast and display it at the annual Firemen's Carnival the next week. They apparently did not succeed in this bold plan.

On the evening of Sept. 19, John Malady "and his expert mechanic," while returning from Swedesboro, saw a strange object crouching alongside the road in the woods at the hollow near Charles Magin's farmhouse. As the car neared the object, it rose on its hind legs and appeared to be about eight feet tall. When the car passed the creature, it attempted to jump onto the running board but was unsuccessful due to the automobile's quick acceleration. The Jersey Devil followed the car for a short distance but soon fell out of view as Malady put the pedal to the metal.

Thereafter, Rider ordered Lock to utilize the stone and concrete road when going to Swedesboro. As the roads were "too high for good railbird shooting," though, the Shoot and Miss Gun Club planned to organize a search party to scour the woods in the vicinity of the hollow.

Malady, touted by the Woodbury Daily Times as "one of the living witnesses to see the Jersey

Devil," was driven to capture the monster. By Oct. 6, he was busily engaged in perfecting his own trap to catch the slippery beast, assisted by Rider. As there was no further news, we can assume that neither Malady nor the dedicated Shoot and Miss Gun Club ever succeeded in trapping or killing the infamous Jersey Devil.

Other Wild Men

The Wild Man of the Woods is a legendary character that dates back to the late medieval period in Europe and appears to have been carried over by settlers who arrived in North America. However, the American Wild Man was many different things. Sometimes he was a hermit, often afflicted with mental illness, living outside society in the forest. Like his European counterpart, his solitude in nature often resulted in him regressing to a feral state, complete with the physiological change of growing hair all over his body and acting like an animal. But in many cases, the Wild Man was described as straddling the line between man and gorilla, especially after French-American zoologist Paul Du Chaillu introduced the latter to the Western world in 1861. Throughout the 19th and early 20th centuries, a number of Wild Men were described as being apelike and close in appearance to the Bigfoot popular today, complete with a tall stature, a body covered in hair, and traits such as great strength and speed, aversion to humans, and the emittance of eerie noises like whistling.

One of the strange traits of Salem's Wild Man is that none of the witnesses could decide if he wore clothes or not, although he was consistently described as hairy. This reflects a number of 19th century Wild Man reports in which witnesses could not determine if what they encountered was man or beast. Like a missing link, it was recognizable as being human-like but displayed traits associated with other primates. Perhaps Salem's Wild Man was just a large, hairy human who had gone back to nature. But it is fun to imagine that fleeting sightings of an unknown hominid covered in a thin coat of fur might generate such confusion.

Salem's bogeyman wasn't the only case of a Wild Man in New Jersey during this period:

- On Aug, 20, 1927, just a week before the first appearance of the Salem Wild Man, the Millville Daily Republican in Cumberland County (bordering Salem County) reported the capture of a Wild Man by New York City police. This particular Wild Man, decidedly a human being, had been frightening female berry pickers in the vicinity of South River in northcentral New Jersey for several weeks. City police contacted South River Chief of Police Charles Eberwein, who traveled to

New York City with one of the berry-pickers to try and identify the man, who was being held at Pier A, Marine Police Precinct 71. Wild Men (and apparently Jersey Devil) sightings are often associated with berry-picking, perhaps owing to the remote nature of the activity during the 19th and early 20th centuries.

- In October 1927, a possible "Wild Man," described as tall with a heavy black beard and wearing a dirty shirt and trousers, appeared out of the woods which fringed the farms at Beasley's Point in the shore town of Ocean City, New Jersey. "Women and children ran screaming to their homes and when their husband and fathers would appear, the man scurried into the dense thickets," wrote the Camden Morning Post. Many sleepless vigils in strongly barred farmhouses ensued. On the afternoon of Oct. 6, Henry Clouting saw the strange man on his farm. State police at Tuckahoe were notified and Trooper McGuire hastened to the scene, but the interloper had by then disappeared. Local farmers organized a posse and followed "Black Beard's" footprints into the woods. After proceeding several hundred yards, the trail was lost.

- On May 28, 1928, Woodbury Sheriff John B. Stratton and local police were hot on the trail of a "Wild Man" seen in the Dickerson woods at the southern end of the Gloucester County city during the previous few nights. Employees of the West Jersey and Seashore Railroad claimed they had spotted a man running about in the woods, scantily clad and hiding behind trees. The railroad workers stated that the man was about six feet tall and had bushy hair and a long beard. They said that every time they looked into the woods at him, he would jump behind a tree. Shortly before noon on May 28, Sheriff Stratton, Undersheriff Tryon, Chief of Police McGee and Policeman Hampton conducted a thorough search of the woods in that locality but were unable to locate the Wild Man. They did, however, find numerous footprints.

- On Nov. 18, 1928, Joseph Stout of Swedesboro reported to NJ State Police that he had seen two gaunt and unshaven "Wild Men" lurking in the high marsh grass between Pennsville and Penns Grove in Salem County. What followed was what the Camden Morning Post called "the strangest investigation within memory of local authorities." Police hoped it might be their first real lead in the search for two Delaware men—Wilbert Croes, 21, and Horace Walker, 17—who had disappeared on Election Day after setting off in a small boat for a duck-hunting trip in the Jersey marshes. The young men had been given up for dead after their abandoned rowboat was found on the mud flats near Pennsville. Stout's report, coupled with ramshackle bungalows and extinguished campfires police discovered in the marshes, offered hope that Croes and Walker might still be alive, though having become "lost and demented as they roamed the swamps." However, this promise dissolved when Walker's body was found on a Delaware River beach on Nov. 22. His head and left arm were missing, which police suggested could have been due to contact with the propeller of a river steamer. On Nov. 27, Croe's corpse was discovered lodged in a jetty in the Delaware River. Authorities believed that the hunters' boat had overturned and they drowned. Whoever the two Wild Men were was never solved.

The Jersey "X-Files"

Does anyone remember an early episode of "The X-Files" called "The Jersey Devil"? I recall being disappointed that the titular monster was not presented in the standard fashion of a winged, horse-like chimera but rather as a people-eating, Neanderthal-esque relic hominid living in the New

Jersey Pine Barrens. I never would have guessed that Chris Carter might have been onto something, presenting a Monster of the Week more akin to the Salem Wild Man of 1927!

Look, speaking as a New Jersey native, the Devil is always going to come first. But there is plenty of room, even today, amongst the sprawling farmland and dense Pine Barrens of southern New Jersey for our very own Wild Man.

So, the most pressing question:

Who do *you* think would win in a battle between Bigfoot and The Jersey Devil?

SALEM'S "WILD MAN"

A short time ago we were bold enough to write that we believed unqualifiedly in August freaks, but that was before the alleged appearance of a "wild man of the woods" on the outskirts of Salem, New Jersey. We rise quickly to say that we are willing to believe in any other kind of a freak, but in a South Jersey "wild man"—never. We trust that all other good Jerseymen will join us. Too long have we placed our faith in the regular seasonal appearance of that strange dun-coated hybrid, the "Jersey Devil," to allow ourselves to be carried away by Salem's flimsy makeshift, which is entirely too human and runs every time one looks at it.

The rivalry is on! - Atlantic City Daily Press, Aug. 29, 1927

Bigfoot vs. The Jersey Devil

SOURCES:

"Bridgeport." *Woodbury Daily Times* [Woodbury, NJ], 10 Aug. 1927, p. 4.

"Bridgeport." *Woodbury Daily Times* [Woodbury, NJ], 25 Aug. 1927, p. 4.

"Bridgeport." *Woodbury Daily Times* [Woodbury, NJ], 6 Oct. 1927, p. 3.

"Dead Gunner Ends 'Wild Man' Mystery." *Morning Post* [Camden, NJ], 23 Nov. 1928, p. 1.

"Discovery of Second Body Ends Salem Swamp Mystery." *Morning Post* [Camden, NJ], p. 6.

Guhl, Kevin J. *An Anthology of American Strangeness, Vol. 1: Thunderbirds, Lost Temples and Skeleton Ghosts.* 2024.

"It Barks and Hoots, Has Feathers; What Is It?" Paterson *Evening News* [Paterson, NJ], 5 Aug. 1927, Section 3, p. 5.

"Items of Interest to Local Folks." *Woodbury Daily Times* [Woodbury, NJ], 8 Aug. 1927, p. 4.

"'Jersey Devil.'" *Daily Home News* [New Brunswick, NJ], 4 Aug. 1927, p. 12.

"The Jersey Devil (The X-Files)." *Wikipedia*, https://en.wikipedia.org/wiki/The_Jersey_Devil_(The_X-Files). Accessed 23 Feb. 2025.

"Jersey Devil Beats Salem's Wild Man." *Evening Courier* [Camden, NJ], 3 Sep. 1927, p. 14.

"Jersey Devil Is Back Again." *Woodbury Daily Times* [Woodbury, NJ], 2 Aug. 1927, p. 4.

"Jersey Devil Sighted by Local Men." *Woodbury Daily Times* [Woodbury, NJ], 20 Sep. 1927, p. 4.

"Missing Hunter Believed Drowned." *Morning Post* [Camden, NJ], 24 Nov. 1928, p. 2.

"Reports of 'Wild Men' in Salem Swamps Renew Search for Hunters." *Morning Post* [Camden, NJ], 19 Nov. 1928, p. 4.

"Salem County Staging Hunt for 'Wild Man." *Evening Courier* [Camden, NJ], 27 Aug. 1927, p. 3.

"Salem County's 'Wild Man' Steals Tomatoes at Shirley." *Morning Post* [Camden, NJ], 7 Sep. 1927, p. 3.

"Salem Sheriff Boy Again on Farm of Barefoot Days." *Morning Post* [Camden, NJ], 9 Jul. 1927, p. 2.

"Salem Wild Man Turns Up in Rain at Cemetery." *Morning Post* [Camden, NJ], 29 Aug. 1927, p. 3.

"Salem's 'Gorilla Man' Steals Automobile Tire." *Morning Post* [Camden, NJ], 10 Sep. 1927, p. 3.

"Salem's 'Wild Man.'" *Atlantic City Daily Press* [Atlantic City, NJ], 29 Aug. 1927, p. 9

"Seek 'Wild' Man in South Jersey." *Atlantic City Daily Press* [Atlantic City, NJ], 31 Aug. 1927, p. 2.

"Them Kangaroo B'ars." *Atlantic City Daily Press* [Atlantic City, NJ], 12 Aug. 1927, p. 13.

Universal Service. "Seek 'Wild' Man Roaming South Jersey; Wrecks Bike, Chases Boy." *Atlantic City Daily Press* [Atlantic City, NJ], 29 Aug. 1927, p. 2.

"'Wild Man' Believed to Have Been Captured." *Millville Daily Republican* [Millville, NJ], 20 Aug. 1927, p. 1.

"'Wild Man of the Woods' Gives Salem a Merry Chase." *Morning Post* [Camden, NJ], 27 Aug. 1927, p. 1.

"'Wild Man of the Woods' Keeps Salem Guessing." *Atlantic City Sunday Press* [Atlantic City, NJ], 28 Aug. 1927, p. 6.

"'Wild Man' Reported in Woodbury Woods." *Morning Post* [Camden, NJ], 29 May 1928, p. 6.

"Wild Man Scares Salem Residents." *Millville Daily Republican* [Millville, NJ], 30 Aug. 1927, p. 1.

"'Wild Man' Terrifies Coast Farm Wives, Houses Are Barred." *Morning Post* [Camden, NJ], 7 Oct. 1927, p. 2.

Headless Ghosts, River Monsters and Petrified Corpses: An Exploration of Shoddy & Sensational 19th Century Journalism

Lancaster, PA had a crowded media landscape in the 1880s, and one newspaper wasn't afraid to lean into the lurid to survive.

"The Headless Ghost Which Affrights the People of Manor Township, PA.—A Spook Which Can Unbutton Its Head."—Illustrated Police News, Jan. 10, 1885

Did you know that Lancaster County, Pennsylvania, famed for its rural beauty and Amish community, was once a terrifying nexus of the paranormal? That's the impression one might glean from reading 1880's editions of the daily Lancaster New Era newspaper, which published lurid reports of strangeness such as headless ghosts, water monsters and petrified corpses. It's a case study not only on the infamous trend of newspaper sensationalism in the late 19th century, but on the pushback from other journalists over the very soul of their craft.

The New Era printed one of its spookiest tales just before Christmas on Dec. 23 1884:

MYSTERY AND MEANNESS.

A HEADLESS AND A HEARTLESS MAN.

The Story of a Headless Spectre, as Told and Believed In by Certain People

About half a mile distant from Pittsburg school house, in Manor Township, is a section of country where at long intervals appears a something which truly rivals the horrible spectre which so badly terrorized the redoubtable school teacher of Sleepy Hollow, Ichabod Crane, one of Washington Irving's Sketch Book heroes. The ghost of that tale swept along on horseback, while the Lancaster County spectre, probably less proud or wealthy, stalks majestically along on foot, carrying its head in one of its hands. It was first seen one night many years ago by the Rev. Daniel Witmer, still a resident of Manor Township, and M. H. Kauffman, the latter being in the company of two ladies at the time. All were returning from attendance at a religious meeting which had been held that evening in the Pittsburg school house, where the Rev. Witmer had preached. A short distance away from the fence which divided the fields belonging to farms owned now by Jacob Habecker and Joseph Brenneman, the reverend gentleman separated from Mr. Kauffman and the ladies and started homeward on a near cut across the fields. He had only gone about a hundred yards from his late companions, carrying in his hand a lantern, for the night was dark, when Mr. Kauffman and his lady friends saw him approached by what they supposed to be another man, who also carried a lantern. The two walked on together and finally disappeared from the view of Mr. Kauffman and his companions. The following day the former met the minister, whose look was serious and gloomy. When asked who his companion of the night previous had been he recounted this startling piece of information: "After leaving you last night, I started across the fields and had gone but a short distance when I saw the approach of what I supposed to be a man carrying a lantern. It came directly towards me, and when near enough I was almost paralyzed with horror to perceive that no head crowned the body. The object was a moving body without a head, but when it came quite close to me my terror was increased still further by seeing the head carried in one of its hands. The fearful object took its place by my side and accompanied me to my very door. How I managed to retain consciousness and reach home I don't know. It was the most fearful experience I ever had, and I hope I may never have the like again."

Since the time referred to this same object, whatever it may be, has been seen several times again, the last time being within the year. We hazard no opinion as to what the illusion may be, but simply give the story as related by Mr. Kauffman, and corroborated by others of the vicinity. Of course there is some natural cause for this spectral appearance—and that some peculiar illusion has *been seen is evident from the character of those seeing it—but it would be difficult to make some people of the neighborhood believe that it was anything else than a supernatural object.*

Geographical Note: Manor Township, located near the southeastern border of Pennsylvania, has a neighborhood named Pittsburg Valley, not to be confused with the city of Pittsburgh in western Pennsylvania.

It's not so easy to wave off this story as pure fiction when one considers that the primary witness, Rev. Daniel Witmer, was an established religious leader in the community. For several years, he preached in German at the Evangelical Church at Creswell in Manor Township. He resided in Creswell until his death at age 78 on April 2, 1893, although by that point he had been an invalid for many years, "paralyzed and helpless," per his obituary. Would the New Era risk libel by spinning a complete fairy tale about the reverend, who still resided in the community? Reading between the lines, it seems more likely that Kauffman shared the entire story with the New Era, including a secondhand account of what Witmer saw, and the newspaper printed it without much question. It does not sound like the New Era consulted the reverend himself, although it is unclear if he was in good health at that time. The paper did claim it corroborated accounts of the headless ghost with other locals. By this point, though, it was an old story, one that might have grown into urban legend as its circulated throughout the community and others claimed to had seen the headless spirit. The New Era concluded by downplaying the haunting as a natural phenomenon that had ignited the imaginations of superstitious residents. This would become a pattern for the New Era—printing genuine hearsay without, it seems, digging too deeply into the facts.

Whatever the provenance of Manor Township's headless ghost, the Illustrated Police News brought the story to national attention with a stunning drawing of the incident in its Jan. 10, 1885 edition. (See the header image.) The Lancaster Weekly Examiner and Express, one of the New Era's rival newspapers, was starkly unimpressed by the special attention its competitor had received. "In the long run, foolish newspaper sensations do not pay," wrote the Examiner and Express. "The *Police News* considers the smallest paper in Lancaster, the *Era*, a very esteemed cotemporary indeed. This week the *News* has an illustration of the *Era's* headless ghost. Next week it will have a picture of Frankford's death scene. We congratulate the *News* upon the fact that it has so good a source to obtain horrible stories from, as is afforded by our Lancaster cotemporary." (The reference to Frankford is explained later in this article.)

News of the Headless Ghost of Manor Township made it all the way to Australia, where the Sydney Daily Telegraph seemed delighted. "It is somewhat refreshing in these days of vulgar 'spiritual manifestations' to hear of a good old-fashioned ghost without a head, of whose blood-curdling qualifications there is no mistake. These headless ghosts were once common enough in this country, but have of late years become almost extinct. Perhaps they have all gone to America."

The Dec. 27, 1884 edition of the New Era published two other incredible tales in tandem, both from Fulton Township: James B. Fry was digging a ditch in a low, marshy area of his farm when he uncovered a perfectly "petrified human body." Some old residents of the neighborhood suspected it might be the remains of a drover who was moving livestock from Rising Sun to Wakefield and disappeared 50 years earlier. At the time, locals suspected the drover had been murdered for his money and his body concealed. According to the New Era, "the petrification is so perfect that the skull plainly shows a fracture which may have been done by some heavy weapon." Fry sold the body to exhibitors from Philadelphia for $1,000. Meanwhile, a boy in the vicinity of Rock Springs, a small village adjacent to the Pennsylvania and Maryland line, was trying to unearth a skunk when two feet down he discovered a "bright, glittering mineral." He excitedly snatched a lump of it and ran home to show his father, who solicited the expertise of two former California miners to declare it was gold. The father and son were frequently pestered about the "gold mine's" location but refused to tell.

"The Director of the Mint is preparing a report on the production of gold and silver during the year 1884. Has he been properly informed of the *New Era's* gold mine in Fulton Township, discovered a few weeks since?" sniped the competing Lancaster Inquirer.

Continuing their landmark run of solid reporting, the New Era announced in bold letters on Dec. 29 that notorious "one-eyed" horse thief and jailbreaker John Frankford was dead. According to a letter sent by Frankford's half-brother, Martin Kline of Akron, Ohio, to the criminal's adult daughter, Maggie Rittenhouse of Fulton, the fugitive had died on Oct. 22 "after an illness of nine weeks from brain fever." This infection stemmed from a horrible wound in Frankford's eye, sustained when a guard shot him in the face during an attempted escape from Lancaster County Prison via a ventilating flue. Immediately, the New Era faced criticism from competing newspapers and locals who said their main source, Kline, had actually died years ago.

The Lancaster Daily Intelligencer not only debunked Kline's presence on the mortal plane, but could find no one who had seen Frankford in Akron during the past five years, including Kline's widow. The New Era defended itself the next day, admitting its error in attributing the letter to Kline instead of his son. Responding to jabs by the Intelligencer, the New Era published an interview with Rittenhouse on Jan. 6, 1885 in which she confirmed her belief that her father was dead. She explained that she had heard the news from a visitor and had not received any letters from her father since his last clandestine visit to her on Nov. 13, 1883. "Whenever our slow-going contemporaries of this city miss an important item they think the next best thing is to question the truth of the item," protested the New Era. "Life is too short to take much notice of their snarls."

The New Era was forced to eat crow when Frankford turned up alive in November 1885, having been arrested in Philadelphia. The New Era poked fun at itself, headlining their next article "Not Dead, But Sleeping." Upon his return to Lancaster County Prison, the "gentle" horse thief cordially greeted his jailers. He was met by a New Era reporter, who asked him, "Didn't you know you were dead?" Frankford replied, "I didn't until I read it in your paper." It is unclear if Frankford's relatives knew he was alive and lied to protect him, or were truly in the dark about his whereabouts. Fifteen months were added to Frankford's original 19-year sentence for horse theft, of which he had served just under five years between two separate jailbreaks. He was sent to the more secure Eastern State Penitentiary in Philadelphia.

Lancaster had a crowded newspaper business in the late 1800s, and it can't be ruled out that some of the attacks on the New Era's veracity arose from professional rivalry. However, the indignation over the New Era's alleged lack of journalistic ethics is clear. The Lancaster Inquirer wrote, "The story, originating with our sensational contemporary, the *New Era*, about the exhuming of a petrified man, in Fulton Township, supposed to be the body of a drover, murdered some fifty years ago, proves on inquiry to be utterly without foundation. The same is true of the story concerning the finding of gold, from that source. These, with the Manor ghost story, and the report of Frankford's death, indicate that our contemporary, forgetful that fact is news and fiction isn't, cares more to print a sensation than to tell the truth."

The Intelligencer raked the New Era over the coals on Jan. 5, 1885 for reporting an assassination attempt on Col. James Duffy, of Marietta, Pennsylvania, when in truth a stray bullet had accidentally passed through his bedroom window. "The *New Era* falsely states that it was their supposition 'that the person who fired the shot saw some person at the window through the heavy lace curtains, and, supposing it to be Colonel Duffy, fired in the hope of striking him.' The idea originated with the same reporter who, suffering from a fit of holiday indigestion, saw a headless ghost walking over the Manor hills, found the petrified corpse of a murdered peddler in the Fulton swamps, and had a vision of John Frankford in the spirit," wrote the Intelligencer, who added that Duffy's family had never entertained the idea that there was an assassination attempt. In fairness, no one could determine who had recklessly shot the stray bullet—perhaps an overenthusiastic New Year's reveler?—so the New Era was hazarding a conspiratorial guess.

The New Era kept its chin up and remained open to printing the latest poorly-sourced sensation. On May 27, 1885, it pieced together vague reports of a strange animal in Bainbridge in order to suggest the community had its own river monster:

A MONSTER OF THE WATERS.

A Curious Fish or Animal That Is Exciting the Residents of Bainbridge.

The fishermen and the people in general at Bainbridge are greatly agitated over the presence of a strange fish or animal that has made its appearance in the river at that place. It was first seen on Saturday afternoon about midway between the shore and the island plunging and diving about, and has since been noticed on frequent occasions acting in the same strange manner. From an eye witness who had a close view of it on Sunday afternoon, at which time it came to the surface of the water, just opposite the landing, it is described as being of a deep black color, very much resembling in appearance a big black dog. It was thought to be about four feet in length and when it appeared it swam for a short distance, then, lashing the water to a foam, immediately disappeared. It was seen again on Monday, near the point of the island, opposite Bainbridge, where it continued the same maneuvers for several minutes, after which it finally disappeared from view. The fishermen are at a loss to account for its presence, they never having seen anything of the kind in all their experience. They give as their opinion, from the description given of it, that it is an otter, and is all probability the same one that was reported as having been seen in the Conewago Falls last winter. The canal boatmen, who have had an extended experience on the bays and other waters, give a quite different opinion as to its name or origin, and claim it to be a fish or water animal, which frequents the bay and is commonly known as a "sea dog." Its presence has had the effect of creating an unusual interest in its behalf, and at all hours during the day, and more especially in the evening, there can be seen numbers of town people standing on the river bank, who out of curiosity wait and watch for hours anxious for a glimpse at the monster. It has not only been the cause of arousing the interest above mentioned, but has as well had a disastrous effect on one of the small boy's most enjoyable pleasures, which is that of bathing in the river. The reports current in regard to the animal, whatever it is, are greatly exaggerated, and have caused the boys to give the river a wide berth.

Again, the New Era hedged its bets by raising a skeptical flag at the article's conclusion. But the headline was enough to pull in readers and spark a legend, even if a likely identity for this mysterious beast was simply a river otter. (Where have we heard that before?)

Surprisingly, this isn't the only report of a mammalian monster in the Susquehanna River. Columbia, Pennsylvania, about 15 miles downstream from Bainbridge in Lancaster County, was excited in April 1878 over the appearance of an animal variously described as a sea lion, an otter or a seal. It was spotted standing on its rear legs in the river near the Wrightsville shore. The animal was at least seven feet in length with a head like a dog. It had a thin neck about a foot long, and a body with a one-foot diameter around its thickest section. The creature possessed small eyes and had something like a fan, with claws or fins, on each side of its head. Where did this story run? In the Lancaster Intelligencer, of all places!

My friend and Clinton County, Pennsylvania historian Lou Bernard has written about a Susquehanna River monster of this era that he has affectionately dubbed the "Susquehanna Seal." As related by the Lock Haven Daily Democrat in 1897, there were generations of stories, dating back to indigenous inhabitants, about a strange aquatic beast contained to the West Branch of the Susquehanna River, immediately above the mouth of Kettle Creek on the northern end of Clinton County. As the legend goes, this "marine animal or sea monster" entered the Susquehanna River via its mouth in

Chesapeake Bay at Havre de Grace, Maryland during the early decades of the 18th century, before the construction of any dams along the river. The beast became trapped inland but was so awash in delectable shad and other fish that it "continued to wax in size until he equaled the bulk of an ox or hippopotamus." The animal grew so large as the seasons passed that no ordinary flood provided sufficient water to carry it over the shoals. So, it continued to inhabit the river depths along the big, black rocks at the bottom of the Susquehanna.

Witnesses who encountered the creature claimed it had a terrible roar and disturbed the waters greatly, lashing them to foam. Per the Daily Democrat, "He was not the form or image of anything on earth. Some claimed, by his roar, that he was a sea lion; some that he was a monster cuttlefish; and again, some thought that he might possibly be an only survivor of some (thought to be extinct order of sea or river monster, a labyrinthodon, an ichthyosaurus, a ramphorhynahus [Ed. Note: They likely meant rhamphorhynchus, an aquatic pterosaur.], or a hadrosaurus). Others claimed he was a species of whale or shark. But the majority of people believed him to be a sea lion, as his actions resembled that animal more than any other they had ever heard or seen." Locals began referring to the animal as a dugong, not so much after the actual herbivorous marine mammal, but the dangerous behemoth described by Jules Verne in his books "The Mysterious Island" and "Twenty Thousand Leagues Under the Seas."

The Susquehanna dugong was said to be a voracious consumer of both water and land animals—*man, included.* Children were warned to look out for the monster when swimming in the river.

Some thought the dugong departed during the big river flood of 1889, the water finally rising enough to carry it back to the Atlantic Ocean. Others thought it remained, possibly having discovered subterranean passages that allowed it to come and go as it pleased. Actual dugongs are confined to coastal waters in the Pacific and Indian oceans, but interestingly they can live up to 70 years, fitting the Susquehanna monster's longevity.

The Susquehanna River is one of the world's most ancient rivers, at about 200 million years old. It meanders for 444 miles from its origin point at Otsego Lake near Cooperstown, New York, emptying into Chesapeake Bay and the Atlantic Ocean at Havre de Grace, Maryland. It is the largest commercially non-navigable river in North America, exceptionally shallow with an average depth of 15-20 feet at its mouth and only a few feet upstream. Its abundance of jutting bedrock and waterfalls also restrain its commercial viability. Until the introduction of hydroelectric dams in the early 1900s, the Lower Susquehanna enjoyed an onrush of migratory fish in the spring, with locals easily catching shad by the hundreds.

The Nautilus crew battles a giant dugong in Jules Verne's "20,000 Leagues Under the Seas."

Ken Maurer, licensed fishing guide along the confluence of the Susquehanna River's north and west branches in Northumberland County, had several encounters with a mystery animal for a couple of years around 2001. In his regular Outdoor column in the Sunbury, Pennsylvania Daily Item, Maurer wrote that the creature appeared to be at least five or six feet long, larger than any carp he'd ever seen. It pushed a wake that caused waves to lap on the shoreline, and always sunk out of sight before it got close enough to be observed clearly. A friend of Maurer's who witnessed the creature described the thing swimming in the river like "a small submarine about to surface." Another witness suggested it might be a mammal like a seal or otter, but Maurer disagreed because the animal never surfaced to breathe. Adam Zurn, writing about the Susquehanna River's strange aquatic menagerie on Uncharted Lancaster, asked, "Has the Kettle Creek Monster moved downriver?"

The Intelligencer continued to serve watchdog duties on the New Era throughout 1885. For example, in August, a small earthenware battery cup that looked like a flower pot, of the type used in burglar alarms at the time, was found in the alley behind a new building in town. The finder was unable to identify the object and one townsperson suggested to a New Era reporter that it was a dynamite cartridge. This was enough for the newspaper to proclaim in bold type, "Was it Dynamite?" and suggest a plot to blow up the new building, worrying the community. "All were surprised at finding what the alleged infernal machine really was, but it is not known whether the reporter has yet discovered his mistake," wrote the Intelligencer.

In another instance the following month, the New Era announced that elderly Joshua Potts, a local doctor serving a five-year sentence at Eastern State Penitentiary for performing an abortion, was gravely ill. This was the first notion his family had of any illness, and the prison soon reported back that Dr. Potts was in good health. "The Potts story must be added to the long list of 'exclusive' sensational stories for which our e. c. is responsible," concluded the Intelligencer.

Also in September 1885, the Lancaster Weekly Examiner and Express accused the New Age of exaggerating the fungal rust infection of some early patches of tobacco plants into a full-blown "calamity" that threatened the entire crop of Lancaster County's most profitable agricultural product.

"Sensational journalism and lying go hand-in-hand like twin brothers, but it seldom happened that journalists resort to downright lying to mitigate humiliation as is the case with the *New Era* in the Hoffert shooting affair," the Lancaster

Weekly Examiner wrote on Sept. 28, 1887. "The world will laugh at the headless ghost story, or be amused at a sea-monster in the Susquehanna; may be disgusted at a gold mine in Fulton Township, or at apples growing on grape vines, for no one familiar with the geology and history of the country will allow himself to be hoodwinked, if his intelligence is insulted. Like an overloaded gun the man who handles it is kicked. So we think that most of the harm, aside from the immoral effect of it, is done unto the journalists who do the lying."

The incident that riled up the Examiner happened in the early morning of Sept. 19, when a private watchman named Hoffert was walking his beat on Mary Street in Lancaster and saw what he thought was a thief acting suspiciously. Hoffert yelled at the man to stop, but the supposed robber ran away at full speed. Hoffert fired his pistol twice in the man's direction. It turned out the "thief" in question was actually Prof. Richard C. Schiedt, of Franklin and Marshall College, who had just returned home to Lancaster from Philadelphia. He had run after mistaking Hoffert for a highwayman who intended to mug him. Thankfully, Schiedt was uninjured, despite one bullet whizzing past his head. After some angry words with the overeager night watchman, the professor returned home. Amusingly, Hoffert mistook Schiedt for a rampant peach thief that had been plaguing Lancaster.

19th Century Journalism

The Examiner said it was the only newspaper to print a full and accurate account of the shooting. It tooted its own horn, sharing compliments it received from Schiedt about the accuracy of its story, and praising "the energy and enterprise of the young men of the EXAMINER staff." The paper decried the conduct of the "ignorant watchman," as well as the New Era, "with its usual lack of trustworthiness" in omitting Schiedt's identity and simply referring to him as a "suspicious character" who escaped into a nearby house. When the New Era wrote a follow-up, it explained that it had purposely declined to name Schiedt, "supposing that he would prefer to have it that way." The Examiner didn't buy this attempt to obfuscate what it considered "the work of a slow-going journalist and a bungling specimen of a botch." To be fair, the Intelligencer reported the incident similarly to the New Era, but printed a correction after Schiedt contacted them to provide his side of the story.

Yellow Journalism, the "Fake News" of the late 19th century, arose when Joseph Pulitzer's New York World and William Randolph Hearst's New York Journal engaged in a war of one-upmanship to garner the highest circulation. Journalistic standards were trumped by a burning desire to churn out stories that were more sensational and salacious than whatever their competitor had written the day prior. This intense feud reached its ugly apex when both newspapers printed "unsubstantiated claims, sensationalist propaganda, and outright factual errors" following the explosion of the USS Maine in Havana Harbor on Feb. 15, 1898, per Public Domain Review. Hearst in particular fueled anti-Spanish sentiment in the U.S. by claiming Spain was responsible for the Maine's destruction, without any evidence, leading to the beginning of the Spanish–American War later that year.

However, American newspapers had been printing fantastic tales of the strange long before Pulitzer and Hearst ignited a war, reveling in much less harmful topics such as ghosts, sea serpents and Wild Men of the Woods. "Tall tales were a long American tradition, especially on the frontier. Newspaper hoaxes were also a long tradition," wrote Don Lago in the Grand Canyon Historical Society's The Ol' Pioneer magazine. "Readers didn't even bother to call such stories a hoax, for their truthfulness was beside the point. One was supposed to admire their talent of imagination."

"In the good old times when the telegraph service was not so extensive as at present, it was the duty of the telegraph editor to draw upon his imagination and write up horrors, supposed to have happened in faraway places," wrote the Examiner and Express on May 5, 1886. "This kind of journalism has passed away in most well-regulated offices. Our cotemporary, the *Era*, however, keeps up the ancient custom."

J. M. W. Geist, editor of the New Era, co-founded the newspaper in April 1887 after resigning as editor of the Examiner, owing to a difference in views between himself and the publisher over the paper's political policy. Geist always held firm in his stance that journalism and office-holding were incompatible with the independence necessary to inspire reader confidence. Geist, a veteran journalist, edited and published his first newspaper in 1844 when he was only 19. He enjoyed a long career as editor of the New Era, up until shortly before his death in 1905 at age 81. "He had always been a hard worker, and his voice and pen were always arrayed on the side of right," read the news report of Geist's death.

Geist, presumably, laid out the New Era's reporting philosophy in an unsigned editorial on May 15, 1885. It offers a remarkably candid insight into the mind of a newspaper editor of this era who was unopposed to utilizing a bit of sensation to sell papers:

THIS IS EMPHATICALLY an age of exaggerations. It seems almost impossible for newspapers to give a plain unvarnished statement of any ordinary or extraordinary occurrence. In the desire to make the paragraph attractive the widest liberty is taken with the actual facts. No actual misstatements may

J. M. W. Geist

*be made, but the facts are so given that almost any
inference may be drawn from them. They are
furthermore so surrounded by ifs and possibilities
as to verge on the ridiculous. This is a sensational
age, and this exaggerated style of serving up news
is only in strict accordance with the public demand.
It is simply a catering to the general taste. The
accounts of some tragedy or the details of some
exciting occurrence that are dished up in the most
exciting and sensational way are the ones that find*

most favor with the majority of readers. Of course, all this has nothing to recommend it, and ought to be condemned, but so long as the reading community demands it so long will the practice continue in favor. Only a higher and purer public standard will do away with the evil.

The Examiner and Express replied with a withering, "Our cotemporary, the *Era,* has at last come to the conclusion that the public loves to be gulled and excuses its part in giving the public horrible tales about 'petrified men,' 'headless ghosts,' etc."

The key here is that the New Era, in Geist's view, wasn't purely making up stories. It was reporting what it was told and filtered out little because Geist felt the public demanded a rousing good tale. The New Era often defended its reporting, although it appears to have been brazenly sloppy and sensational during much of the 1880s. The New Era might have shrugged and distanced itself in reporting the crazier tales that came its way, although giving them space at all offended its competitors. But Geist was unwilling to pull any punches in the highly competitive Lancaster media landscape, and his candor about embracing sensationalism to sell more papers is strangely refreshing. One also wonders if there remained some bad blood between Geist and his former employer, the Examiner.

While it seems the New Era eventually toned down its sensational reporting habits, its reputation lived on. Throughout the early 1890s, any "tall tale" that made its way into Pennsylvania newspapers was compared by the New Era's competitors to the former's days of reporting on headless ghosts and the like.

Amusingly, the Examiner ran its own headless ghost story on Apr. 2, 1890: "A headless ghost has made its appearance at Reading, Pa., which the family of William Ruppert and others have identified as that of the murdered Mrs. Lebo. Mrs. Ruppert relates how she heard groans in the alley beside her house and went out into the moonlight, when she saw the headless body of the murdered woman swaying to and fro on the spot where she was shot. Many people of the neighborhood are willing to corroborate this statement." Granted, this was on the heels of All Fools' Day and the Examiner couched the story in folksy narration, writing, "All bosh, you exclaim, old boy. Of course it is. But will you be kind enough to tell me why you put your right shoe on first; why you hate to see the salt cellar upset and why you will not sit down to a table of thirteen guests? Why, my dear old boy, three-fourths of our actual or accepted beliefs are ghost stories and how dearly we love them! Don't laugh at the Reading woman till you can put on your left shoe first and not think of that absurdity called luck."

The New Era, having merged by this time with the Examiner, reported on another headless ghost in 1922. The story recalled an incident that happened in the late 1800s. For weeks, an abandoned "spook house" on the 500 block of West Chestnut Street was a matter of controversy in Lancaster. Family after family had been driven from the house, scared off by the ghost of a headless man seen at all hours of the night and sometimes during the day. "Spook parties" gathered there with hopes of seeing the phantom. Dr. R. C. Schiedt of Franklin and Marshall College—the very same man who had a precarious encounter with an overzealous night watchman in 1887—was called in for a scientific examination of the house, accompanied by Dr. Stanley L. Krebs, pastor of Calvary Reformed Church in Reading, Pennsylvania. Krebs was an authority on psychic phenomena and a well-known exposer of fraudulent mediums, whose work was printed in publications such as the Journal of the Society for Psychical Research. The pair spent two nights in the house and, as claimed by the Examiner-New Era, "what they found is not for the lay mind to comprehend." Frustratingly vague, the report stated that the ghostly visitor was witnessed, brought forth by an unnamed medium who was then a student at the Reformed Theological Seminary and later became a prominent pastor in Buffalo, New York. After this medium departed, none of the subsequent residents saw the shade and the story died out.

In the end, the Lancaster New Era simply shook off the scathing criticism from its competitors. It merged with the Examiner in 1920, hyphenating their names until dropping "Examiner" and once again becoming just the New Era in 1928. (Geist, had he been alive, would surely have smirked at that.) The New Era merged with the Intelligencer Journal (itself the result of a merger between the Intelligencer and The Lancaster Journal) in 2009. Today, the New Era and its former competitors exist as one united newsroom, branded LNP Media Group. As far as I can tell, it's been a while since they reported on any headless ghosts.

SOURCES:

"About Us." *Lancaster Online*, https://lancasteronline.com/site/about.html. Accessed 3 Feb. 2025.

Begos, Kevin. "On Ancient Susquehanna, Flooding's a Frequent Fact." *PHYS*, 10 Sep. 2011, https://phys.org/news/2011-09-ancient-susquehanna-frequent-fact.html. Accessed 12 Jul. 2025.

Bernard, Lou. "Seal of Approval: The Monster of the Susquehanna." *Pennsylvania Wilds*, 6 May 2019, https://pawilds.com/monster-of-the-susquehanna/. Accessed 8 Feb. 2025.

"Death of J. M. W. Geist." *Morning News* [Wilmington, DE], 19 Jan. 1905, p. 2.

"'Dr.' Potts Is Not Sick." *Lancaster Weekly Intelligencer* [Lancaster, PA], 23 Sep. 1885, p. 6.

Dubbs, Joseph Henry. *History of Franklin and Marshall College*. Franklin and Marshall College Alumni Association, 1903.

"Dugong." *Oceana*, https://oceana.org/marine-life/dugong/. Accessed 9 Feb. 2025.

Ellis, Franklin and Samuel Evans. *History of Lancaster County, Pennsylvania, with Biographical Sketches of Many of Its Pioneers and Prominent Men*. Philadelphia, Everts & Peck, 1883.

"Excursion to Cresswell." *New Era* [Lancaster, PA], 29 Dec. 1883, p. 8.

"A Female Ghost." *Morning News* [Lancaster, PA], 15 Dec. 1892, p. 1.

"Frankford's Return." *New Era* [Lancaster, PA], 24 Nov. 1885, p. 4.

"Further Experiments Relating to Dr. Hodgson Since His Death." *Journal of the American Society for Psychical Research*, vol. 1, no. 2, 1907, pp. 125-148.

"A Headless Ghost." *Daily Telegraph* [Sydney], 28 Feb. 1885, p. 10.

Illustrated Police News. 10 Jan. 1885, p. 5.

"Indigestion, or Inveracity?" *Lancaster Intelligencer* [Lancaster, PA], 3 Jan. 1885, p. 1.

"John Frankford." *New Era* [Lancaster, PA], 6 Jan. 1885, p. 4.

"John Frankford Dead." *New Era* [Lancaster, PA], 29 Dec. 1884, p. 4.

"John Frankford's Death." *New Era* [Lancaster, PA], 30 Dec. 1884, p. 4.

John of York. "The Dugong." *Daily Democrat* [Lock Haven, PA], 27 Feb. 1897.

John of York. "The Dugong." *Daily Democrat* [Lock Haven, PA], 1 Mar. 1897.

John of York. "The Dugong." *Daily Democrat* [Lock Haven, PA], 2 Mar. 1897.

"Journalistic Lying." *Lancaster Weekly Examiner* [Lancaster, PA], 28 Sep. 1887, p. 2.

Krebs, Stanley L. "A Description of Some Trick Methods Used by Miss Bangs, of Chicago (Illustrated)." *Journal of the Society for Psychical Research*, vol. 10, no. 175, 1901, pp. 5-16.

Lago, Don. "'Looks Like a Mulhatton Story': The Origins of the Grand Canyon Egyptian Cave Myth." *Ol' Pioneer*, vol. 20, no. 2, 2009, pp. 3-11.

"Lancaster Had Headless Ghost." *Examiner-New Era* [Lancaster, PA], 10 Mar. 1922, p. 1.

Lancaster Inquirer [Lancaster, PA], 31 Jan. 1885, p. 2.

Lancaster Weekly Examiner and Express [Lancaster, PA], 7 Jan. 1885, p. 4.

Lancaster Weekly Examiner and Express [Lancaster, PA], 20 May 1885, p. 4.

Lancaster Weekly Examiner and Express [Lancaster, PA], 5 May 1886, p. 2.

"Local News in Brief." *Daily Times and Dispatch* [Reading, PA], 27 Feb. 1890, p. 4.

"A Look Back at Hunting, Fishing & Trapping." *Susquehanna National Heritage Area*, https://www.susquehannaheritage.org/hunting-fishing-trapping/. Accessed 12 Jul. 2025.

Mauer, Ken. "Mystery of the 'Thing' Deepens." *Daily Item* [Sunbury, PA], 16 Aug. 2009, p. C7.

"A Misunderstanding." *Lancaster Weekly Intelligencer* [Lancaster, PA], 21 Sep. 1887, p. 6.

"A Monster of the Waters." *New Era* [Lancaster, PA], 27 May 1885, p. 4.

"More Sensations Spoiled." *Lancaster Daily Intelligencer* [Lancaster, PA], 5 Jan. 1885, p. 4.

"Mystery and Meanness." *New Era* [Lancaster, PA], 23 Dec. 1884, p. 4.

New Era [Lancaster, PA], 15 May 1885, p. 2.

"No More Jail Breaks." *New Era* [Lancaster, PA], 12 Sep. 1885, p. 1.

"Northwest Lancaster County River Trail." *TrailLink*, https://www.traillink.com/trail/ northwest-lancaster-county-river-trail/. Accessed 9 Feb. 2025.

"Not Dead, But Sleeping." *New Era* [Lancaster, PA], 23 Nov. 1885, p. 4.

"The Obituary Record." *Morning News* [Lancaster, PA], 4 Apr. 1893, p. 1.

PA Department of Conservation and Natural Resources. "Susquehanna River Basin Facts." *Watershed Education,* https://watersheded.dcnr.pa.gov/training/assign ments/dcnr_20031260.pdf.

"Potts Gets Five Years." *Lancaster Weekly Intelligencer* [Lancaster, PA], 29 Apr. 1885, p. 5.

R. B. R. "Observed and Noted." *Lancaster Weekly Examiner* [Lancaster, PA], 2 Apr. 1890, p. 3.

"Ready for the Great Change." *New Era* [Lancaster, PA], 20 Apr. 1878, p. 5.

"A Reporter's Vivid Imagination." *Lancaster Daily Intelligencer* [Lancaster, PA], 25 Aug. 1885, p. 4.

"A Reportorial Dream." *Morning News* [Lancaster, PA], 16 Apr. 1892, p. 1.

"Rhamphorhynchus." *Wikipedia*, https://en.wikipedia.org/wiki/Rhamphorhynchus. Accessed 9 Feb. 2025.

"River Roots: Power of the River." *Susquehanna National Heritage Area*, https://susqnha.org/riverroots-power-of-the-river/. Accessed 12 Jul. 2025.

"The 'Sea Lion.'" *Lancaster Daily Intelligencer* [Lancaster, PA], 29 Apr. 1878, p. 2.

"Stanley LeFevre Krebs." *Wikipedia*, https://en.wikipedia.org/wiki/Stanley_LeFevre_Krebs. Accessed 2 Feb. 2025.

Stoltzfus, Lee J. "Willis Geist: A Small-Town Teacher / Printer Becomes a Media Giant." *The Black Art*, https://www.lancasterlyrics.com/j_m_w_geist/. Accessed 2 Feb. 2025.

"A Stray Bullet." *Lancaster Intelligencer* [Lancaster, PA], 2 Jan. 1885, p. 1.

"Susquehanna River Basin." *SRBC*, https://www.srbc.gov/portals/susquehanna-atlas/data-and-maps/susquehanna-basin. Accessed 9 Feb. 2025.

"They Tell Wild Tales." *Lancaster Daily Intelligencer* [Lancaster, PA], 28 Aug. 1890, p. 4.

"Two Discoveries." *New Era* [Lancaster, PA], 27 Dec. 1884, p. 6.

Verne, Jules. *The Mysterious Island*. Chicago, Belford, Clarke & Co., 1884.

Verne, Jules. *Twenty Thousand Leagues Under the Seas; Or the Marvellous and Exciting Adventures of Pierre Aronnax, Conseil His Servant, and Ned Land, a Canadian Harpooner*. Boston, Geo. M. Smith & Co., 1875.

"Wanted—Another Calamity." *Lancaster Weekly Examiner and Express* [Lancaster, PA], 9 Sep. 1885, p. 4.

"Yellow Journalism: The 'Fake News' of the 19th Century." *Public Domain Review*, 21 Feb. 2017, https://publicdomainreview.org/collection/yellow-journalism-the-fake-news-of-the-19th-century/. Accessed 8 Feb. 2025.

Zurn, Adam. "Cryptid: Legend of the Kettle Creek Monster." *Uncharted Lancaster*, 18 Oct. 2024, https://unchartedlancaster.com/2024/10/18/cryptid-legend-of-the-kettle-creek-monster/. Accessed 8 Feb. 2025.

Zurn, Adam. "Mystery On the River: Legend of the 1878 Wrightsville 'Sea Lion' Monster." *Uncharted Lancaster*, https://unchartedlancaster.com/2024/02/09/mystery-on-the-river-legend-of-the-1878-wrightsville-sea-lion/. Accessed 9 Feb. 2025.

The Blissville Banshee

A spectral voice, a brutal street thug, and the death spirit of the Emerald Isle stalked and disturbed a Long Island community in this true and harrowing tale of 19th century New York City.

The Blissville Banshee (Artist: Robert Jacob Woodard)

Long Islanders, particularly those of Irish descent, were tormented in 1884 by a disembodied voice they attributed to a Banshee, a wailing omen of death that had trailed them from their home country to New York City. What followed was a mystery, a manhunt and a mire of tragedy revealing dark forces, both tangible and ethereal, at work in late 19th century America.

Among Irish fairy-folk, the Banshee is the spirit of death, watching over families of historic lineage and persons gifted with music and song (said to be talents bestowed by the spirit race). Lady Jane Wilde, the mother of Oscar Wilde, wrote, "Sometimes the Banshee assumes the form of some sweet singing virgin of the family who died young, and has been given the mission by the invisible powers to become the harbinger of coming doom to her mortal kindred. Or she may be seen at night as a shrouded woman, crouched beneath the trees, lamenting with veiled face; or flying past in the moonlight, crying bitterly; and the cry of this spirit is mournful beyond all other sounds on earth, and betokens certain death to some member of the family whenever it is heard in the silence of the night... The Banshee even followed the old race across the ocean and to distant lands; for space and time offer no hindrance to the mystic power which is selected and appointed to bear the prophecy of death to a family."

The Blissville Banshee

Blissville, Laurel Hill and the suburban hamlets of Long Island City, adjacent to Calvary Cemetery, were haunted in March 1884 by a perambulating sound resembling a human voice. At about 10 p.m. on Thursday, March 6, James Flaherty, a wealthy florist of Blissville, was walking home from Laurel Hill. As he passed some unoccupied buildings on the road leading from Blissville to the Bohemian settlement on Thompson Avenue, he was startled by a loud, soprano voice that cried, "Oh, ho!" From the peculiar sound of the voice—if indeed it was a human voice—Flaherty thought it was a female in distress and entered the empty, two-story frame house from which it emanated.

This was a brave move on Flaherty's part, for the building was long reputed to be haunted. The house had been formerly occupied by the Gleason family, but had been untenanted for three years. A German resident had committed suicide in one of the neighboring homes a few years earlier, as had a man named Daley, owner of the nearby Windsor Hotel in Long Island City, seven or eight years prior. A neighborhood barn, the site of a murder some years earlier, was another candidate for spiritual activity. All in all, the area was spook central.

The florist searched the house from cellar to garret but did not discover the source. As he stood, puzzled, on the upper floor, he suddenly heard the noise again, coming from the vacant lot behind the house. From the window he saw nothing, and later admitted he was from that moment "a little frightened."

Flaherty headed home and told his family about the strange experience. His son, John, a strapping young man, seized his shotgun and summoned 10 of his peers from the neighborhood. Together, the determined group set off in pursuit of the "strange creature."

The group walked about a quarter of a mile when they heard the odd voice call out from the direction of Calvary Cemetery. The young men separated into pairs (splitting up as any foolish mortals would do in a horror movie) and searched the entire graveyard to no avail. At about 10 minutes to midnight, the voice grew faint and seemed to die out in the center of the sprawling cemetery. Unsuccessful at tracking the disembodied voice, the group returned to their respective homes.

The next morning, Flaherty, his son, and the other posse members learned that fellow residents of the village had heard the weird sounds but were afraid to speak of them openly. The group spread the word to nearly all the young men residing in Blissville and Laurel Hill to be ready on Friday night to run down the "Banshee" or ghost, or whatever else it might be.

The Blissville Banshee

Calvary Cemetery in Queens, New York, circa 2006. Original photo taken by Plowboylifestyle at en.wikipedia, Public Domain, via Wikimedia Commons.

At 9 p.m. on Friday, the party of over 100 met at the bar at Bradley's Hotel in Blissville, each man armed with a six-shooter or shotgun. Flaherty told his account of the previous night, and the group decided to separate into three patrols, led by Ex-Alderman Murray, Judge Patrick Kavanagh and James McWilliams, each taking a different route and meeting at a given point. Scarcely had they left the hotel when they heard "Oh ho!" in the same house that Flaherty had previously explored. The vigilantes surrounded the house, finally selecting 10 of their number to go inside. Just as the search began, the voice called out from the cemetery fence. The entire party charged in that direction but were just as unsuccessful as the smaller group that scoured the graveyard the previous evening. Discouraged and disheartened, they dispersed to their homes.

On Saturday, a Brooklyn Eagle reporter visited Flaherty at his home to learn more about the invisible spook. "There is something very strange in this thing," Flaherty told the journalist. "I don't believe in ghosts or 'banshees,' but I'm sure the voice I heard was not the voice of any living creature." Flaherty declined further comment and directed the reporter to other Blissville residents who had shared the same experience. Kavanagh, Murray, Alderman White and others backed up Flaherty's claims and asserted their belief that the voice belonged to no living being, but a ghost.

However, Kavanagh revealed that when he first heard the soprano voice, he identified it as belonging to a barber from Laurel Hill, who was reputed to possess "the strongest voice of any man on Long Island." But the barber himself was among the search party, so Kavanagh ruled him out as the true identity of the Banshee.

It should be noted that none of the reporters that covered this story and its fallout could agree on the barber's name, although he was consistently stated to be African-American. The barber was variously named Jackson, Thomas Williams, Peter Johnson, Andrew Johnson, Rolland S. Johnson and, most commonly, Rollins Johnson. The 1880 U.S. Federal Census shows a Rowland Johnson, a 26-year-old Black man and barber, living on Grand Street in New York City, although it is unclear if this was the same individual.

Another official on the search committee, Supervisor Joseph McLaughlin, also suspected the barber and cautioned him to discontinue the annoyance. Some citizens theorized that Johnson was a ventriloquist who was throwing his voice to bedevil the community. These accusations incensed Johnson, who threatened to "brain" the next man who pointed the finger at him.

"I am no more the ghost than you are. I haven't been out of my house at night since the spook came around here," Johnson told the New York Sun. "I am afraid to be out after dark. You can say that Rollins Johnson is a gentleman's barber and no spook."

"It must be an owl," Kavanagh concluded. He claimed that he saw this owl in the old barn, "large as a goose, with eyes as large as a dessert plate." The barn was checked Monday morning, but the owl was not present. The Brooklyn Eagle added, "No one believes the Judge."

"It's an owl, or Johnson, the barber, imitating an owl," conceded McLaughlin. "There are no such things as ghosts or banshees."

Michael Powers, the sexton of St. Raphael's Church, admitted to hearing the voice but stated it was unlucky to discuss it any further. John Hipple, assistant superintendent of Calvary Cemetery, fully corroborated Flaherty's story. A police officer named Fantry, who resided close to the cemetery, opined that it was just young men who were out gallivanting late at night.

Nonetheless, the community was uneasy and the night watches continued. A local man who had emigrated from Ireland, and refused to be named, told the Brooklyn Eagle, "In the [Old] Country [when] the banshee came around, the handsomest-looking girl in the neighborhood was sure to die within a period of four weeks. I don't [mean] to say that any of the young ladies in this village will die—God forbid it—but it doesn't look right to me."

A number of locals agreed with the supernatural hypothesis. As reported by the Brooklyn Eagle, "They have all seen a wee woman with fiery red hair curled down her back, who vanishes from sight into the old barn, and the old inhabitants say the figure is like the corpse of the woman who, they allege, was murdered in the building. That crime has always remained a mystery. Others think it is the spirit in distress of some person buried in Calvary, and still others think it the spirit of Mrs. Collier, who was recently killed by arsenical poisoning."

The Blissville Banshee

John Powers, proprietor of a hotel directly opposite St. Raphael's Church, said, "A few nights ago, when I was on my way home from the City Hall, I met a little woman on the road back of the De Bevoise homestead. I thought it was strange that a woman should be out alone at that hour of the night. I stopped when she passed me and said: 'Good evening.' She made no reply, and I passed on. Soon afterward I turned around and she had disappeared. Where she could have gone to, I don't know. There are no houses or fences on the road, and she must have disappeared into the bowels of the earth."

Blissville resident Thomas Culvert, Jr. also ran into such a woman on Saturday night but did not speak to her. "She had red hair with long curls down her back. She seemed to be about 25 or 30 years old but was only about three feet in height. I ran home as fast as I could." Both John Powers and Culvert said the woman was dressed all in black, the latter man also noting her stony blue eyes and expression of deep melancholy.

Patrick Hughes described an even weirder experience: "I was coming home late on Saturday night, and when about halfway from Hunter's Point I saw a little man, riding a pig across the lot, going in the direction of the water works. I didn't look behind me, and you can bet that I ain't out late any more at night."

The vigilante committee decided on stronger measures for Monday, March 10. "If the specter reappears tonight and vanishes into the rickety barn, fire will be applied to it," reported the Brooklyn Eagle. "Lights are to be placed in the Gleason house. It is said that one light was left there last night which was mysteriously extinguished, the smoke from the wick creating an odor of brimstone. Every man who passes halts to make the sign of the cross as a protection against the apparition."

Perhaps tongue-in-cheek, the Brooklyn Eagle stated that a Protestant who joked the phantom was "an escaped prisoner from purgatory" narrowly escaped violence from insulted Catholics. Nevertheless, an Episcopalian minister offered to join a Catholic priest in reading prayers to banish the annoying spirit, although the priest regarded the affair humorously. "There will be music in Blissville tonight," mused the Eagle.

Another barber, August Heffner from Hunter's Point, offered his services as a ghostbuster. "I will bet any man in Blissville $5 that I can catch the ghost. I have seen a good many ghosts in Germany, and I know how to handle them." Heffner had arrived in Laurel Hill and Blissville on Sunday afternoon, only to be disappointed when the ghost hunt was called off due to a storm. But he promised to be on hand when the search resumed on Monday.

The Blissville Banshee

Monday night, at 10 p.m., the Blissville Ghost was finally "treed." John Flaherty, whose father had first investigated the strange voice, was on the way from Laurel Hill to his home in Blissville when he heard the familiar "Oh ho!" coming from behind a large tree a short distance in front of him. Flaherty quickly drew his pistol and ordered the banshee to surrender or he would "kill it dead." The phantom threw up its hands and exclaimed, "Don't shoot... I am the ghost!" Squinting through the dark of night, Flaherty immediately recognized who stood before him—Johnson, the barber with a voice of gold.

The young man demanded an explanation from the barber, who made light of the situation and admitted he had quite enjoyed the ruse. Flaherty angrily thrashed the barber and made him pledge he would discontinue his midnight prowling around Laurel Hill and Blissville. Johnson acquiesced, and Flaherty sent him home.

On Tuesday, a New York Times reporter caught up with Johnson and asked about his motive. The barber admitted he did it for fun. "I didn't think I was going to scare anybody, but you can bet that I'll never holler again as long as my name is Rollins Johnson." (As indicated earlier, "Rollins" might have been a misspelling by the reporter.) A later New York Times report claimed that Johnson said he conducted his prank "[just] to frighten the

Irish," presumably playing on Banshee lore they had carried with them from Ireland.

One unavoidable fact to mention here is that, while New York City has a long history as a melting pot, the prejudices of the era are evident when reviewing the news coverage surrounding the Blissville Banshee. While some of the articles treated Johnson respectfully, other stories quoted him in caricatured dialect (as well as with outdated racial terms). Irish accents were conveyed in a similar fashion. In instances included in this article, I made and noted corrections within brackets.

Johnson, who apparently WAS a skilled ventriloquist, soon faced what he believed was retribution from indignant members of the community over his shenanigans. On March 15, he filed a complaint with Judge Kavanagh in Long Island City Court against John Powers, the Blissville hotel owner. Kavanagh soon issued a warrant for Powers' arrest on charges of assaulting Johnson on the highway and threatening to kill him.

"I was on my way from Dutch Kills about 10 o'clock on Friday night," Johnson told the Brooklyn Eagle. "I wasn't yelling or thinking about ghosts. I met Powers and a man named Blake. Powers ran at me and said, 'I'll kill you.' He then hit me and knocked me down, and when I was down, he kicked me. He pulled out his revolver and fired two shots but he must not have intended to kill me, or he could have done so. I lost $2.75 out of my pocket, but I don't think Powers took it. He had no reason to hit me unless he was mad because I turned out to be the ghost. I ain't going to play ghost any more, but I don't want to be knocked down every time I go on the street."

Powers denied the charges and said he had accidentally stumbled against Johnson in the dark. He also told the New York Times that he did strike a Black man who assaulted him while on his way home on Friday night. "I did not know who it was, as I never saw Johnson. I fired two shots to frighten him. I did not intend to hurt him, and I intended that he should not hurt me." Powers was scheduled for trial on Monday, March 17, but the outcome does not appear to have been reported.

This story took an awful and tragic turn when, on Aug. 18, 1884, Johnson drowned in Bowery Bay under suspicious circumstances. According to press accounts, Johnson and a group of white men headed out onto the bay in a boat that morning. They became intoxicated and started horsing around when the boat suddenly overturned, causing Johnson to fall into the water and drown. A rumor began circulating that the other men in the boat with Johnson—John Schroeder, Beaman (no first name given), Frank

Beck and John Farrel—were members of the notorious Dutch Kills gang. The Brooklyn Eagle reported that the men were heard to say that if they did not catch any fish, they would drown Johnson. Beaman, though, stated that the group was "cutting up" in the boat when it upset, causing the accident. A local man named James McDonald found Johnson's body in shallow water. He stated that the other men exerted no effort to recover Johnson's body and left the scene as soon as they reached the shore. Johnson's body was transported to Hunter's Point Morgue and the matter was scheduled for a coroner's inquest on Friday, Aug. 22. Again, New York papers do not appear to have reported on the outcome. In the coverage of his death, Johnson was remembered as a well-known barber with a shop in Dutch Kills, as well as the "Blissville Banshee."

The Dutch Kills gang was feared in Long Island City during the late 1800s and early 1900s, allegedly committing burglaries, assaults and murders. Victims included other gang members, citizens and the police. The Beaman involved with Johnson's death was likely John Beaman, a young, six-foot-one-inch-tall "tough of toughs" in Dutch Kills. Beaman was reported to have committed several violent crimes throughout the 1880s but routinely escaped justice. Among his alleged offenses were bludgeoning an "old and inoffensive man" named John Loeffler to death with a bedpost during a drunken row in Dutch Kills on New Year's Night, 1882; brutally beating a young German mechanic, Gottlieb Clymer, nearly to death with a chair in his own Dutch Kills home on Sep. 23, 1883, after a drunken Beaman and a companion chided the man for sawing wood in his yard on the Sabbath and the man told them to mind their own business; and, along with another tough, assaulting a Chinese laundryman, called Ah Ting by the press, so ferociously in October 1886 that it looked like the victim had been "dragged through a thrashing machine."

Finally, in October 1887, justice succeeded in catching up with Beaman. Queens County Judge Cullen sentenced Beaman to seven years in prison for, along with several other men, beating and robbing Max Halfmann of his silver watch and chain as he walked home from a late summer picnic at Schuetzen Park. The young tough's criminal record as a frequent offender factored into his sentence.

"Justice in Queens County, however slow, is sure-footed and overtook yesterday John Beaman..." the Brooklyn Daily Eagle reported on Oct. 15, 1887. "Things have changed in Queens County and indictments are no longer pigeonholed or disposed of by mock trials, as used to be the case. A good many old offenders have come to judgement latterly, and Beaman is about the last of the men who were privileged to commit offenses and go scot free."

Unfortunately, Beaman and another inmate, arsonist Charles Ricket, escaped from Dannemora Prison in upstate New York on the morning of Oct. 11, 1890. (Dannemora was the site of another infamous double prison break by inmates Richard Matt and David Sweat in 2015.) The pair, part of a work detail that was making repairs to the warden's house, jumped from a second-story window and slipped away, not being missed until dinner time. Despite a $100 reward for each of the escaped convicts, no trace of them was found.

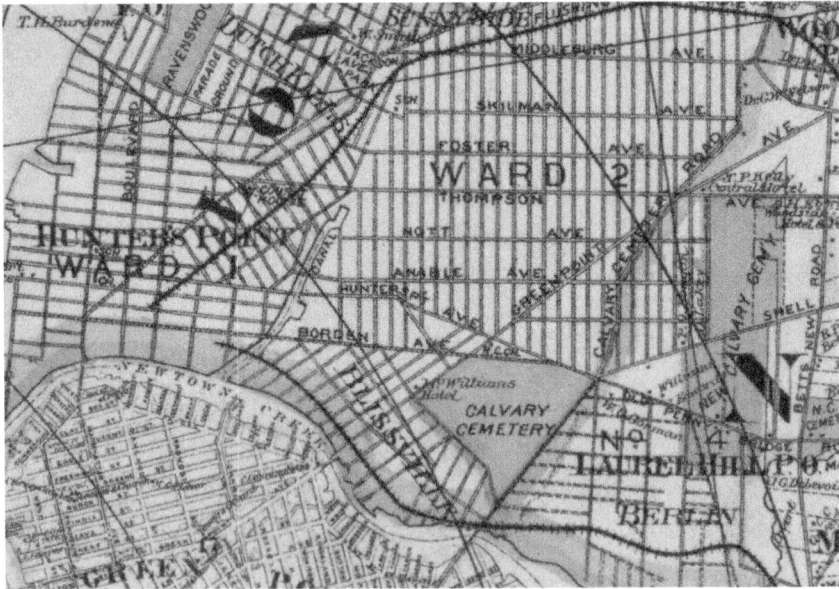

Map of Blissville and surrounding areas on Long Island, 1886.

The Blissville Banshee

Blissville, the Second Ward of Long Island City, was founded by Neziah Bliss, although it was considered less prosperous than surrounding areas at the turn of the 20th century. It was part of the old Dutch Kills section, a locality which had by then passed out of existence legally, only persisting in local tradition. Bliss developed Greenpoint and later purchased a large tract of land on the further side of Newtown Creek in Dutch Kills. Despite the ominous-sounding name, "Kill" is Dutch for "little stream," referring to a tributary of Newtown Creek, per the Dutch Kills Civic Association. According to the 1898 book "Leslie's History of the Greater New York," the name Blissville was "most mournfully out of harmony with its appearance and actual residential conditions."

By the mid-19th century, Blissville became a center for heavy industry such as glue factories, smelting and fat-rendering plants, refineries and foundries, according to Brick Underground. Many Irish laborers followed the work opportunities and settled in Blissville, per Brownstoner. Nearly 800,000 Irish immigrants arrived in New York during the devastating potato famine that swept their home country from 1845-1852. They established working-class settlements all around Manhattan, including Long Island City in Queens, many finding work in labor-intensive jobs.

Today, wrote Brick Underground, Blissville is "a rough-hewn, mostly forgotten outpost of New York City." The aging section lies along the Long Island Expressway and is occupied by warehouses, auto repair shops, some factories, and a smattering of housing and storefronts. Calvary Cemetery, one of the historic haunts of the Blissville Banshee, stretches along the length of Greenpoint Avenue, a sea of green in an urban landscape. Established in 1848 to compensate for a shortage of burial ground in Manhattan, Calvary Cemetery has been expanded over the years to encompass 365 acres and has the largest number of interments of any cemetery in the United States. The Blissville Banshee remains part of local folklore, although it is generally conveyed without the greater historical context and human identity of the phantom.

However, the case of the Blissville Banshee isn't fully solved with Johnson's admission to throwing his voice to prank his neighbors. It doesn't explain the reports that veer into high strangeness, such as the "wee woman with fiery red hair" who appeared to vanish into thin air before various eyewitnesses, and the little man riding a pig. These accounts are more in line with fairy-beings of Irish lore, much like the Banshee. Fairies have been said to ride a variety of steeds, including ponies, deer and dried stalks of weeds magically transformed into flying horses. The 1884 reports suggest a contemporary belief in the manifestation, by either supernatural means or imagination, of fairy folk who followed Irish immigrants across the Atlantic Ocean from the Emerald Isle to New York City.

Strangely, the tale of the Blissville Banshee has striking parallels to a story collected and presented by Lady Wilde in her 1887 book, "Ancient Legends, Mystic Charms, and Superstitions of Ireland." It also tells of a Banshee who followed Irish immigrants to the New World:

A branch of the ancient race of the O'Gradys had settled in Canada, far removed, apparently, from all the associations, traditions, and mysterious influences of the old land of their forefathers.

But one night a strange and mournful lamentation was heard outside the house. No word was uttered, only a bitter cry, as of one in deepest agony and sorrow, floated through the air.

Inquiry was made, but no one had been seen near the house at the time, though several persons distinctly heard the weird, unearthly cry, and a terror fell upon the household, as if some supernatural influence had overshadowed them.

Next day it so happened that the gentleman and his eldest son went out boating. As they did not return, however, at the usual time for dinner, some alarm was excited, and messengers were sent down to the shore to look for them. But no tidings came until, precisely at the exact hour of the night when the spirit-cry had been heard the previous evening, a crowd of men were seen approaching the house, bearing with them the dead bodies of the father and the son, who had both been drowned by the accidental upsetting of the boat, within sight of land, but not near enough for any help to reach them in time.

Thus the Ban-Sidhe had fulfilled her mission of doom, after which she disappeared, and the cry of the spirit of death was heard no more.

While Johnson might not have been Irish, he was gifted with a powerful voice. A superstitious person could surmise that, in invoking the ancient spirit of the Banshee haunting his Irish neighbors, the mischievous barber of Dutch Kills might have unleashed its fatal foresight on himself, leaving him drowned in the waters of Bowery Bay only five months later. And that tragedy survives in some form to this day in the legends and lore of Long Island.

SOURCES:

"Ah Ting Will Get Even." *Brooklyn Daily Times* [Brooklyn, NY], 20 Oct. 1886, p. 1.

"Alleged Robbers on Trial." *Brooklyn Daily Times* [Brooklyn, NY], 31 Aug. 1887, p. 1.

"The Banshee of Blissville." *New York Times*, 17 Mar. 1884, p. 2.

"The Blissville Banshee." *Brooklyn Eagle* [Brooklyn, NY], 9 Mar. 1884, p. 1.

"The Blissville Ghost Treed." *New York Times*, 12 Mar. 1884, p. 8.

"The Blissville Mystery Unsolved." *New-York Daily Tribune*, 11 Mar. 1884, p. 8.

Briggs, Katharine M. *The Vanishing People*. B. T. Batsford Ltd., 1978.

"Calvary Cemetery (Queens)." *Wikipedia*, https://en.wikipedia.org/wiki/Calvary_Cemetery_(Queens). Accessed 20 Apr. 2025.

Cohen, Marjorie. "Pirates, Glue Factories, and Mob Graves: Blissville Is Queens's Dumping Ground." *Brick Underground*, 14 Nov. 2017, https://www.brickunderground.com/live/blissville-queens-history. Accessed 19 Apr. 2025.

"The Day's Minor News." *Brooklyn Daily Eagle* [Brooklyn, NY], 19. Aug. 1884, p. 4.

"Detective Murdered in Long Island City." *New York Times*, 17 Jul. 1902, p. 14.

"The Dutch Kills Gang Again." *Brooklyn Daily Eagle* [Brooklyn, NY], 20 Aug. 1884, p. 4.

"The Dutch Kills Ruffians." *Brooklyn Daily Eagle* [Brooklyn, NY], 24 Sep. 1883, p. 3.

"Giving a Banshee Good Evening." *Sun* [New York], 10 Mar. 1884, p. 4.

"History of Dutch Kills." *Dutch Kills Civic Association*, http://dutchkillscivic.com/history/. Accessed 19 Apr. 2025.

"Hunting a Voice." *Buffalo Evening News* [Buffalo, NY], 13 Mar. 1884, p. 3.

Casey, Marion R. "Irish (from the Encyclopedia of New York City)." *Virtual NY*, https://virtualny.ashp.cuny.edu/EncyNYC/Irish.html. Accessed 20 Apr. 2025.

"Irish American Heritage at the William Floyd Estate." *National Park Service*, https://www.nps.gov/fiis/learn/historyculture/irish-american-heritage-at-the-william-floyd-estate.htm, Archived: https://web.archive.org/web/20250409023505/https://www.nps.gov/fiis/learn/historyculture/irish-american-heritage-at-the-william-floyd-estate.htm. Accessed 20 Apr. 2025.

"Jane Wilde." *Wikipedia*, https://en.wikipedia.org/wiki/Jane_Wilde. Accessed 20 Apr. 2025.

KHN. "That Ghost." *Brooklyn Eagle* [Brooklyn, NY], 10 Mar. 1884, p. 4.

"Killed by Gangsters." *Sun* [New York], 26 May 1909, p. 6.

"Knocked Out in One Round." *Brooklyn Eagle* [Brooklyn, NY], 16 Mar, 1884, p. 12.

Lady Wilde. *Ancient Legends, Mystic Charms, and Superstitions of Ireland.* Boston, Ticknor and Co., 1887.

"Late News." *Rutland Daily Herald* [Rutland, VT], 4 Jan. 1882, p. 1.

"Long Island." *New-York Daily Tribune*, 11 Oct. 1883, p. 8.

"Long Island." *New York Times*, 19 Aug. 1884, p. 8.

"Long Island." *New York Times*, 20 Aug. 1884, p. 8.

"Long Island." *New York Times*, 30 Dec. 1885, p. 8.

"Murder in L. I. City." *Brooklyn Daily Eagle* [Brooklyn, NY], 26 May 1909, p. 18.

"A New Year's Tragedy." *New York Herald*, 19 Jul. 1882, p. 5.

"News from the Suburbs." *New-York Daily Tribune*, 10 Mar. 1884, p. 8.

"News from the Suburbs." *New-York Daily Tribune*, 17 Mar. 1884, p. 8.

"Notes." *Brooklyn Daily Times* [Brooklyn, NY], 24 Sep. 1883, p. 1.

"On Long Island." *Brooklyn Daily Eagle* [Brooklyn, NY], 15 Oct. 1887, p. 1.

Portrait and Biographical Record of Queens County (Long Island) New York. Chapman Publishing Co., New York, 1896.

"A Red-Haired, Blue-Eyed Ghost." *New York Times*, 10 Mar. 1884, p. 8.

"Remarkable Double Escape." *Buffalo News* [Buffalo, NY], 13 Oct. 1890, p. 1.

Ross, Peter. *A History of Long Island, from Its Earliest Settlement to the Present Time, Vol. I.* Lewis Publishing Company, 1902.

"Rowland Johnson in the 1880 United States Federal Census." *Ancestry,* https://www.ancestry.com/search/collections/6742/records/38843228. Accessed 17 Apr. 2025.

"Sherlock and Beaman." *Brooklyn Daily Times* [Brooklyn, NY], 2 Sep. 1887, p. 1.

Singleton, Bob. "Grim Tales from Old LIC." 21 Nov. 2011, https://qns.com/2011/11/grim-tales-from-old-lic/. Accessed 19 Apr. 2025.

"Two Clinton Prison Convicts Escape." *Morning Star* [Glens Falls, NY], 14 Oct. 1890, p. 4.

Van Pelt, Daniel. *Leslie's History of the Greater New York, Vol. II.* Arkell Publishing Company, New York, 1898.

"Various Matters." *Buffalo Express* [Buffalo, NY], 19 Aug. 1884, p. 1.

Waxman, Mitch. "The Blissville Banshee." *Brownstoner*, 10 Oct. 2013, https://www.brownstoner.com/history/the-blissville-banshee/. Accessed 19 Apr. 2025.

Young, S. R. *The Wollaton Gnomes: A Nottingham Fairy Mystery*. Pwca Books and Pamphlets, 2023.

Did Edgar Allan Poe & Mark Twain See Giant Birds in Pennsylvania?

Two of America's literary giants and legends of immense, black birds have become mixed together in the savory stew of Pennsylvania folklore.

The raven statue on the grounds of the Edgar Allan Poe National Historic Site in Philadelphia (Midnightdreary, Public domain, via Wikimedia Commons)

Poe and Twain

If Pennsylvania folklore is to be believed, Mark Twain once spotted an immense, black bird while writing on a rock on the present-day grounds of Ravensburg State Park in Clinton County. Edgar Allan Poe encountered a similar remarkable creature while visiting the Poe Valley (possibly named for his ancestors) in Centre County. Did these two icons of American literature come face-to-face with The Keystone State's legendary Thunderbirds? These brief anecdotes from "regional lore" were published by Thunderbird researcher Gerald Musinsky, who took a great interest in northcentral Pennsylvania's reports of abnormally large, unidentified birds of prey. Musinsky, who sadly passed away in 2008, possibly collected these tales while interviewing local residents, as earlier written sources about these giant bird sightings are as yet evasive. But these stories didn't arise from nothing; Twain and Poe are indeed entangled with Pennsylvania history and legend.

In the late 1860s and the 1870s, Twain embarked on national lecture tours that included several stops throughout Pennsylvania. He made a one-day visit to the Lock Haven Opera House in Clinton County to perform "Roughing It" on Jan. 16, 1872. It's certainly feasible that Twain could have visited the nearby, future site of Ravensburg State Park (established in 1933) on this or another trip. Twain is known to have stayed at the Fallon Hotel in Lock Haven.

Situated within Rauchtown in Crawford Township, Ravensburg State Park is indeed known for its rock ledges (on which Twain perhaps wrote) and the ravens that roost upon them. My good friend and Lock Haven-based historian Lou Bernard documented an unfinished story collected by prolific Pennsylvania folklorist Henry W. Shoemaker about the doomed Philip Rauch, whose family founded their namesake place. The tale recounts Rauch's tragic love life and the jealous and murderous ghost of an ex-girlfriend. Circling ravens portended these events, leading searchers to find Rauch's broken body—thrown from his horse after something or *someone* spooked it—near present-day Ravensburg State Park.

There are several disagreements in Pennsylvania folklore and history about where and how Poe came to pen his beloved and atmospheric poem, "The Raven." In one account, Poe visited Poe Valley in 1839 and experienced an intense, unrequited romance with a mountain girl, Helen Hallferty Park (aka Helena Halit or Hallett). Mind you, he was married to his teenaged cousin, Virginia Clemm, at the time. According to the story, Poe wrote "The Raven" and dedicated it to Helena, which either happened in the immediate aftermath of this adventure during a sleepless night at the Old Fort Hotel in Centre Hall, Pennsylvania, or once he returned home to Philadelphia.

This version (or versions) of events is, of course, disputed. In 1941, Pennsylvania journalist Agnes Selin Schoch exposed the holes in the tale, such as the fact that Poe never dedicated "The Raven" to any Helena. "It is a good story but we do not believe a word of it," wrote Selin Schoch, aware she was draining the fun from a saucy folktale.

Ravens (H.koppdelaney, CC BY-SA 3.0, via Wikimedia Commons)

The Edgar Allan Poe National Historic Site, a red brick house Poe rented during his years in Philly,

Quoth the Raven, "You sure look tasty!" (Artist:
Krisnasatriafeb)

did at one point claim to be where he wrote "The
Raven." It might align with the first publication of
the poem in January 1845 but not necessarily the
earlier Poe Valley story. Poe lived in several homes
during his 1837-1844 stay in The City of Brotherly

Love and wrote many of his great works there. But he only resided in the current historic site from 1843-1844.

The Poe family then moved to New York City, where today plaques and a large raven statue on 84th Street commemorate the demolished Brennan Farmhouse, where in 1844 Poe wrote, or at least "finished writing," per one of the plaques, "The Raven."

Shoemaker recorded a slightly different version of Poe's time in Poe Valley. In the folktale "A Modern Petrarch," the young poet's quest to seek his inheritance fell by the wayside after his "brief and tempestuous courting" of the beautiful Helena Walters. She was the daughter of a leading farmer in the valley, who ended up choosing another man (Abram Halit) that Poe considered "his inferior." Poe despondently left the area, soon afterward visiting the prophetically named Raven Hotel in Milroy, Pennsylvania and strolling along the scenic banks of Alexander's Stream. He sat down on a log, where he "could faintly hear the cawing of ravens in the tops of the tall oaks on the apex of the cliff which overhung the fountain" and proceeded to write a mournful poem inspired by Helena—which was decidedly NOT "The Raven," but a different poem he would later discard!

Mary E. Phillips, in her 1926 biography, "Edgar Allan Poe: The Man," wrote that Helena was actually Helena Elizabeth Liddell, whose family mansion Poe had stayed at while seeking an inheritance of timber and farming acres left by his ancestors in Poe Valley. Poe and Liddell, who was then 18, took an interest in one another, with Poe quickly becoming infatuated. It was poor timing, as he was already married to Virginia Clemm and Helena was secretly betrothed to a man named Jacob Weaver. Liddell was unmoved by Poe's literary pursuits and began to find him odd, so she frostily rejected his declaration of love and married the stalwart Weaver. About seven years later, the married Mrs. Weaver received an anonymous envelope containing an exquisitely handwritten copy of "The Raven." She found it "heavy, tiresome" and didn't get past the first verse. Phillips wrote that Shoemaker, anxious to meet the woman who claimed to have known Poe, paid a visit to her estate. Shoemaker noted that the former Miss Liddell, then 78, had aged gracefully, remarking, "I complimented her appearance and turned sadly away from a beautiful mask with a skeleton steel within."

An interesting parallel to this article's topic: Quoting Shoemaker's letters, Phillips wrote that Shoemaker told of seeing majestic golden eagles soaring over Poe Valley. Shoemaker wrote, "I will never forget Povalley one lowering autumn afternoon. There had been a storm. We had come to a vast open country. Out of a thicket flew two superb golden eagles so near that the whirring of their wings frightened our horses. The majestic birds shot upward with the velocity of biplanes to the near touch of the storm clouds, then began tremendous circles in their flights. Masters of high air, they triumphantly disappeared through its storm-tossed embattlements." Phillips observed (via the work of Pennsylvania poet John H. Chatham), that golden eagles would have been numerous in Poe's time, and she pondered if they might have inspired the nature-loving poet. She wrote, "It is interesting to think how their mighty flights must have enthralled his attention, while a pinion of their imperialism fluttered to his feet for his own, in 'The Raven' and other pen-inspirations."

Trough Creek State Park in Huntington County, Pennsylvania also makes a claim that Poe was influenced by its resident, cliff-dwelling ravens in writing his famous poem.

While it's hard to say if Mark Twain or Edgar Allan Poe ever saw "immense black birds in Pennsylvania," as Musinsky claimed, there's no doubt that the two authors AND the local population of *Corvus corax* have left an indelible mark on residents of The Keystone State. Perhaps we will one day stumble upon these elusive monster tales in some "quaint and curious volume of forgotten lore."

SOURCES:

Bernard, Lou. "The Jealous Ghost of Crawford Township." *The Express*, 28 Oct. 2020, https://www.lockhaven.com/news/local-news/2020/10/the-jealous-ghost-of-crawford-township. Accessed 13 Jul. 2021.

Bernard, Lou. "Lou's View: The Fallon in its Prime." *The Record Online*, 28 Jan. 2021, https://therecord-online.com/site/archives/66059. Accessed 13 Jul. 2021.

"Edgar Allan Poe." *Wikipedia*, https://en.wikipedia.org/wiki/Edgar_Allan_Poe. Accessed 10 Jul. 2021.

Edgar Allan Poe National Historic Site. *Wikipedia*, https://en.wikipedia.org/wiki/Edgar_Allan_Poe_National_Historic_Site. Accessed 10 Jul. 2021.

Esper, George. "Edgar Allen Poe Museum in Philadelphia Lures Few." *Daily Record* [Stroudsburgs, PA], 21 Feb. 1964, p. 7.

Musinsky, Gerald. "Return of the Thunderbird: Avian Mystery of the Black Forest." *Reflections on Cryptozoology*, 1 Jul. 1999, http://www.cryptozoologicalrealms.com/english/reflections/return.html. Archived: https://web.archive.org/web/20010119101500/h

ttp://www.cryptozoologicalrealms.com:80/english/reflections/return.html. Accessed 10 Jul. 2021.

"Trough Creek State Park." *Pennsylvania Department of Conservation and Natural Resources.* http://www.dcnr.state.pa.us/stateparks/findapark/troughcreek/index.htm. Archived: https://web.archive.org/web/20111107162049/

Phillips, Mary Elizabeth. *Edgar Allan Poe, The Man, Vol. I.* The John C. Winston Co., 1926.

"Ravensburg State Park." *Wikipedia*, https://en.wikipedia.org/wiki/Ravensburg_State_Park. Accessed 13 Jul. 2021.

Schmidt, Barbara. "Chronology of Known Mark Twain Speeches, Public Readings, and Lectures." Twain Quotes, http://www.twainquotes.com/SpeechIndex.html. Accessed 13 Jul. 2021.

Shoemaker, Henry W. *In the Seven Mountains: Legends Collected in Central Pennsylvania.* The Bright Printing Company, 1913.

Selin Schoch, Agnes. "Yesteryears." *Selinsgrove Times* [Selinsgrove, PA], 11 Sep. 1941, pp. 1,4.

Young, Michelle. "Where Edgar Allan Poe Wrote 'The Raven,' Published 175 Years Ago." *Untapped New York*, 20 Feb. 2020, https://untappedcities.com/2020/02/20/where-edgar-allan-poe-wrote-the-raven-published-175-years-ago/. Accessed 10 Jul. 2021.

Haunted Televisions

The advent of TV brought with it new pathways to the paranormal. Technological explanations for these phenomena did little to quell the natural human tendency to find terror in the latest electronic marvel.

Haunted Television (Artist: Orila Id)

In 1982, Steven Spielberg gave us the indelible nightmare fuel of a ghostly hand reaching out from a staticky television screen as a little girl sat before it, creepily announcing, "They're here…" In 1998, the international "Ring" franchise debuted with its first Japanese installment, terrifying audiences with a cursed videotape and a malevolent female spirit who crawled out of a well and stepped right through the doomed viewer's television screen. These petrifying poltergeists are thankfully just movie magic, right? You might be surprised to learn that there are real-world analogues, cases in which unsettling specters appeared on TV screens and cast a dark pallor over the living rooms of American families. Many of these cases can be chalked up to a lack of understanding about a bold new technology that rapidly invaded homes and became the center of daily entertainment. But the television also acted as a mirrored portal in its early days, drawing us into simulated life while simultaneously reflecting back our timeless fears.

Television developed rapidly during the 1920s and '30s. Moving images of then U.S. Secretary of Commerce Herbert Hoover were broadcast over phone circuits from Washington, D.C. to New York in 1927. American inventor Philo Taylor Farnsworth created the first working all-electronic television system the same year, which RCA then copied, starting a legal battle, per Elon University.

Haunted Televisions

NBC and CBS made the leap from radio to building experimental TV broadcast stations in New York during the 1930s. Despite the technology stalling during the Second World War, in 1946 RCA introduced Americans to the first mass-produced cathode-ray tube (CRT) home television, the 630-TS, fondly remembered as the "Model T" of its medium. Approximately 8,000 U.S. households owned television sets in 1946, and that number grew to 45.7 million by 1960, according to Elon University.

RCA Model 630-TS, the "Model T" of televisions. Photo by Fletcher6, CC BY-SA 3.0, via Wikimedia Commons.

As early as 1927, Bell Telephone Laboratories was examining the phenomena of "ghosts" that appeared on television screens. These weren't of the supernatural variety, but rather faint or negative duplicates that haunted a broadcast image. A 1944 report on the future of television compared radio waves that followed the contour of the Earth to television signals transmitted in a straight line, giving them a range no greater than 100 miles. TV signals were prone to reflecting off mountains or tall buildings, with these reflected signals arriving with a slight delay, causing ghosting in the televised program. TV repair shops were quick to capitalize on the "ghost" phenomenon. "Haunted by 'ghosts' in your television receiver? Call Reception Unlimited," advertised a New Rochelle, New York business in 1948, dubbing themselves "Professional 'Ghost' Catchers."

GET
RID OF GHOSTS
ON YOUR TELEVISION SCREEN

A 1954 ad for Inman's Sales & Service, offering TV repair to eliminate "ghosts" and other problems. Printed in the March 14, 1954 State Journal of Frankfort, Kentucky. Included here on a Fair Use, educational basis.

Haunted Televisions

In 1950, New York City TV broadcasters pooled their resources to construct a new television tower atop the Empire State Building, expected to increase transmission range by 52 miles and curb the metro's pervasive "ghost" troubles (decades before the Ghostbusters). Safety helmet "cocked rakishly over one eye," wrote the New York Daily News, Mayor William O'Dwyer stood 1,250 feet above Fifth Avenue on Jul. 27 and used a compressed air hammer to drive home a gold spike into the television tower's foundation. Lt. Gen. Hugh A. Drum, president of Empire State, Inc., dramatically declared, "For centuries a ghost was something that haunted houses. Today it is something that haunts television screens. In a sense, we are here today to perform witchcraft—to exorcise that ghost from television viewers in the great Metropolitan Area."

But these were technical ghosts, a mere nuisance to the average viewer. What about ghosts of the classic ethereal type, the unexpected presence that raises the hairs on your arm and blows a chill down your spine?

Dr. Louis K. Anspacher of the American Society of Psychical Research suggested the possibility of tuning in to "atmospheric spooks" by means of television during a 1934 address at the Hotel Kimball in Springfield, Massachusetts. "If I told you, 25 years ago, that this room was full of music, you would have doubted my sanity and yet now any person with a radio can tune in on it. Perhaps you'll be able to tune in on invisible ghosts by television." Clearly, TV was already imagined this early on as a possible window to another realm.

Graphic representation of how "ghosts" of television experiments make their appearances.

A 1927 illustration of technical TV "ghosts," printed in the April 30 Hanover, Pennsylvania Evening Sun.

Haunted Televisions

By 1937, the prospect of television had excited the American populace, although the reality of practical household units was still some years off. People had odd misconceptions about TV, equating it more to telephone than the radio, and thinking strangers on the other side of the picture tube would be able to see them. (They were several decades ahead of themselves in that notion.) "Are we really going to have television? I hope not," one woman was quoted in The American Weekly. "It would be awful if I answered the phone by mistake when I wasn't dressed."

According to The American Weekly, television companies were already having strange encounters with callers who imagined they were being menaced by the nascent technology, which was already crossing the airwaves in New York City, despite few people having receivers. One young woman residing on the outskirts of the city complained to a local TV company official that people on the other side of the television were spying on her day and night. Assured that she would need a camera and broadcasting equipment in her home for this to even be possible, she confided, "They see me through the mirror. I hate to say so and you won't think it's nice, but they— they even look at me when I take a bath. I want you to help me find out who they are." Only a week or two later, the same official was visited by another woman, neatly dressed, who insisted that local gangsters had hidden a camera in her room, watching her disrobe and operating through TV signals. "They come through my mirror at night," she added. "They watch me all the time. Then they come out and stick pins in my arm and burn me." Even local police and politicians joined in the terrifying mirror shenanigans, she claimed. Other concerned citizens told similar stories, most of them suspicious that forces in the television were planning to rob them of some vague fortune. A California television executive described a woman who entered his station and announced that her child had been kidnapped through the television; investigation proved she never had a child. A Long Island woman claimed to see television pictures, bathed in green light, on her bedroom ceiling every night. The American Weekly pointed out that scientists and doctors of the day attributed these types of beliefs to mental health disorders. "Such subjects always keep up with the latest development in science and fasten their delusion on that," wrote the magazine. "Just now it's television; before that it was radio."

Hugh Gernsback, editor and publisher of Radio Electronics magazine, was unmoved when Newsday asked him in 1953 about the prospect of ghosts in the TV machine. "Gernsback views phenomena stoically," wrote Jo Coppola of Newsday. "He cited authenticated cases of people receiving radio programs through their teeth, housewives getting music from the running faucet, a frying pan which gave forth music and a cave in California which vibrated with 'Hot Time in the Old Town Tonight,' or some such radio music years ago."

Out of the Mirror in the Privacy of Her Bedroom, the Deluded Woman Insisted, Crept Leering Gangsters, Miraculously Transported by Television.

A 1937 drawing in American Weekly illustrated irrational fears of new television technology. Included here on a Fair Use, educational basis.

As it turned out, 1953 and 1954 were banner years for TV spooks.

Mr. and Mrs. Ernest Rode of Ft. Lauderdale, Florida were haunted for a few days in May 1953 by the face of a man that appeared on their television screen whether it was on or off. The couple at first noticed a black spot on the screen that suddenly enlarged to become a man's gaunt face with eyes, nose, ears, mouth, eyebrows and hair clearly visible. Straight black lines appeared to radiate from the figure's head and eventually a shape that resembled a vase of flowers formed beneath the man's chin. When the set was turned on, the man's face remained faintly visible, "looking out from the picture like a double exposure," according to the Ft. Lauderdale News. "It looks like Abe Lincoln," said Mrs. Edward Rode, cousin and sister-in-law of Mrs. Ernest Rode. A neighbor, Mrs. E. L. Moon, said the phantom on the television resembled her husband when he was 19. "I asked him what he was doing on Mrs. Rode's television set and he had to come over to see it before he'd believe it," she said. Although local television servicemen told the Rodes that the image was impossible, WFTL-TV engineer R. P. Northey explained that the image of the man had burned into the "memory" of the phosphor coating as ultra-high-speed electrons beat against the picture tube. Northey said that this phenomenon happened frequently on live-camera tubes. While he had never heard of it happening with a home set, he guessed it was possible if there was a defective tube with the wrong mixture of phosphor.

In the days leading up to Halloween 1953, Lt. Carl Neill of the Birmingham, Alabama police department patiently recorded a complaint from an elderly man who insisted that his television screen was bewitched. No matter which program he chose, there was always the same face of a woman staring back at him, along with the outline of a hand. The owner of the haunted TV was referred to a doctor, although similar cases suggest a TV repairman might have been more effective!

In December 1953, Blue Point, Long Island resident Jerry Travers and his family were surprised by the unmoving face of an eerie but beautiful woman peering out from the right side of their 17-inch television screen, lips puckered for a kiss. At 10 a.m. on Tuesday, Dec. 8, six-year-old Carolyn Travers sat down to watch "Ding Dong School" with her younger brothers, Michael and Jimmy. The girl soon complained to her mother, Emily, that they couldn't see the children's program because, "A face is in the way." Emily suspected the apparition might be the face of singer Francey Lane, who had just performed on NBC's Morey Amsterdam program. The couple had watched Amsterdam's show the hour before Carolyn reported the ghost image. According to one news dispatch, "Mrs. Travers investigated and agreed that the bosomy Miss Lane was out of place in the decorous atmosphere of the Ding Dong School." Jerry later joked, "I thought it was one of my old girlfriends coming back to haunt me." The three Travers children were so terrified by the TV tube phantom, who remained in place no matter the channel or brightness, that their parents turned the set toward the wall.

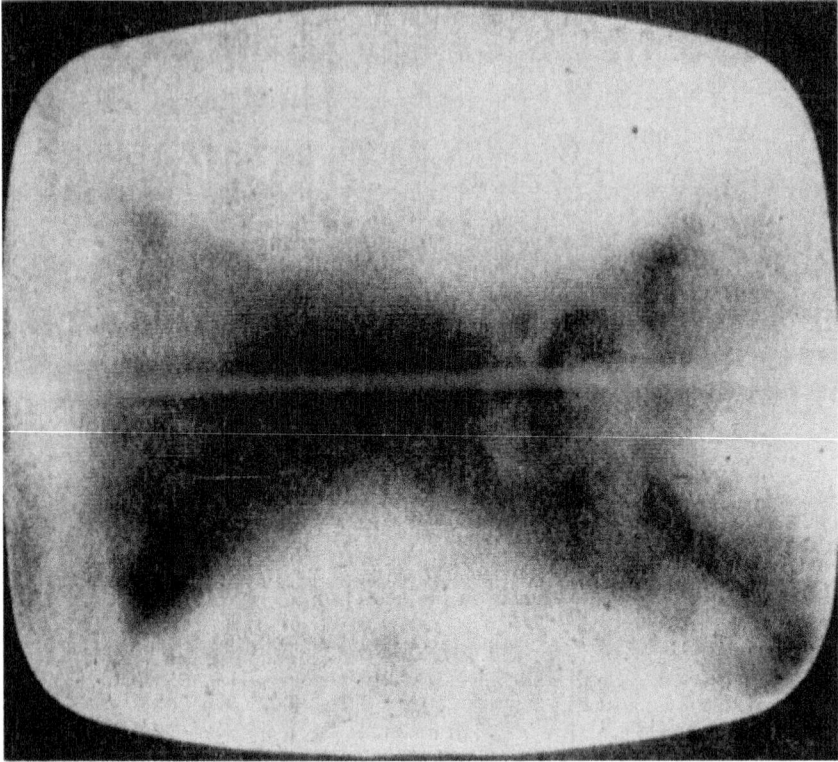

The Travers TV Ghost, supposedly the frozen image of singer Francey Lane. Published in several newspapers in December 1953. Included here on a Fair Use, educational basis.

Experts from the Zenith Company and General Electric took interest in the phenomenon, with some engineers and repairmen suggesting that a burst of electrons could have branded the face of a television personality into the inner phosphorescent coating of the tube, likely due to faulty equipment. Before the lady shade appeared, Jerry had noted a cross in the picture, a symptom of ions causing a "gassy" cathode tube, according to Ray Clurman, chief engineer at Telechrome Color Television Laboratory in Amityville (yes, THAT Amityville), New York. Pioneering Newsday TV columnist Jo Coppola investigated the "Case of the TV Face" and concluded, after speaking with a number of electronics experts, that the root cause of Francey Lane's TV phantom was a power failure that affected Blue Point the morning of Dec. 8, followed by a power surge as electricity returned at the precise time the singer was belting it out to Morey Amsterdam.

About 50 visitors dropped by to examine the TV ghost, creating a hectic scene and a media frenzy in the Travers household. After 51 hours, the mysterious face fizzled into a "cobwebby bunch of lines and we can't seem to get her back," said Jerry. Although too late to see her spooky doppelgänger, Lane herself visited the Travers family accompanied by a retinue of press agents. Presented with a Newsday photograph that showed the formerly hexed television, Lane said, "Well, I never thought I'd stop a TV set."

A month went by and the Travers family pulled the old television out of the basement. Jerry was sore at never receiving a new set he said that NBC had promised them, and at getting a runaround from the manufacturer, Zenith. It didn't take long for another girl to appear frozen on the set, this one an actress from a British film. The set went straight back into the cellar.

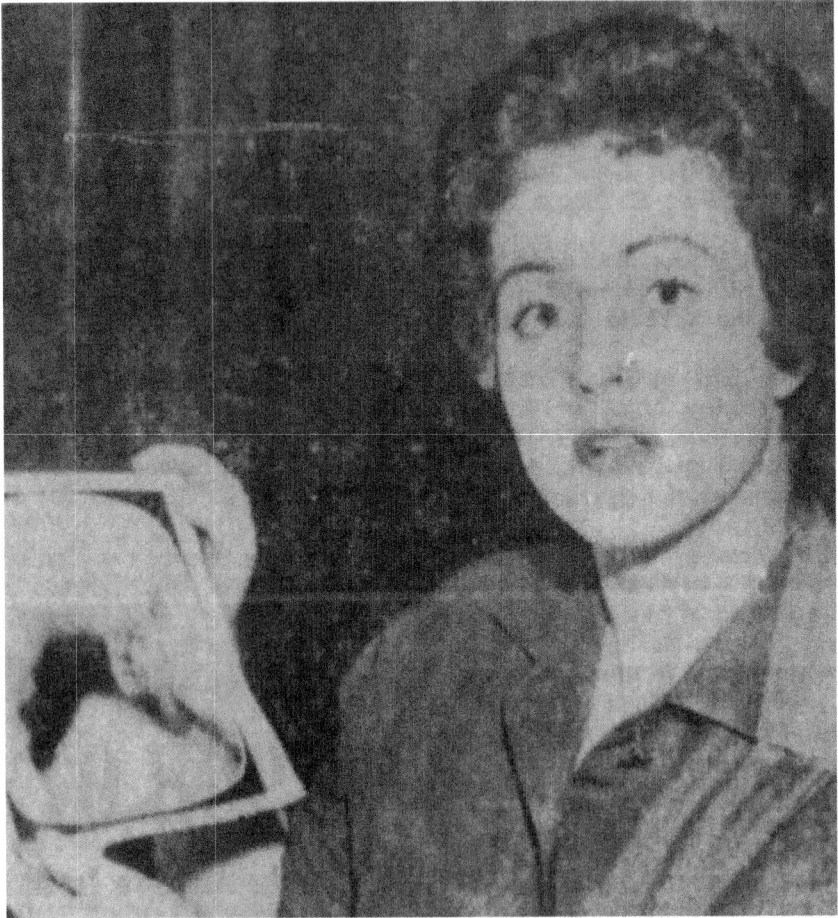

Francey Lane holds a photo of her spooky TV doppelgänger. Published in several newspapers in December 1953. Included here on a Fair Use, educational basis.

A Dec. 14 editorial in the Petersburg, Virginia Progress-Index playfully rejected the technical explanations for Francey's ghost double as a cover story, promoted by TV experts who were waking up to the "mysterious monster in the living room" they had created. "Yes sir, it could be that ghosts are finding television an excellent medium of physical expression," the article stated. "Not many folks believe anymore in white-clad spooks that run around making weird sounds. So, isn't it conceivable that a smart old ghost would try to confuse and scare the living by staring at them silently and soundlessly from the TV screen?"

"I'm going crazy," said Virginia Mackey of Indianapolis in September 1954, convinced that the ghost of her dead grandfather was haunting her TV set. She and her husband, John, were watching a Friday night network drama broadcast live from New York when the apparition of George Shots, who had died four months prior, materialized on the screen. The phantom image grew in intensity the following day and remained frozen in place no matter where the dial was set or whether the unit was switched on or off. Once turned off, a flashlight aimed at the darkened screen revealed the clearly visible face. The "ghost" resisted all efforts to wipe it off. Virginia, her husband, mother, a neighbor, and other relatives all immediately recognized the mustached gentleman on the television as the deceased grandfather—he was even wearing the suit in which he was buried. "Father!" exclaimed

Virginia's mother, Marie Johnson, when she saw the figure. Afraid to leave his wife alone in the house with the television set, John called the Indianapolis police department on Sunday. Police could do little more than confirm the persistent existence of the shadowy figure of an elderly man shown from the chest up on the TV tube. The face was about eight inches tall, less distinct on its upper part and more clearly delineated below the eyes. Shots had never watched the set, a 17-inch table model, which had been purchased two months after his death.

Police took the television, the mysterious face "still staring stolidly from the lower half of the screen," back to headquarters and disassembled it piece-by-piece in the property room. When put back together, though, the face was still there, clear as before. Nearly the entire police force as well as about 400 visitors stopped by the station to witness the strange phenomenon. Electronics experts and engineers who examined the TV advanced the theory that the figure of an actor who resembled Shots might have been burned into the phosphorescent backing of the picture tube by an abnormal stream of electrons, a temporary surge in the beam. Paul McAllister, an engineer with Indianapolis television station WISH-TV, recalled cases in which a test pattern was burned into a picture tube by an excess flow of electrons.

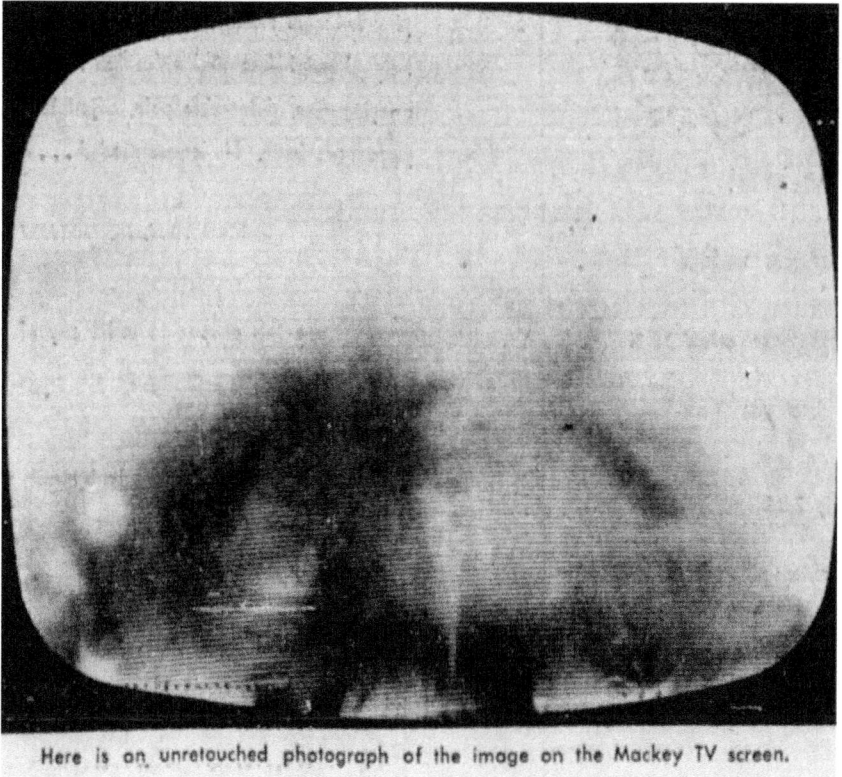

Here is on unretouched photograph of the image on the Mackey TV screen.

A not-so-clear newspaper photo of Grandpa's ghost seen on the Mackey family's television. Printed in the Sep. 13, 1954 Indianapolis Star. Included here on a Fair Use, educational basis.

Virginia doubted this reasoning at first, owing to the man's suit and tie being a match for her grandfather's burial clothes, but ultimately accepted the scientific explanation. "I guess it was just a coincidence, but it will always be on my mind," she said.

WISH-TV reported on the strange incident and it was learned that other Indianapolis residents reported the same face burned into their own TVs.

WISH newscaster John Frame arranged to have a new picture tube installed in the Mackey's TV, with the "haunted" tube sent back to the manufacturer for examination. Although the traumatized Virginia was initially happy to be rid of the cursed device, her tune changed when the repaired set arrived the next week. "It's certainly hard to get along without one, once you get used to it," she admitted.

Across the pond, George Leek and family in the town of North Shields, England, were beleaguered by a poltergeist that, while not *in* the TV, seemed to like viewing it. By August 1960, the Leeks had already endured several months of the invisible, chuckling spook that regularly invaded television time in their upper flat, located in a block of council houses in Red Burn View, Percy Main. Unable to find another flat, the family begrudgingly accepted the ghost as a "sort of unwelcome lodger," telling only a few close friends about the spiritual infestation. But then the ghost increased its repertoire to touching George, his wife Margaret, teenaged daughter Vivian, and baby David. On one occasion, Margaret was admiring a woman's hat on an afternoon TV program when the spirit brushed right across her face. "The noises were bad enough but this is going too far," George snapped.

The poltergeist caused mayhem outside of TV time, as well, making cracking noises and repeatedly grabbing, shouting at, and evoking a body-wide feeling of "pins and needles" in George and Margaret as they tried to sleep in their bedroom. The phantom tromped down the hall and up the stairs outside the family's bedroom doors, and once tapped on a window, sending Vivian running from the flat. After several weeks of fear, George decided to consult the local vicar, Rev. Clement White. After interviewing the family about the unsettling events, the clergyman stated, "I have suggested that the house should be given the ministrations of the Church, to exorcise any spirits." He intended to return later in the week, following strict exorcism protocol. Margaret declared she would petition the council for new housing if it failed. "The ghost bothers us night and day," she lamented. "This awful spook will drive us all to destruction." Locals joked that if Rev. White was unsuccessful, the Leeks should charge the phantom a pro rata share of the $11-per-year TV license.

The Leek case made history, according to journalist Robert Musel, as the first-reported ghost associated with television viewing, as well as one of the few spirits to haunt a new home, the building being only three years old at the time. George believed the eerie incidents tied back to an old legend regarding the "haunting" of Red Burn dene. The stories dated to when the vale was still in its natural state, a deep and narrow river valley surrounded by woods, before it was filled in and the council house built on top of it. Perhaps the results of Rev. White's exorcism are documented in a Church of England archive, for the final fate of the Redburn Spook went sadly undocumented in the press.

One weekend in 1964, Charlie Williams of Baltimore was puzzled when his TV set repeatedly turned itself on to show a children's program, "Hector Heathcote." Williams realized that, rather than his television having a preference for Saturday morning cartoons, the trigger was his telephone. Every time someone called, "the pitch or harmonics of the telephone ring" switched on the television due to an identical frequency to the TV's remote-control unit. Until he could have either device adjusted, Williams muffled the phone with a pillow.

According to a 1964 account, a Miami woman discovered that when she whistled to her cat, calling the feline from its perch atop her warm TV, the noise would reliably change the channel. It seemed that her whistle was perfectly tuned to the frequency the set used for remote control, even though she didn't have such a device.

"John Prigg knows his TV isn't haunted. He also knows his dog snores, but it took a while to connect the two," wrote the Paris, Texas News on Sep. 12, 1979. One night, Prigg heard voices in the living room shortly after retiring to bed. He rose for a quick check and found the TV blaring with his boxer, Jojo, soundly snoring in an armchair. Assuming his wife had forgotten to turn off the TV, Prigg switched it off and returned to bed. Minutes later, the set snapped to life again and Prigg trudged back in to turn it off. After this happened a third time, Prigg—an amateur radio operator with 18 years of experience—developed a theory as to why his television was persistently returning to life. It seemed that Jojo's snoring had hit just the right pitch to trigger the TV's remote-control box. Sure enough, Prigg watched in disbelief as Jojo began snoring madly and the television flickered on once again. "I thought I was going to die," said the bemused dog owner. Prigg—and the snoring Jojo—soon returned to nights of sound sleep with the removal of the remote-control box.

In more recent years, possessed televisions have been blamed as the impetus behind horrific crimes and tragedies associated with mental illness. In May 1992, attorney Allan Focarile attempted to convince a New York Supreme Court jury that his client, Walter Carlaftes of New Rochelle, had heard voices coming from his television on the night he killed and dismembered his sister, Maria Caputo. Carlaftes, a diagnosed schizophrenic, pled insanity, claiming he believed that Caputo and other family members were alien clones sent to rob his mind. He was sentenced to 28 1/2 years to life in prison. In June 2004, Constantin Deaconu, a serial arsonist from Bellevue, Washington, allegedly believed he heard voices coming from his television and set it and resultingly his own house ablaze, before calling 911 to report it, stated police. Deaconu had previously been arrested for setting fire to two different Bellevue apartment complexes in which he resided, in one case leaving 30 of his neighbors homeless. He was ruled innocent by reason of insanity in 1997 for fires he started the previous year. Alex Tilghman, a gunman who wounded three people when he randomly opened fire through the door of an Oklahoma City restaurant in May 2018, had posted videos on Facebook and YouTube in which he claimed his television was possessed by the devil, as well as his refrigerator and even a squirrel that followed him around the zoo. "I am under hardcore demonic attack," said Tilghman who, similar to Carlaftes, believed that most of the people around him had been replaced by "demons in cloned transsexual bodies," and thought that he was living in a simulation like "The Matrix." Tilghman, suicidal and lonely, begged for help from a "real human." Intervention sadly did not arrive before Tilghman went on his violent rampage and was himself killed by two armed bystanders to prevent a greater tragedy. Even with the extensive reach of the internet, it can still feel quite lonely on our side of the screen.

Haunted Televisions

In 1994, Sherry Hart claimed that her home on Fourth Street in Elyria, Ohio, constructed in 1850, was haunted by the ghost of a little girl named Hazel. Hart first noticed strange activity after she turned off her television and left the house, only to return and find "Sesame Street" playing on the set. Hart struggled to turn off the TV, with the picture persisting without the sound, only succeeding after several tries. At other times, Hart heard a voice calling for "Mommy." Hart investigated the attic and discovered a 1902 birth certificate for a girl named Hazel, who she assumed was the spirit enjoying Big Bird on her TV.

Like most new technologies, early television was a Rorschach test, a shiny new fulcrum for our ever-present anxieties and fears. It provided an unprecedented illusion of life, tricking our eyes and ears into perceiving a connection to the world instead of a box filled with cold mechanics. It is understandable to imagine the picture tube facilitating two-way transmission, whether to a studio on the other end, or to a phantom realm that now had its own way to tune in... *to us.*

SOURCES:

"13 Local Haunts." *Morning Journal* [Lorain, OH], 30 Oct. 1994, p. 8.

A modern-day haunted image, courtesy of AI.

"1920s – 1960s: Television." *Elon University*, https://www.elon.edu/u/imagining/time-capsule/150-years/back-1920-1960/. Accessed 15 Mar. 2025.

"Attempt to Explain 'Ghost' Image on Television Screen." *York Daily News-Times* [York, NE], 13 Sep. 1954, p. 1.

"Bellevue: Arsonist Suspected in House Fire." *Herald* [Everett, WA], 1 Jul. 2004, p. B8.

Bergmann, Art. "Francey's TV 'Ghost' Fades Out Before She Can See Herself." *Newsday* [Long Island, NY], 12 Dec. 1953, p. 5.

Bergmann, Art and Dick Aurelio. "Face on TV Screen Haunts LI Family, Puzzles Nation." *Newsday* [Long Island, NY], 11 Dec. 1953, pp. 3, 42.

"Cathode-Ray Tube." *Wikipedia*, https://en.wikipedia.org/wiki/Cathode-ray_tube. Accessed 20 Mar. 2025.

Coppola, Jo. "Case of the TV Face." *Newsday* [Long Island, NY], 14 Dec. 1953, p. 40.

"Couple Demands Removal of TV 'Ghost Lady.'" *Evening World-Herald* [Omaha, NE], 11 Dec. 1953, p. 3.

Cross, Phil. "Restaurant shooter: 'I am under hardcore demonic attack...'" *Fox 25* [Oklahoma City], 25 May 2018, https://okcfox.com/news/fox-25-investigates/restaurant-shooter-i-am-under-hardcore-demonic-attack. Accessed 15 Mar. 2025.

"'Dead Man's' Image Haunts TV Set." *Indianapolis Star*, 13 Sep. 1954, pp. 1-2.

"Deceased Grandpa 'Haunts' TV Screen." *Brooklyn Eagle* [Brooklyn, NY], 13 Sep. 1954, p. 3.

Dickerson, Eula K. Letter. *Plain Dealer* [Cleveland], 12 Jan. 1964, p. 7-AA.

"Do You Live in a Haunted House?" *Standard-Star* [New Rochelle, NY], 30 Mar. 1948, p. 3.

"Dog Snores; Television Not Haunted." *Paris News* [Paris, TX], 12 Sep. 1979, p. 13B.

The Emerging Technologies. David Sarnoff Research Center, 1993.

"Face Stares Permanently from TV Set." *Alameda Times-Star* [Alameda, CA], 11 Dec. 1953, p. 2.

Fleming, Mildred. "Television Prospects for the Postwar." *Daily Worker* [New York], 14 Aug. 1944, p. 11.

"Francey Lane Out of Place on 'Ding Dong School' Skit." *Daily Dispatch* [Moline, IL], 12 Dec. 1953, p. 5.

"'Ghost' on TV Set Not a Relative." *Evening Republican* [Columbus, IN], 13 Sep. 1954, p. 2.

"Ghosts in Television Follow Image Taken." *Wilmington Morning News* [Wilmington, DE], 21 Apr. 1927, p. 19.

"Ghosts Make Appearance on Television Screens." *Marion Chronicle* [Marion, IN], 22 May 1950, p. 7.

Golding, Bruce. "Carlaftes Gets 5-15 for Rape." *Standard-Star* [New Rochelle, NY], 23 Jul. 1994, p. 5B.

Gray, Kevin. "Man Heard Voices Before Killing Sister, Lawyer Tells Jury." *Standard-Star* [New Rochelle, NY], 7 May 1992, p. 5.

"Guardsman Gives Account of Faceoff with Gunman." *Waco Tribune-Herald* [Waco, TX], 29 May 2018, p. 3A.

"Haunted TV, Dead Bodies Bother Police." *Birmingham News* [Birmingham, AL], 22 Oct. 1953, p. 66.

"Haunted TV Mopes, Family Hopes." *Newsday* [Long Island, NY], 16 Jan. 1954, p. 3.

"Indiana Woman Convinced that Kin Hasn't Appeared from Dead on Her TV Set." *Cincinnati Enquirer*, 14 Sep. 1954 (final edition), p. 1.

"Is There a Spook Network?" *Progress-Index* [Petersburg, VA], 14 Dec. 1953, p. 8.

"Jo Coppola." *Wikipedia*, https://en.wikipedia.org/wiki/Jo_Coppola. Accessed 18 Mar. 2025.

Journal Reporter. "Vicar Will Try to Exorcise Red Burn 'Ghost.'" *Journal* [Newcastle upon Tyne, England], 8 Aug. 1960, p. 5.

"Man Solves the Case of Spooky TV Set." *Evening Sun* [Baltimore], 13 Jul. 1964, p. B3.

Musel, Robert. "Ghost Haunts New House, Enjoys TV Programs." *St. Catharines Standard* [St. Catharines, Ontario, Canada], 9 Aug. 1960, p. 2.

"New 'Ghost' Girl Shows Up on Haunted Television Set." *Times Herald* [Washington, D.C.], 16 Jan. 1954, p. 1.

"O'D. Puts Gold Rivet in Empire State TV Mast." *Daily News* [New York], 28 Jul. 1950, p. C6.

"Persistent Ghost Confronts Police on TV Screen." *Hartford Courant* [Hartford, CT], 13 Sep. 1954, p. 9.

"'Persistent' TV Face Identified; Francey Lane's." *Des Moines Tribune* [Des Moines, IA], 11 Dec. 1953, p. 16.

"'Phantom Lady' of TV Screen Identified." *Brooklyn Eagle* [Brooklyn, NY], 11 Dec. 1953, p. 3.

"Philo Farnsworth." *Wikipedia*, https://en.wikipedia.org/wiki/Philo_Farnsworth. Accessed 20 Mar. 2025.

"Spectral Spook Haunts Television Screen." *Ft. Lauderdale Daily News* [Ft. Lauderdale, FL], 14 May 1953, p. 8-B.

"Television Ghost Gone After Repair Job." *Leader-Tribune* [Marion, IN], 19 Sep. 1954, p. 7.

"Television Ghosts." *Wilkes-Barre Record* [Wilkes-Barre, PA], 18 Nov. 1949, p. 19.

"Television Set." *Wikipedia*, https://en.wikipedia.org/wiki/Television_set. Accessed 20 Mar. 2025.

"Television Set Ghost Removed." *Leader-Tribune* [Marion, IN], 18 Sep. 1954, p. 13.

"Today's Television Program." *Newsday* [Long Island, NY], 8 Dec. 1953, p. 50.

"Tortured by Television, Say Victims of Strange Phobia." *San Francisco Examiner*, 14 Mar. 1937, American Weekly supplement, p. 6.

"Tuning in on Atmospheric Spooks by Television Termed Possibility." *Springfield Daily Republican* [Springfield, MA], 13 Nov. 1934, p. 4.

"TV Image May Not Be Ghost of Grandpa, Woman Decides." *Rushville Republican* [Rushville, IN], 13 Sep. 1954. pp. 1, 3.

Santa Claus Is Coming to Town in a Mystery Airship

On Christmas 1896, holiday traditions merged with the craze of proto-UFOs that had been sweeping the skies over the United States.

Christmas Airships

A wave of mystery airship sightings emerged above California in November 1896, ultimately working its way eastward across the U.S. during the first half of 1897. Occurring just seven years before the Wright Bros. soared over Kitty Hawk, this weird epidemic immediately presaged the dawn of powered flight. Numerous newspapers recorded encounters with everything from strange lights to large propellered craft hovering in the night-time sky. The pilots were theorized to be secretive inventors testing prototype craft, although in some cases they were said to be visitors from other worlds. In many ways, the phenomenon is eerily similar to the mystery drones that began buzzing New Jersey and other states in the last couple months of 2024. In 1896, the mystery airships made such an impact on the public consciousness in California that they infiltrated the jolliest of holidays—Christmas, itself!

At the Methodist church in Vallejo, Santa Claus made an unexpected entrance, said to have arrived on an "airship." To shouts of mingled surprise and welcome from the children who filled the church, J. Hartman in the guise of St. Nick entered through a window at the peak of the ceiling and slid down a rope to join the festivities below.

Meanwhile, Police Judge Campbell rode in as Santa on a bicycle to entertain about 500 kids at the First Christian Church at 13th and Jefferson

streets in Oakland. Santa nearly took a header off
the bike several times until Rev. Edwards Davis
leapt forward and wrestled the wobbly, two-
wheeled steed to a halt.

POLICE JUDGE CAMPBELL AS SANTA CLAUS.

Santa disembarked near the Christmas tree at the
pulpit and told the crowd, "I'm a little late, but it's

all right. I've had a long, hard ride. At 5 o'clock I left my workshop, just above Sitka, Alaska. Now I am going to tell you a secret. I'm the mysterious inventor of the airship. I've just come in on it from the North, stopping at Vancouver, New Westminster, Portland and other places, where I filled up boys' and girl's stockings—good boys and girls. I was delayed, because I lost a feather out of one wing of my airship. At Portland I caught a seagull, got a feather out of his wing, put it in my machine's wing and came flying along. Why, I take a fly every night across the bay to my Berkley home. This airship business is a great thing. I am going to take a long trip tonight if I do not lose any more feathers. And do you see these whiskers, children? Well, they are all mine and known as the finest in the land."

Santa then distributed presents to the old and young and rode off on his bicycle into the rain... presumably to rendezvous with his airship.

The mystery airship made its appearance over, fittingly, Santa Cruz at 9:30 a.m. on Christmas morning. Spectators gathered to observe the hovering craft, which was shaped like a torpedo, about 10 feet long and entirely red. On each side were wings and at the stern was a propeller which revolved in the wind. It was the work of boys from the Y.M.C.A., who suspended their handcrafted Christmas decoration from two poles on the top of the organization's building. Weather permitting, they planned to light the Christmas airship in the evenings.

Jake H. Ring, a druggist in Ferndale, placed a model airship in his store's front window. "Take a look at it," urged the Ferndale Enterprise, "for he sails tonight—Christmas night—for the planet Mars."

Fiel's Variety Store in Folsom advertised, "Have you seen the airship? We have it, filled with candies!" Apparently, this was another model airship. Every 25-cent purchase at the store earned the customer a guess at the number of sweets within, the closest guess winning a large supply of Christmas goods.

Of course, what would Christmas be without a genuine airship sighting? However, it happened all the way across the country—as the reindeer flies—near Wilmington, Delaware.

Ezekiel Sergeant, a "grizzly" farmer and milkman from Brandywine, claimed to have seen an airship sailing through the air shortly after daybreak. It was filled with people and illuminated with multi-colored lights. Music drifted down from the brass band that played onboard, and some of the passengers were singing melodies. Sergeant and a helper had just finished milking the cows and were returning to the farmer's house holding "buckets brimful of the foaming liquid" when they were stunned by the spectacle. The airship was about a half-mile up and floating toward the northeast. A powerful searchlight beamed from the vessel, revealing it to be a huge machine shaped like a fish, "with wide-spreading wings and a mighty tail."

While the two men watched, something crashed to the ground just outside the doorway, flying glass scattering in every direction. Suddenly, the airship extinguished its lights and turned about, making a complete circle and darting off to the southeast. Sergeant and his helper scoured the ground for the missile which had fallen from the clouds. After a few minutes, they discovered a broken bottle that displayed the name "J. Krause & Co., Salt Lake City Utah." While the top of the bottle had broken, the label and lower part remained intact. Inside was a slip of paper that contained the following message:

On board the air-ship Icarus. Thursday afternoon, December 24, 1896. The air-ship Icarus, Captain James Dashiel, with Thomas Murphy as companion, et al., Salt Lake City 10 P.M. Tuesday, December 8, bound for Cuba. Wind due east, blowing at the rate of sixty miles an hour. At an altitude of one mile we found a steady current. Machinery working to a charm. All well. Provisions sufficient for a week longer. Will land in the neighborhood of Jacksonville, Fla. Send word, collect, to Hatcher & Mills, bankers, 720 South Second Street, Salt Lake City, Utah.

JAMES DASHIEL, captain.

THOMAS MURPHY.

Sergeant brought the bottle and message into Wilmington, where it caused quite a stir. He entrusted the airship evidence to Anton Hauber of Sixth and Shipley streets, where it was to be further examined.

The Icarus being bound for Cuba reflects an article that ran in the San Francisco Call on July 19, 1896, detailing a daring plan to support the Cubans against the Spanish in the former's war of independence. A Frenchman, Captain E. Lagrifoule, had supposedly improved upon aerial navigation innovations discovered by Dr. Rufus Gibbon Wells and was about to begin work on an airship that could carry 125 men, 1,000 rifles, a half million rounds of ammunition, ingredients to make dynamite, and medical supplies.

Lagrifoule planned to construct the airship in a secluded grove in Florida before sailing to Cuba's aid. It was to consist of a boat-shaped car, 100 feet long and 50 feet wide, held solidly between a cluster of five balloons inflated with a secret, lighter-than-air gas "made of chemicals by electric power." An immense screw propelled the ship, and sails aided in steering. The aluminum car would have nine windows on each side and a series of long, narrow openings, closed with aluminum bars, which run around the upper guard, which runs around the upper deck of the boat. Inside would be comfortable accommodations, an electrical engine room and kitchen, bedrooms, a smoking room and observatory. Water was captured from the clouds. Lagrifoule boasted that the airship could deposit men and arms in Cuba before lifting safely away from enemy fire. This, he believed, would bring a quick end to the war. It is unclear what became of this doomsday vessel, as the Cuban War of Independence waged on through 1898.

A FRENCHMAN'S INVENTION FOR CUBAN WARFARE.

*"A Frenchman's Invention for Cuban Warfare."
Illustration published in the Montanian newspaper,
Sep. 19, 1896.*

Back in California, a loud explosion rocked the business district of Chico at about 9:40 p.m. on Christmas Eve. Police and amateur detectives had to spend their Christmas day tracking down evidence of the mysterious blast. According to the Chico Daily Enterprise, "One prominent citizen suggested that maybe the air-ship passed over Chico and let fall one of those deadly dynamite shells in our midst, but if such is the case we have heard of no damage resulting. Another 'maybe' was that the steam boiler on the air-ship had blown up, but this theory cannot be held for the reason that the ship does not use steam power."

The San Francisco Chronicle, meanwhile, paid tribute to the holiday airship mania in verse:

Solved at Last.

Twinkle, twinkle, little star.

Now we all know what you are,

Up above the world so high—

You're an airship in the sky.

Happy Holidays, Humans!

SOURCES:

"An Airship." *Santa Cruz Surf* [Santa Cruz, CA], 24 Dec. 1896, p. 4.

Ash, Clarke. "Castro Hasn't Seen Anything." *Miami News*, 11 Mar. 1968. p. 18.

Christmas Airships

"Christmas Festivals." *Vallejo Evening Chronicle* [Vallejo, CA], 26 Dec. 1896, p. 3.

"A Great Airship to Free the Cubans." *San Francisco Call*, 19 Jul. 1896, p. 29.

"Have You Seen the Airship?" *Folsom Telegraph* [Folsom, CA], 26 Dec. 1896, p. 3.

"Local News." *Ferndale Enterprise* [Ferndale, CA], 25 Dec. 1896, p. 5.

"A Mysterious Explosion." *Chico Daily Enterprise* [Chico, CA], 25 Dec. 1896, p. 1.

"Mystery Airship." *Wikipedia*, https://en.wikipedia.org/wiki/Mystery_airship. Accessed 22 Dec. 2024.

"Police Judge Campbell as Santa Claus." *Examiner* [San Francisco], 24 Dec. 1896, p. 8.

"Saw an Air-Ship." *Philadelphia Times*, 28 Dec. 1896, p. 5.

"Solved at Last." *Atchison Daily Globe* [Atchison, KS], 26 Dec. 1896, p. 2.

"That Airship." *Santa Cruz Surf* [Santa Cruz, CA], 26 Dec. 1896, p. 1.

"Wonderful Ship." *Montanian* [Choteau, MY], 19 Sep. 1896, p. 3.

Also by Kevin J. Guhl:

Thunderbirds, Lost Temples and
Skeleton Ghosts
An Anthology of
American Strangeness,
Vol. 1

The Unnatural History of
Man-Eating Plants

(coming soon)

Printed in Dunstable, United Kingdom